PEOPLE IN CITIES

Environment and Behavior Series

Editors

DANIEL STOKOLS
University of California, Irvine

IRWIN ALTMAN
University of Utah

PEOPLE IN CITIES
The urban environment and its effects

EDWARD KRUPAT

Massachusetts College of Pharmacy and Allied Health Sciences, Boston

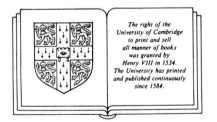

The right of the
University of Cambridge
to print and sell
all manner of books
was granted by
Henry VIII in 1534.
The University has printed
and published continuously
since 1584.

CAMBRIDGE UNIVERSITY PRESS

CAMBRIDGE

NEW YORK   NEW ROCHELLE   MELBOURNE   SYDNEY

Published by the Press Syndicate of the University of Cambridge
The Pitt Building, Trumpington Street, Cambridge CB2 1RP
32 East 57th Street, New York, NY 10022, USA
10 Stamford Road, Oakleigh, Melbourne 3166, Australia

First published 1985
Reprinted 1987

Printed in the United States of America

Library of Congress Cataloging in Publication Data
Krupat, Edward.
People in cities.
(Cambridge series in environment and behavior)
Bibliography: p.
Includes index.
1. City and town life – Psychological aspects.
I. Title. II. Series.
BF353.5.C53K78   1985   155.9′42   84–21488
ISBN 0 521 26544 4 hard covers
ISBN 0 521 31946 3 paperback

To NEW YORK, BOSTON, and SAN FRANCISCO

CONTENTS

SERIES FOREWORD

In recent decades the relationship between human behavior and the physical environment has attracted researchers from the social sciences – psychology, sociology, geography, and anthropology – and from the environmental-design disciplines – architecture, urban and regional planning, and interior design. What is in many respects a new and exciting field of study has developed rapidly. Its multidisciplinary character has led to stimulation and cross-fertilization, on the one hand, and to confusion and difficulty in communication, on the other. Those involved have diverse intellectual styles and goals. Some are concerned with basic and theoretical issues; some, with applied real-world problems of environmental design.

This series offers a common meeting ground. It consists of short books on different topics of interest to all those who analyze environment-behavior links. We hope that the series will provide a useful introduction to the field for students, researchers, and practitioners alike, and will facilitate its evolutionary growth as well.

Our goals are as follows: (1) to represent problems the study of which is relatively well established, with a reasonably substantial body of research and knowledge generated; (2) to recruit authors from a variety of disciplines with a variety of perspectives; (3) to ensure that they not only summarize work on their topic but also set forth a ''point of view,'' if not a theoretical orientation – we want the books not only to serve as texts but also to advance the field intellectually – and (4) to produce books useful to a broad range of students and other readers from different disciplines and with different levels of formal professional training. Course instructors will be able to select different combinations of books to meet their particular curricular needs.

Irwin Altman
Daniel Stokols

PREFACE

By way of introducing this book, let me offer some autobiographical and environmental commentary. It is a widely acknowledged fact that human beings are products of their social and physical backgrounds. We reflect the groups and places we are or were once a part of, and judge present and future experiences in the context of our past experience. I was born and raised a "New Yorker" as surely as I was born into certain sex, class, race, and religious groupings. It is part of my identity, as each of the others is, and sometimes I am proud of it whereas at other times I try to live it down. Yet I have lived in, and identified with, many places (Ann Arbor, Michigan; New Brunswick, New Jersey; Berkeley, California; and now Boston, Massachusetts); and as the places around me have changed, so have I. If you were to ask me today where I am from, I would answer, "Boston"; and this is a reflection of not just my identity but my values, my ways of looking at the world, and my behavior as well.

This is all to say that the physical context in which one grows up and the places in which one lives are every bit as important as one's genetic endowment or social class in determining behavior. The city, as a context for behavior, is the topic of this book. As a place that houses more and more of the world's population every day, it is a place that needs to be studied and discussed. It influences people and their behavior for better and for worse; and its influence, whether subtle or explicit, immediate or delayed, is always there.

This is a book about understanding cities and, therefore, about understanding people – how people act and why they act as a function of their past and present environments. I have written it to be useful to a wide variety of readers, students and professionals alike. I have not included any discussion of complex statistical techniques or sophisticated methodologies that might befuddle those without the proper expertise or background. In addition, I have tried to avoid detailed debates about the validity of one or another theoretical position that might be of interest only to proponents of those positions. Instead, my purpose has been to gather and summarize current knowledge and to synthesize and analyze in a critical manner, all within a social psychological framework. For the advanced undergraduate and the graduate student, I hope I have supplied the building blocks with which to comprehend urban life and generate a more sophisticated understanding of the relationship of environment to behavior and the reasons why city people act the way they do. For the professional scholar and practitioner, I hope I have offered something new in emphasizing the multiple and contrasting realities of city life and in bringing together the psychological and sociological literatures in a way that has not been done before.

Although the phrase has become a cliché by now, I want to thank many people whose efforts went into the making of this book. It is a project that took more time to produce than I would like to admit. My greatest debt is to the editors of this series, Dan Stokols, Irv Altman, and Larry Wrightsman, who stuck with me and encouraged my work even when it was going slowly or not well. Their moral support and confidence made the writing of the book a possibility, and their intellectual support, their comments, and their patience with early drafts allowed me to fill out incomplete ideas and discover just what my own perspective on the city was.

Thanks go to Claire Verduin at Brooks/Cole for staying with the project for many years; and to Susan Milmoe, Rhona Johnson, and other editors at Cambridge University Press for taking on the project and seeing it through to publication. At Massachusetts College of Pharmacy and Allied Health Sciences, I want to acknowledge Mary Chitty and Peg Hewitt for much help in the late stages of bibliographic work, Donna Boardman for her efficient typing and cheerful manner, and Sumner Robinson and Amy Lezberg, who provided me with the time and support to complete the book.

A number of others, some of whom I am glad to call friends, some of whom I have dealt with only professionally, and others whom I have never met, have influenced my thinking about environmental issues and cities in important ways. At the risk of naming so many people that I give no one sufficient credit and at the simultaneous risk of leaving out others whom I consider important, let me acknowledge Andy Baum, Kenneth Craik, Yak Epstein, Claude Fischer, Jeff Fisher, Charles Holahan, Chuck Korte, Kevin Lynch, William Michelson, Stanley Milgram, Rudolf Moos, Douglas Porteous, Amos Rapoport, Ralph Taylor, and John Zeisel. Each in his own way has provided me with new ideas, interesting concepts, and useful perspectives. I hope I have done their work and ideas justice. In addition, although he is not aware of it, Leonard Reissman's book *The Urban Process* deserves much of the credit for initially stimulating my thinking and making me want to pursue the city as a topic of study.

Through a succession of cities, one constant influence has been my family. I want to thank my father, who was witness to the beginning of this project but not its completion, and my mother, who oversaw my early dealings with the city and taught me to profit from its variety of experiences. As well, I owe a great debt of thanks to my wife, Barbara, who provided me with the emotional support to complete this project, as well as my sons, Jason and Michael. Their combined presence makes any environment, city or town, suburban or urban, far more livable.

PART I
THE IDEA OF THE CITY

1
THE CITY AS ENVIRONMENT: AN INTRODUCTION

"You see, I'm an environmental psychologist and I –"

"Pardon me, you're a what?"

"An environmental psychologist. It's a new field concerned with the ways in which actual physical settings affect human behavior. You know, like cities. In fact, that's why I came to talk to you about –"

"That's a nice idea. I'm glad to hear there are people into that."

– Conversation between the author and an urban official

The city is the ultimate creation of the human mind. It is an aggregation of people and activities unparalleled in the history of civilization. Yet the city is only a recent invention. Its development and the spread of its influence have occurred so quickly that we have often failed to look at it carefully and see just what effect it has on its people. In modern times, this influence goes well beyond its physical boundaries. The city's products, values, and lifestyles affect us all regardless of where we live or work. Whether you live in the city or as far away from one as you can get, whether you love it or hate it, it cannot be ignored. This is a book about cities or, more accurately, about *people and cities*. In it I will describe the nature of the urban experience from close up, considering how city people cope and adapt, and why some thrive and others do not.

Multiple and contrasting realities

To understand something as large and involved as the modern city requires an approach that allows us to account for the full complexity of this gigantic creation. The general perspective taken here is that of environmental-social psychology, and some of its organizing principles will be dealt with in the next few pages. As important as this general framework is, however, there is another perspective that is equally important to spell out. Much of the discussion of the city has been phrased in extremes, in debates of an either-or nature. Examples abound: the city as a place that isolates people or integrates them; as a home for rich versus poor; and, most generally, as a ''good'' or a ''bad'' place to live (Sternlieb & Hughes, 1983).

It is suggested here that simple answers to these issues are not possible, not only because value positions on both sides of each question can be sup-

3

ported by personal experience but also because scientific conclusions based on careful data collection can also be used to support both sides. The mere fact that both experience and common sense, science and statistics, can be called upon to support both sides suggests that we should not be looking for answers that lie on a single point of a continuum. Rather, I propose that the city is a place of *multiple and contrasting realities*. It contains within it the possibility for both ends of the continuum to exist – and to exist simultaneously. To understand the city is to understand it not in terms of good *versus* bad but in terms of good *and* bad. Cities have the potential to pull people apart and to bring them together, to produce constraints and to create opportunities. We shall see this duality constantly throughout the book. As a result, cities are good for some people and bad for others, better at certain times and worse at others, good for certain purposes but not very good for others. Both extremes – and several shades of gray – exist side by side.

For the most part, we lack concepts in our language that incorporate two extremes. Clinical psychologists sometimes describe people as passive-aggressive in referring to the different elements of their personalities. Yet a pitcher of water is thought to be hot or cold, not both. And if we place the two extremes in a single container the result is still identified at a single point in temperature somewhere in between.

There are a few exceptions to this sort of unidimensional classification of people and places. In looking at the concepts of masculinity and femininity, for instance, psychologists have recently come to recognize that they are not mutually exclusive. Rather, people can have a number of traits that are masculine and also a number that are feminine. We refer to such people as androgynous (see Bem, 1974).

I believe that this state of affairs holds for the city as well. Those elements that please and satisfy can exist independently of those that frustrate and disturb. The advantages and costs of urban living reside side by side. Therefore there is no contradiction, logically or experientially, between the simultaneous existence of both positive and negative aspects of city living. And although I do not intend to propose any single new term to depict the city in this manner, I will describe the city from a hot–cold, multiple- and contrasting-realities perspective throughout this book in order to deal with questions and debates about the nature of urban life.

Environmental-social psychology and the city

Before we go any farther in our discussion of the city, it might be best to take a step back and ask just what it is that the field of *psychology* can bring to this topic. After all, it is a widely held stereotype that psychologists are concerned with the inner workings of the individual, that they study the drives, motives, habits, and personalities of *people* – not of cities. The city is the realm of the sociologist, the historian, the political scientist, and the economist. What can a psychologist contribute to knowledge about cities, except perhaps to the study of community mental health?

To respond to this question, it would be reasonable to take a brief, if not highly superficial, look back at the roots of psychology and some of the directions in which the field has branched out. As members of a discipline concerning itself with individual behavior, psychologists have tended to look within the person, analyzing their subject for the most part as if it were isolated from its social surroundings. From early introspectionism to mental and personality testing to the study of memory, perception, and psychopathology, the primary focus was on looking inward rather than to what was around as a source of explanation for behavior. Although there were certainly some other trends in the field, it would be difficult to deny that this was the predominant orientation of psychology. It was not really until after World War II, and especially after the pioneering work of Kurt Lewin (1951), that the external context in which the individual functioned was considered very fully as a determinant of behavior. Lewin proposed the formula $B = f(P, E)$, defining behavior as a function of the person and the environment. Out of the acknowledgment that external forces determine behavior in interaction with internal forces, the field of social psychology grew. It emphasized not the characteristics of different kinds of people or the qualities of different settings but, rather, the relationship between the person and the environment, the interaction between the two.

Although it expanded the scope of psychology's interest by placing emphasis upon the external determinants of behavior, social psychology's conception of environment was still quite narrow. It was phrased largely in terms of other people or what has been called the *social* environment. For the most part, social psychology lost sight of the possible effects of the *physical* environment, the ecological context in which behavior was embedded. But, as a result of a number of important trends that converged most clearly in the 1960s (e.g., the desire to apply social psychological knowledge, a general concern with the state of the environment), the field of environmental psychology came to be defined.

This is largely where we come in: the city as environment, the city as a setting for behavior. What should be made clear about the perspective of this book is that I have no intention of trying to demarcate the world into physical as opposed to social things; even if I could, my interest would be not in one or the other but in both. In fact, this social-physical thing, the city, may be delineated quite usefully according to its cultural, economic, or political characteristics as well. Thus, while I shall maintain a psychological perspective on the city, it is possible to avoid being narrowly psychological by recognizing that behavior in the city is often a function of architectural and design features, of one's place in the social structure, and of political and economic pressures.

Our topic is urban behavior – the behavior of people in cities. All of those factors that determine it are of relevance to us. Yet what distinguishes this as a psychological approach is that our critical unit of analysis is still the *individual* or, to speak in terms of environmental psychology (Altman, 1973, 1976), the individual-in-the-city. In the course of this book we are likely to confront urban problems and the city's social and political organization, but it should be understood that these are of relevance to us only to the extent that they bear on individual behavior in the city.

Person-in-environment relationships: levels of analysis

Before we move along any farther into an exploration of the effects of the city on behavior, it is important to spell out more fully the framework that we will be using to account for the general relationship of environment to behavior. This framework or model has been called by some a filter model (Rapoport, 1977; Warr & Knapper, 1968), and it also bears resemblance to the organismic-developmental model of Seymour Wapner, Bernard Kaplan, and Saul Cohen (1973). This type of model suggests that there are a number of levels at which the environment may be described. The first of these is the *physical* or *objective* level – the "real world" out there. This type of objective description involves units that are well defined, can be counted, and do not depend on any personal evaluation. At this level a place could be defined according to its latitude and longitude, its average monthly temperature or rainfall, its square mileage, or its population size. The nature of the environment as described at the physical level may be an important determinant of behavior, certainly at extremes such as those of heat, cold, or density. But this is true more because it makes certain forms of behavior unlikely or impossible than because it requires that certain specific forms of behavior occur.

But places have meanings: They are seen and interpreted through a social-cultural filter. A structure made of two hundred thousand bricks and three tons of mortar that reaches two hundred feet in the air may have a name – *church* – and this name would bring to it a new and different significance. Defining a place at the social-cultural level endows it with certain characteristics known to most if not all of the members of a given social group. At this level of description, we can speak of signs, symbols, and meanings. Congregants of the church know where they should go and where they should avoid going, when to stand and when to be seated, when to be silent and when to chant in full voice. They are also likely to feel uplifted and inspired by the contents of the service. However, to those who speak a different cultural language, people who are outsiders to this culture, the patterns of behavior and messages will fail to be communicated. They may be misinterpreted or may simply make little or no sense. It is like the mythical observer from outer space who encounters the planet Earth for the first time at 5:00 P.M., hovering above a Los Angeles freeway. Noting what those within the culture would call a traffic jam, the extraterrestrial reports back that earthlings must have a highly advanced technological society: ''After all,'' the being reports, ''how else could they engineer and maintain such beautifully precise lines and intricate formations?''

Description at this level, therefore, accomplishes two things. First, as just stated, it gives meaning and significance to places. Second, it implies what forms of behavior are appropriate and encouraged (a place's prescriptive characteristics) and what forms of behavior are inappropriate and discouraged (its proscriptive characteristics). These messages, however widely held within a culture, are still likely to evoke little or no meaning for members of a different culture. The problems that places designed for members of one culture present for members of another will be discussed more fully in Chapter 7.

Further, places and things with specific definitions for a culture in general may take on different meanings for certain of its members as a result of the personal or subjective filters through which they pass. Depending on the differing needs, goals, interests, expectancies, past experiences, or emotional states of a pair of individuals, the same ''thing'' out there may be perceived quite differently. To an atheist the church has meanings quite different from those it has to the true believer; to a group of student radicals the university administration building has meanings very different from those it has to the college president. The environment as experienced may be common to a wide set of individuals because of its shared physical, structural, administrative, social, and cultural properties; but it is unique to each individual because each one perceives and organizes the world in ways that are idiosyncratic to him or her.

In Figures 1.1–1.3 we can see three very different views of Boston. In Figure 1.1, an aerial shot, we are afforded an objective mapping of at least part of the city. We can see its bridges, highways, and buildings and can gauge exact distances between different points. It is a view that would come out the same whether photographed by a native of Boston or a first-time visitor. Its language is physical and therefore universal.

In Figure 1.2 we get a different kind of mapping. It is also objective in one sense, but the kind and amount of information it conveys and the messages it implies are very different to members of the culture (Bostonians) and to those who are not members. The Bostonian will know which trolley lines are underground and which are not, which are more reliable than others, which are safe to ride at night; and as the Kingston Trio once sang about Charlie on the MTA, how much one has to pay and whether one has to pay extra to

Figure 1.1. The objective level of description: Boston as seen from an aerial photograph. Landslides/Alex S. MacLean.

get off ("Will he ever return?"). It says to the native that Arlington is the stop for the Public Garden and that North Station is where to get off for the Italian festivals. To the nonresident it communicates far less.

In Figure 1.3 we have my own personal map of Boston. Just as a fingerprint is unique, no other map of Boston would be exactly the same, since this is the product of one individual's experiences and knowledge. It is neither accurate nor complete, and it distorts scale and direction. Some parts of the city are left out completely, whereas other parts are depicted in some detail. How personal cognitive maps are developed and the role they play will be discussed in Chapter 4.

This basic distinction between the "perceived" and the "actual" environment is not new. In 1935 Kurt Koffka, one of the leaders in the Gestalt school of psychology, distinguished between the geographical (objective) environment and the behavioral (subjective) environment. At about the same time Henry Murray (1938), a leading personality psychologist, was referring to external conditions (presses) that have effects on behavior. The distinction he made between an alpha press (the environment as it actually is) and a beta

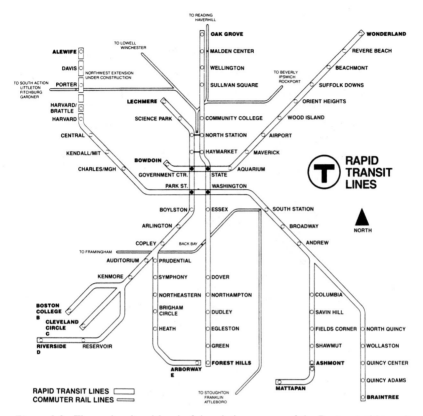

Figure 1.2. The sociocultural level of description: a map of the Boston rapid transit system. (C) MBTA 1982. Reproduced by permission of the Massachusetts Bay Transportation Authority.

press (the environment as interpreted by the person) closely parallels that of the Gestaltists. Lewin, influenced by the Gestalt school himself, made the same distinction. In fact, the E of his $B = f(P,E)$ formula refers not to the objective environment but to the environment as it is perceived.

Figure 1.4 represents a version of this model, of which there are a number of important features. First, whereas the determination of behavior must begin with the constraints of the real world and whereas these may be very strong, their effect is still indirect. That is, the physical environment has its effect through social-cultural and personal definitions of a situation. It is the individual's interpretation and assessment of a situation that ultimately and most directly determines his or her behavior. And although it may prove to be almost as accurate and far more efficient to predict behavior in the aggregate by disregarding the subjective level, we must still recognize its role concep-

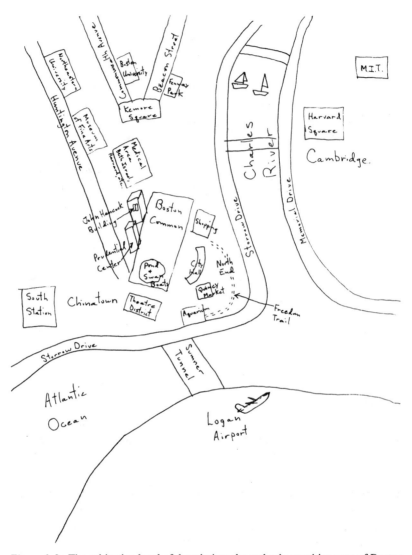

Figure 1.3. The subjective level of description: the author's cognitive map of Boston.

tually. In addition, one level does not merely superimpose meanings on the last; rather, each level provides input and feedback to each adjacent level (note the dotted lines in Figure 1.4).

Let us take an example directly pertaining to the experience of the city. Natives of New York often develop an incurable case of New York-centrism. Native New Yorkers such as me think Philadelphia is small and Boston quaint.

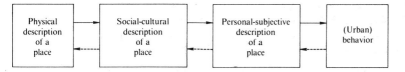

Figure 1.4. Levels of description and their relationship to behavior.

When I arrived fresh from New York in Ann Arbor, Michigan (population approximately ninety thousand then), to do my graduate work, I was overjoyed to find it was a pleasant, easygoing, clean, friendly *small town*. It was easy to get from one place to another, and in addition the town was safe at all times. And my perception had clear effects on my behavior. Although I had three locks and chains on my door on the Lower East Side of New York, I often did not bother to lock my door when I went out in Ann Arbor. Also, I could not get over the ease of the pace and the politeness of the drivers ("Imagine, they actually stop at stop signs here").

I naturally assumed that my view of Ann Arbor was universally shared until I began comparing notes with a friend from a small town in rural Kansas. I first noticed that he locked his car at all times, even if he were going to leave it for just a moment. He commented that people didn't do that at all back in Kansas, but that in a *big city* like Ann Arbor a person couldn't be too careful. He also said that it was quite an adjustment to get used to the traffic, the pollution, and the impatience of the people on and off the road.

One might think that we were living in two different places, and in a certain sense we were, although in other ways we were not. The world each of us was acting upon was a subjective or personal world of impressions and interpretations. The total range of cues, signs, and stimuli available to each had been filtered so that some of the information was amplified, whereas some was weakened or eliminated. In short, for each of us the data on the environment were transformed in a unique pattern with a unique meaning and different behavioral implications.

Yet it is dangerous to go to the extreme in overemphasizing the subjective perspective on behavior in the city. As Joachim Wohlwill (1973) has stated, "The environment is not in the head" (p. 166). There are certain fixed, undeniable properties of any environment that limit the range of interpretations, images, possibilities, and behavior. Although distortion and biases vary as a function of the individual, knowing how individuals differ merely helps us to account for additional variance in their behavior in relation to the "objective" environment. We must remember that behavior, more specifically urban behavior, is the property of a person-in-environment *system* and is not an attribute of a person. As a result, we might even go so far as to say that the most interesting piece of information we can get about an environment involves the degree of agreement or correspondence between objective data and subjective data. When there is a low rate of crime in a neighborhood park as indicated by police statistical reports, but people are still afraid to use it, or when there is a high rate of crime in a particular neighborhood, yet people refuse to leave it, these discrepancies offer us information that analysis at either level alone fails to provide.

Person-environment models

The discussion so far can be rephrased to provide three different views of person-in-environment. These range from the individual as a shaper of the environment, to a more interactive or dynamic exchange approach of person-environment relations, to the other extreme, where the environment is seen as the shaper of human behavior. The last of these, environmental *determinism*, implies that external forces dictate responses and require people to behave in specific ways. Determinists use an extensive battery of causal verbs, which suggest that people are *pushed*, *driven*, or *led inevitably* to certain decisions and behaviors (Sproul & Sproul, 1956). This is a passive view of the individual and downplays the ability to select and choose, to arrange and change the environment to fit one's needs.

At the other extreme, in a position described as *possibilism*, the environment is conceived of as a medium that presents opportunities rather than constraints. According to this model, the ability to make choices and accomplish things through directed efforts is seen as an important characteristic of the person; and it is the environment that is acted upon and determined rather than vice versa. It is as if the environment were a stage and the performance of a play were limited only somewhat by its size and shape. It is a view that sees the actors as capable of improvising action and creating dialogue on their own – of determining their own fate with little help or interference from the surrounding environment.

Finally, the position that we shall adopt involves the idea of dynamic interchange (Ittelson, Proshansky, Rivlin, & Winkel, 1974) and comes closest to what others (Porteous, 1977; Rapoport, 1977) have labeled *probabilism*. According to this view, the environment does not simply determine behavior, nor does it merely provide possibilities, but rather it makes certain choices more likely than others. It supports rather than requires; it discourages rather than prohibits. It can reinforce certain preexisting modes of behavior and can elicit and enable new forms, but it cannot "create" behavior. It can and often does provide limits on behavior, but an environment such as the city can also enlarge one's range of awareness and create greater freedom of choice by making explicit latent possibilities and opportunities. When we think of the environment in these terms, person and environment cannot be separated but rather are thought of as constituting a single system. Moreover, the relationship of person to environment is dynamic rather than static. There is a constant give and take, with each part of the system providing reciprocal influence on the other. We shape our environments and are in turn shaped by them in a never-ending cycle of mutual influence. As a result, we can make generalizations about urban behavior, but we should not conceive of such behavior as having necessary consequences or as providing uniform patterns for all people.

A matter of fit

A final issue concerning this environmental-social approach follows from the Lewinian dictum $B = f(P,E)$ and is consistent with the multiple- and contrasting-realities approach. The Lewinian formula implies that it is inappropriate to refer to something as a good or bad environment, as either the evil, menacing city or the good, idyllic countryside. Rather, certain environments will fit the needs, values, desires, and preferred lifestyles of some people but will be incompatible with those of others. When there is a "good fit" between people and their environment, they are happy, productive, and satisfied. But as the degree of fit between them and their environment decreases, the levels of satisfaction and productivity fall.

There is a great deal of evidence on this point, whether the people are students in a college or workers on the job. Nevitt Sanford (1962), in overstating the case, has said, "An environment must be suited to the species; if it isn't the organisms die or go elsewhere" (p. 727). Although Sanford may have underestimated the ability of humans to effect change in their environments or to adapt to them successfully, there is no doubt what his message is. I myself have moved from New York City (which I dearly love and hate) to a small place just outside a smaller city (Boston). I am quite satisfied there and cannot imagine ever returning to live in New York. When I ask my brother why he continues to live and raise his children in a "bad neighborhood" in New York, he tells me that whenever he leaves it for too long he needs to return in order to thrive on the chaos. We will pick up on this issue of needs for differing input levels in Chapter 5.

Similarly, a well-known social psychologist was complaining one day about the limitations of the university in which he was teaching. I asked him why he chose to teach in New York rather than go elsewhere to a school that he might like better. He replied that although he thought his own institution was a good one, if he were ever given the choice between a second-rate school in a great city or a great university in a second-rate city, he would always opt for the great city. I am sure that there are many readers whose choice would be just the opposite, but it should be clear that the point is not who is right and who is wrong, but – whichever the preference – whether it is right *for that person.*

What is a city?

Now that we have established the nature of our perspective on cities and city life, it is still necessary to take one more step backward before moving forward. That is, we ought to ask ourselves a question that at first glance appears deceptively simple: What is a city? By realizing that we can relate to this question at any number of levels and from a great many professional perspectives we come to recognize that there are many possible answers, each one having different implications for *how* we study urban life, *what* we study about urban life, and even what *answers* we are likely to come up with.

To the geographer or demographer the city represents a specific physical location where large numbers of people are concentrated in a small space. The political scientist sees the city as a unique administrative unit with a given internal power structure and a set of relationships to other political entities. The sociologist sees the city as a particular set of institutions and social organizations; and the anthropologist sees it as a place with certain cultural features and dominant values. Social and environmental psychologists, as I said before, are likely to visualize cities in terms of a set of social behavior patterns and interpersonal orientations. For instance, Harold Proshansky, as part of a definition of the city, referred to it as "a set of *human activities* concentrated in a geographical area" (quoted in Krupat, 1982, p. 330).

If instead of asking professional urban analysts for their definitions we were to ask the typical man or woman on the street, the answers would vary even more widely, according to *where* we asked, *when* we asked, and *whom* we asked. The answers would undoubtedly derive from each person's own relationship to, values regarding, and experience with, the city (i.e., the subjective point of view). For some who live outside the city it may be a place to escape to, a symbol of boundless hope and great opportunity. For others it is a place of evil, temptation, and corruption. Still other outsiders would tell us what a wonderful place it is to visit, adding, "But I wouldn't want to live there." For those who live in the city by choice, it may mean excitement, stimulation, and culture. But for those who feel trapped there it may mean poverty, fear, isolation, and disappointment. Once again, we see the city as a place of multiple and contrasting realities.

Let us take something that is even more basic: We all know that Chicago, San Francisco, and Boston are cities. So too are Indianapolis, Toledo, and Denver. But how about Des Moines, Iowa? Of course it is. It has a population of over two hundred thousand; it has a large art museum; and it is the capital of the state. Just ask anyone living in Des Moines what a thriving metropolis it is. But ask a New Yorker and you might get a different answer. Or ask some of the residents of Alton, Kansas (population two hundred), and compare their answers to those of members of the other two groups.

Regardless of whose perspective we look from, is it right to imply that the city is concentrated in or even limited to a given geographical area? Should we be speaking of a place – the city – or simply of a concept – urbanization? Long ago this question was easy to answer. The city had walls around it; it was a place to conduct trade and seek protection. These walls not only served their primary purpose of keeping invaders out but also kept certain ideas and values in. In more ways than one we could clearly demarcate where the city of the past began and where it ended.

Today, however, with the advent of modern means of transportation and the widespread influence of the media, the matter of where the city starts and stops is far more complicated than locating its physical boundaries. The ideas and values that come with urbanization are pervasive. Leonard Reissman (1970) has gone so far as to state that "the study of the city has become the study of contemporary society" (p. 3). He suggests that the effects of the city so totally engulf us that Thoreau's Walden Pond, the symbol of total retreat from the pressures and tensions of the city, "is only to be reached by a super-highway, through the television antenna forest, and directed all the way by road signs" (p. 9). Therefore, there is a part of the city in all of us, regardless of where we live or where we were raised. Yet the city is such a large and complex entity that its effects on the person and its contributions to personality and behavior are likely to be unique for each person. A discussion of these effects and contributions makes up the subject matter of the rest of this book.

The plan of this book

To this point I have stated a perspective on urban life, the perspective of environmental-social psychology. This point of view implies that my focus is on the *individual* in the city, on the impact and experience of the environment and the person's reactions to the subjective and symbolic meanings it conveys. Yet I will focus not on the individual alone but on the interrelationships and interactions of people in the city, on the individual as a member of social networks. An important feature of this perspective involves seeing the person, the group, and the environment as a single system each part of which constantly influences the others. The city makes certain demands on its residents, and they respond by making certain demands on each other and on the environment itself in an endless cycle.

In addition, I have stated that to understand urban life we must be ready to accept that it is full of apparent contradictions in the coexistence of good and bad, rich and poor, isolation and integration. I have suggested, however, that both positive and negative elements exist independently in such a way that the single most distinctive characteristic of urban life is the presence of both extremes. Therefore, the social reality of urban life can be hot and cold as well as lukewarm, and whenever we approach the issue of good and bad, it must always be considered as a question of the fit among person, purposes, and environment.

In the chapters to follow, I will attempt to describe the nature and experience of urban living within this context. In the rest of Part I – comprising Chapters 2, 3, and 4 – I will pursue a basic path, asking just how the city is seen from a number of points of view. First we will look at the ways in which city and town have been differentiated by social commentators and social scientists; then we will note the distinctive features of life used by various theorists to capture the essence of urban living; and then we will go inside the minds of urban residents themselves to look at their own cognitive images of the city.

Specifically, Chapter 2 addresses an issue so basic that it is often taken for granted. As the example about the status of Des Moines suggests, we have no straightforward, universally agreed-upon dimensions to distinguish city from non-city or even one city from another. This chapter points out that both objective and subjective criteria should be used to describe what cities are, and that a combination of the two is the most useful form of description we can have.

Chapter 3 builds on this discussion. In it we note that whereas cities differ from towns most obviously in size, a full description of urban life must go beyond head counting to consider the broad range of experiential consequences of population size. In this chapter we focus on the distinctive features that various theorists have seized upon and the models of urban life that have grown from these. In particular, we consider the anonymity that size can bring, the potential overload on our eyes and ears that accompanies daily life in the city, the number of behavior settings available to the urbanite, and the ways in which subcultures form – all in addition to the basic demographic facts of size, density, and population heterogeneity.

The focus changes in Chapter 4 from the description of the city by social scientists to the image of the city held by the urban resident. In this chapter we consider how the presence of a clear and consistent cognitive image allows city residents to move about their environs and to feel confident and secure while they are doing so; and we see how this image contributes to the development of emotional attachments and allows for symbolic communication among city people. We then analyze cognitive maps, looking at their various elements and the ways in which they develop. We will note that these maps vary from person to person and city to city, and we will ask why they do so and what consequences this variation can have.

In Part II – comprising Chapters 5–8 – we get closer to the experience of urban living itself and consider how city people deal with their environment. In Chapter 5 stress and coping are the key concepts. We analyze the position that the city is too crowded, too noisy, too overwhelming for people to live in comfortably. In reviewing the research evidence on crowding and noise in particular, we will discover that the evidence about the effects of these factors is anything but consistent. As a result, it will be suggested that depending on past experiences, personal styles, and individual needs, some people may experience high levels of stimulation as unmanageable, overwhelming, and disruptive, whereas others may prefer or even require an exciting and stimulating environment in order to function at their highest level.

Chapter 6 looks at the individual not as an information processor but as a support seeker – in the sense of social stimulation rather than physical stimulation. In this chapter we address the question of whether the stereotype of the lonely, isolated urbanite is an accurate one. Once again, in a critical look at the literature we find a good deal of inconsistency. We note that although the city is such a large place that in absolute numbers there are undoubtedly many people who are lonely and feel alienated, this should not be taken to mean that the ''average'' city person is any less involved in deep and caring friendships than a person living elsewhere. We will note that the distinction between relations in public and in private is an important one, and we will then go on to consider the distribution of urban attachments as well as their quality and quantity. Within this context we will consider the meaning of the terms *neighborhood* and *community* for the urban dweller.

In Chapter 7 we go beyond a consideration of how the city person is affected by other people, either by their numbers (as in crowding) or by their relationships (as in friendships). Here we discuss the city as a physical environment in terms of the arrangement of rooms, housing, neighborhoods. We will look at what architecture, design, and planning can do – and also what they cannot do. We will review a number of ''design disasters'' in order to see why these projects failed and to consider how the findings of social science research could help avoid similar mistakes in the future. It will be noted that good design cannot be expected to solve the problems of the city, nor is bad design the cause of urban crime, fear, or unrest. Rather, we will see how certain forms of design can help facilitate the expression of basic human needs. In particular, we will review examples of social scientist-architect-planner collaboration in the creation of ''defensible space'' in urban public housing.

In Chapter 8 we will briefly review some of the main themes and urban characteristics found throughout the book. Most specifically, we will consider how size brings with it the advantage of diversity and at the same time the disadvantage of loss of control. We will consider some alternatives to the city, especially the suburb and the new town, and see how these fare on diversity and control. Finally, we will examine some suggestions for ways of increasing the amount of control that city dwellers feel they have over their lives, while at the same time maintaining and accentuating the diversity that city living brings.

Suggestions for further reading

Fisher, J. D., Bell, P. A., & Baum, A. 1984. *Environmental psychology* (2nd ed.). New York: Holt, Rinehart & Winston.

Holahan, C. J. 1982. *Environmental psychology*. New York: Random House.

Krupat, E. (Ed.). 1980. Urban life: Applying a social psychological perspective. *Journal of Social Issues*, *3* (Whole).

Porteous, J. D. 1977. *Environment and behavior: Planning and everyday urban life*. Reading, Mass.: Addison-Wesley.

Reissman, L. 1970. *The urban process*. New York: Free Press.

2

URBAN CHARACTERISTICS: CITY VERSUS CITY AND CITY VERSUS TOWN

city/ 'sit-ē/   *a center of population larger or more important than a town or village.*
– Webster's New World Dictionary, *1982*

If we think of this book as a guided tour through urban life via social psychology, we might say that Chapter 1 has taken us from the airport to the city limits. We are now about to encounter this thing called the city at first hand and try to make sense of it. In many ways the goal of the social scientist is the same as that of any visitor. We want to understand and to comprehend this place and then be able to comment on its way of life. We want to see its streets, know its people, soak up its flavor, and then capture all this on paper.

Novelists, poets, and essayists have made this attempt throughout history, and it is largely their descriptions by which cities are known. Although the last thing we would want to do as social scientists is to ignore or dismiss these writings, it is important to realize that we also want to go beyond them. Most important, we want to describe the city and its way of life in ways that can be *systematized*. We want, first of all, to find the means to compare and contrast city with city and city with town. Second, we want to be able to find a way to compare our descriptions with those of others. And third, we want to be able to test our own impressions from one time to another.

In reference to this first and all-encompassing goal, the reader will note that throughout this chapter our focus will vary: Sometimes it will be on ways of comparing one large city with another, and then almost immediately we will be comparing the city with some other type of community. This variation will not be confusing if we keep in mind the essential fact that community types differ by degrees. There is no such thing as a rural-urban *dichotomy*; if anything, there is a rural-urban *continuum* (or, as we will see later, more than one continuum).

This is to say that many different qualities distinguish the city from the town, such as size, density, cultural activities, or even possibly friendliness. These, however, are the very characteristics by which we can distinguish one large city from another. Every community, regardless of what we call it, has each of these qualities to some degree; and it will be our job to identify those which are most relevant so that we can compare communities on a relative basis. Therefore, whatever characteristics one chooses as the essence of "cityness," we can assume that the city has more of them than the non-city – and that some cities have still more than others.

In this chapter we will take a guided tour through a number of American cities looking for these qualities. We will, however, be escorted by two kinds of guides. Our first exploration will be through the eyes of the novelist, poet, and social critic. They will draw us a very rich portrait, but one that is full of ambiguities and conflicting opinions. The second tour will be conducted by the social scientist, who will foresake some vividness of description in exchange for more systematic ways of capturing the environment.

Social commentary on the city: the good and the bad

The idea of city rarely elicits a neutral reaction from people in the twentieth century, whether they live within or beyond the city limits. More often than not the response has been negative. Terms like *urban crisis* and *moral bankruptcy of the city* are hardly uncommon, and when people speak positively about the city it is usually not so much spontaneous praise as a defense against critics. It is quite informative to note the title of the most widely cited volume on urban literature and American history: *The Intellectual vs. the City* (White & White, 1962). Note the relational term used – it is not "*and* the City" or "*for* the City" but clearly a case of an adversary relationship.

A popular children's book, *The Little House* (Burton, 1942), winner of the Caldecott Award for 1942, sums up the prevailing sentiment in the direct way that only a children's story can provide. A cute little house sits happily on a hill in the middle of nowhere. It is quite content until the nearby city stirs and starts moving in. Full of smoke, cars, filth, and giant buildings, it continues to grow until the little house is trapped behind a freeway and between two huge office buildings. The house feels very sad. But of course the ending is a happy one. A couple notices it, buys it, puts it on a truck, and moves it out to the country, where it lives happily ever after among the trees, birds, and flowers.

On a more serious note, Irving Howe (1971), a noted literary critic, points out that antiurban feelings in Western civilization have deep roots going back into the Judeo-Christian tradition. Biblical accounts of life in large human concentrations depict it most often as difficult, unpleasant, or simply evil. Many tales of suffering and trouble derive from these places. Stories featuring evil characters and evil urbanlike places – Sodom and Gomorrah, the tower of Babel, and the whore of Babylon, for example – dot the Old and New Testaments. Then there are particular characters who personify the good and the simple, who embody values that are seen as inconsistent with city life. One such person is Joseph, who is forced to leave his family's pastoral setting and venture into the corrupt Egyptian court. His is the success story of a small-town boy who overcomes temptation and returns to his father and the land. And then there is Jesus of Nazareth, the simple shepherd of his flock.

In literature and in the minds of intellectuals, the city has been seen as a setting that replaces spontaneity with calculation, honesty with deceit, the heart with the head, and the sacred with the secular. Writers such as Emerson, Hawthorne, Thoreau, and Poe preferred the solitude of the wilderness. Their works dealt with themes such as the alienation and loneliness of the city, the breakdown of tradition, the impact of mechanization, and the materialism of urban values. Follow nature, their argument runs – and since life in the city does not, it must be bad (Reissman, 1970).

Yet whereas most people attribute the antiurban bias among intellectuals to the romantic and primitivist complaint that urban life is too civilized, White and White (1962) point out that the city has also been attacked on its other flank. That is, people like Henry James and John Dewey have complained that the American city is *not enough* civilized (i.e., is too "cold" as well as too "hot"). For James and Dewey the American city lacked the sophistication, the history and charm, the elevated conversation and face-to-face communication that they valued. In short, they judged it vulgar, chaotic, and gaudy. But if James felt disappointed with New York, it was because it compared poorly to London and Paris, other great cities, not because he preferred the feel of the soil or the quiet of Walden Pond. Even today, noted social critics (e.g., Nathan Glazer, 1984) assert that European cities such as Paris continue to maintain a sense of vitality – Paris is a "city that works" – whereas American cities such as New York do not.

But in addition to the formal attacks on the city by intellectuals and writers as too much or too little civilized, there are some other, subtle reasons why it has a bad reputation. These reasons are psychological in nature rather than historical or political. The first involves the ways in which information is processed and the noticeability of bad over good. Just as we never pay attention to any of the hundreds and hundreds of safe landings at the local airport but sit up and take notice when there is a single plane crash, so it is in the city that news is always made when something bad happens but rarely when something good does. We take little note of the thousands of people who are polite, pleasant, or at least predictable; but we remember and accentuate our encounters with those who are rude, disagreeable, or strange. In a city, regardless of the ratio of positive to negative encounters, the mere volume of people and interactions almost guarantees that the absolute number of negative encounters will be higher than in a small town. And given the heightened salience of negative information, these impressions tend to be stronger and longer-lasting.

Another aspect of the way we notice the bad more than the good involves the services, amenities, and opportunities that we take for granted in a city.

Just as we never appreciate electricity until the lights go out or moderate temperatures until the mercury hits 90 degrees Fahrenheit, so too we rarely appreciate the educational, social, and cultural opportunities – even the municipal services that the city offers until we leave or lose them. We do not often comment on the efficiency of garbage collection (when it is efficient), but we brood and complain about the sanitation workers' strike; we rarely appreciate the fact that there might be fifty or more movie theaters in a city until we move to a town with only one or two.

For all the antiurban bias (whatever the reason), the city is obviously not without its defenders. For those who prefer nature, there is Edgar Anderson's reply (cited in Cahill & Cooper, 1971): "Nature watching is quite as easy in the city as in the country; all one has to do is to accept man as part of nature" (p. 5). For those who prefer solitude there is Richard Bissell's (1950) rejoinder: "A big dirty city is better than a technicolor sunrise out in the sticks, no matter how many songbirds are tweeting. In the city you may feel lost, but you also figure you are not missing anything" (p. 33). And for those who worry about the more basic needs and deplore the crowds, the noise, and the dirt, there is Lewis Lapham's (1976) defense of great cities:

The freedom of the city is the freedom of the mind and the freedom of expression. So precious is this freedom that the inhabitants of a great city pay an excessively high price to obtain it. What provincial opinion regards as unmitigated evil – bad air, noise, crowds, tenements, dirt, heavy taxes, corrupt government and crime – the residents of the city regard as the cost of liberty. It is the nature of great cities to be filthy, loud and dangerous (cf. Elizabethan London and the Paris of the Enlightenment) but the freedom of the mind allows the inhabitants to ignore and make light of their circumstances. [P. 8]

Box 2.1 illustrates these pro- and antiurban issues further. It shows that for a single city, New York, very strong positive and negative sentiments can come from different observers, even that thoughts of the city can run hot and cold in the same mind. Ambivalence about city living is hardly unusual.

Once you've seen one, have you seen them all?

We recognize at this point that although the city has its supporters, the prevailing trend has been negative. Yet if we take this finding a bit farther we come quickly to a second conclusion: Not all cities are alike. New York is not equivalent to Denver, which is not the same as Dallas, which is not just like San Diego. Some cities have better reputations than others and are often singled out for praise, whereas others are constantly being criticized. Just as there are ethnic jokes, there is also urban humor. There's the one about the contest where first prize is a free trip for one whole week to

The Good

"New York is a skyline, the most stupendous, unbelievable, man-made spectacle since the hanging gardens of Babylon." (*Jacques Barzun*)

"[New York] is the place where all the aspirations of the Western World meet to form one vast master aspiration, as powerful as the suction of a steam dredge. It is the icing on the pie called Christian civilization." (*H. L. Mencken*)

"New York is our last frontier, the place where persons of spirit are drawn together by a magnet. It is the 'moving frontier' of American culture, the most important site of progress and innovation." (*Anselm Strauss*)

"New York has taught me the solace of walls. I feel more comfortable in a subway than a field, more willing to concentrate on something with momentum than on a landscape that will not flicker or revolve." (*Michael Goldstein*)

"New York lays hands upon one's bowels; he grows drunk with ecstasy; he grows young and full of glory; he feels that he can never die." (*Thomas Wolfe*)

The Bad

"New York, where sheer enormity has consumed so much humanity." (*William Marline*)

"You could see for 150 miles in any direction except south. New York had literally gone under a cloud, a cloud of its own making. It grabs you sometimes in the cockpit. You don't need an approach plate [flight map] for New York. You can breathe your way in." (*Pilot Robert Jenkins, on taking off from Albany, New York*)

"New York, city with a heart of nylon." (*Paul Morand*)

"Scoundrels and in some cases ruffians terrified the citizens. Young mothers had to take their babies to Central Park in armored cars. Old women went to the theater in tanks and no pretty women would venture forth after dark unless convoyed by a regiment of troops . . . the police wore bullet-proof underwear and were armed with mortars and 15 inch howitzers." (*James Reston, writing of the New York-to-be*)

The Ambivalent

"New York City, the incomparable, the brilliant star city of cities, the Cyclopean paradox, the inferno with no out-of-bounds, the supreme expression of both the miseries and splendors of contemporary civilization . . . at once the climactic synthesis of America and yet the negation of America." (*John Gunther*)

Box 2.1. New York: the ultimate setting of multiple and contrasting realities

Philadelphia. Second prize, of course, is two weeks in Philadelphia. Or the one that states that if you stop and ask some natives of Indianapolis where to go for a good dinner, they will immediately begin to give you directions to Chicago. The question, and it is a deceptively easy-sounding one, is what makes one city different from or better than another?

Unfortunately, psychologists have few direct answers for this question. It should be noted that within the field of psychology there is a clearly defined subfield concerned with individual differences *between people*, but there is no comparable area of study concerned with individual differences *between places*. The systematic study and classification of environments has not been attempted by psychologists in any great numbers (see Argyle, 1981; Fredericksen, 1972; Magnussen, 1981; and Moos, 1973 for some exceptions).

Yet as Anselm Strauss (1976) has pointed out, "The entire complex of urban life can be thought of as a person rather than a distinctive place, and the city can be endowed with a personality – or, to use common parlance – a character of its own" (p. 14). He adds that cities, like people, have biographies and reputations and can be thought of as having the capacity to act in certain ways and possess particular resources.

How do we capture the personality of a great city? How do we reduce its essence to something manageable, yet meaningful? In the past, social scientists did not even attempt this task; they are only now daring to take the plunge. This has always been the writer's turf. In his book *Images of the American City*, Strauss (1976) has collected a number of striking urban characterizations. There is Milwaukee, "which sits in a complacent shabbiness on the west shore of Lake Michigan like a wealthy old lady in black alpaca taking her ease on the beach" (p. 14). Houston is like "an incipient heavyweight champion in its pimply faced adolescence" (p. 20); and Rochester is "like a successful, well-adjusted individual of middle age" (p. 20). Abler and Adams (1976) refer to Carl Sandburg's Chicago as a "tall bold slugger set vivid against the soft, little cities"; Atlanta, they note, "has the nerve of a great mule. If it could suck as hard as it can blow, it would bring the ocean to it and become a seaport" (p. 247).

At other times a city's personality is captured not so much through its own characteristics as through the traits of another urban center. In Box 2.2 we see a sampling of city-to-city comparisons, each capturing the flavor of one by contrasting it with the other.

The products of the social scientist will never approach the brilliance and eloquence of the writer. The novelist and poet use broad or fine strokes as they please and create urban portraits that are both vivid and subtle. There is a richness in their words that no statistic will ever capture. Yet in exchange for vividness of description, the writer gives up (perhaps quite willingly) the ability to be objective and systematic. Since the writer is free to pick and

"London retains the benefits of the enormous wealth of the nineteenth century, the booty of an empire, which was poured into parks and spacious avenues and wondrous monuments . . . New York's gain from the nineteenth century was the immigrants, and the elevator, which we took as divine revelation that people should be enabled to live 34 stories above the ground." (*Jane O'Reilly*)

"San Diego is the good Los Angeles. There the Southern California paradise still exists – worked over perhaps, but not destroyed . . . San Diego represents a Mark II version of Los Angeles – cleaner, more controlled . . . a paradise not yet lost." (*Robert Montgomery*)

"In Boston they ask, how much does he know? In New York, how much is he worth? In Philadelphia, who were his parents?" (*Mark Twain*)

"New Yorkers stay here because this is where all the thinking is done. You lose an I.Q. point for each year you live in Los Angeles. You know what they talk about out there? They talk about what's going on in New York." (*Rex Reed*)

Box 2.2. City-to-city comparisons

choose the aspects of a city that are treated, and to relate them back to his or her own values, the result leaves us no basis for comparisons across communities, across writers, or even over time. When we consider the accounts of various communities offered by writers, it is impossible to know the extent to which we are discovering something about the *place*, rather than about the *commentator*. The approach of the social scientist is to go beyond one individual's opinion to look at collective opinions, or even to avoid opinion altogether and see if there are not some standard criteria by which urban quality can be judged. In short, social scientists ask what kinds of "data" they can generate about cities and the quality of life in them.

As Reissman (1970) points out, anyone who has ever been to at least two cities and speculated on the differences between them has begun the social scientist's task of imagining some index to classify their similarities and differences. In the rest of this chapter we will consider the two major approaches that have been used to differentiate and classify cities. The first of these utilizes *objective* data to measure urban conditions as they are and draws inferences from these. The second approach emphasizes the use of self-reports, or the *subjective* opinions of large samples of people concerning one or more communities. These contrasting approaches correspond to the distinction discussed in Chapter 1 between studying the "actual" and studying the "perceived" environment.

Objective approaches to urban description

Approaches that are objective rely on events and objects that can be counted and require as little personal evalution as possible. Because the determination of such objective figures is based upon record sorting or head counting, those who use them feel assured that they are accurate or nonbiased indicators.

Early efforts

One of the first attempts at developing an objective scientific index by which to differentiate cities can be traced back to E. L. Thorndike, a psychologist far better known for his classic contributions to the field of learning theory. In *Your City* (1939) and also *144 Smaller Cities* (1940) Thorndike asked himself what makes a city a good place to live and developed a "G" or goodness score for each of 310 large American cities. To derive the criteria for differentiation, Thorndike chose thirty-seven items and summed them into a single score. He justified the selection of these particular items by stating that they represented "those which all reasonable persons would regard as significant for the goodness of life for good people in a city" (cited in Reissman, 1970, p. 84). Items were chosen from five categories – educational opportunities for the public, healthfulness of the city, public recreational opportunities, creature comforts, and degree of literacy – with a sixth grouping of fourteen miscellaneous items.

Among Thorndike's more noteworthy findings was that one-quarter of the variation between cities was a consequence of differences in the wealth and level of income in them. Another two-fifths of the variation could be attributed to what he referred to as "quality of the people" (degree of use of public libraries, per capita number of high school graduates, etc.). Although Thorndike did produce some interesting findings, his techniques were rather crude compared to modern methodologists'. Still, he did provide a model for others (Bechtel, 1973; Berry, 1972) to follow.

Robert Angell, a noted sociologist, thought that the differences in the quality of urban life should not be determined by a mere conglomeration of differing items. Instead, he proposed (Angell, 1951) a conceptual basis for classification that he called *moral integration*, defining this term as the "degree to which there is a set of common ends and values toward which all are oriented and in terms of which the life of the group is oriented" (p. 2).

In operationalizing this concept Angell considered that there ought to be both a positive and a negative reflection of a city's moral integration (or lack of it). On the positive side, he reasoned that the citizens of a city that was morally integrated should have a strong sense of responsibility for their neighbors and should be willing to sacrifice their own private interests for the public good. As a result, such a city ought to have a strong welfare effort. In developing and refining his Welfare Effort Index, he considered the amount raised by local sources in comparison to the quota set by the city and the number of pledgers relative to the number of available families; he corrected these figures by the overall wealth of the community. On the negative side, Angell suggested that the more tightly knit a community was, the less violation of persons and property there would be. Therefore, he derived a crime score from statistics on murder, robbery, burglary, and other felonies.

The findings of Angell's research contain some mild surprises. First of all, the two indexes of moral integration were found to be only moderately correlated; knowing the welfare effort in a given city helped account for only about 15 percent of the variance in crime rate. Second, in contrast to Thorndike's findings, income level was not associated with moral integration – nor, for that matter, were variables such as size of city or church membership. Rather, moral integration was most closely related to the heterogeneity and mobility of the population (i.e., the more heterogeneous the population, the higher the Crime Index and the lower the Welfare Effort Index). Finally, it might be interesting to know that using Angell's 1947 figures the four best cities in the United States were Rochester and Syracuse, New York; Erie, Pennsylvania; and Worcester, Massachusetts. The four worst were Atlanta, Georgia; Miami, Florida; Tulsa, Oklahoma; and Memphis, Tennessee.

Economic-functional approaches

One of the most influential traditions in the classification of cities focuses on their economic base or productive specialization. This approach recognizes that the type of economic activity that predominates in a given city should attract and require certain kinds of people and place certain social demands on the community for needed skills and services. In 1937 W. F. Ogburn developed such a typology by determining the degree to which a specific city deviated from the characteristics of an "average city." For instance, since in the average city 17 percent of the population were engaged in commercial trade, a city with more than 20 percent of the population in this form of commerce was designated a "trading center."

C. D. Harris (1943) took a different approach, defining cities according to their "dominant economic activity." Setting minimum required percentages somewhat arbitrarily, he classified cities as manufacturing, retail, transportation, wholesale, mining, university, resort and retirement, or diversified, the last a broad catchall category in which no single activity was predominant.

This approach has been criticized (Hadden & Borgatta, 1965; Reissman, 1970) on a number of grounds, including the lack of comparability of results across studies: Depending on the system used, a given city might end up being classified in any number of ways. Another problem is that the functional categories used are not mutually exclusive, so that for large cities in which many different kinds of economic activities take place simultaneously, there is no alternative but to use the catchall label.

City classification analysis

Brian J. L. Berry, a geographer whose research is within a tradition known as city classification analysis, has been critical of much of this work because (1) it often generates one-dimensional solutions to urban classification and (2) even when the results are multidimensional, they are based on fairly obvious or "manifest" qualities of cities (Berry, 1972). As a result, he believes that such typologies fit well only where they were obvious in the first place. Berry suggests instead that the manifest similarities between communities may be due to more subtle or "latent" traits.

In order to discover what these latent dimensions are, Berry chose ninety-seven widely varied demographic and economic statistics derived from census and other standard record sources. He analyzed these figures for more than seventeen hundred "urban places," as he refers to them – cities with ten thousand or more people in both 1950 and 1960. Using factor analysis, Berry uncovered fourteen latent dimensions of the American urban system, including the economic power of the city, the socioeconomic status of the residents, recent population growth, and various aspects of the city's economic basis.

Although Berry has rejected the unidimensional classification of cities, his methodological approach leads us to nearly the opposite extreme. His fourteen groupings give us a legitimate, empirically derived classification, but it is still not necessarily a *useful* classification – one that tells us something about the complexity of urban living or the quality of life for its residents.

The quality-of-life approach

In direct response to the need to assess the quality of life in the city, there have been some careful and systematic attempts (e.g., Liu, 1976) and others that have been less well done (Boyer & Savageau, 1981). Ben-Chieh Liu of the Midwest Research Institute has conducted one of the most comprehensive and informative studies of comparative urban quality. Liu collected data on over 120 variables from five broadly defined areas that he judged relevant to the lives of all urban residents:

1. *The economic component.* Personal income and wealth were among the items chosen to reflect individual economic well-being. Community economic health was also considered.

2. *The political component.* Indications of professionalism and performance of local government were measured, as well as the degree of citizen

participation in the political life of the community. Degree of public welfare assistance was also included.

3. *The environmental component.* Measures of air quality, noise, water, and pollution were gathered. Data on outdoor recreational facilities were also considered here.

4. *The health and education component.* Infant mortality and death rate were used to indicate individual health. Community health protection was measured via availability of medical care.

5. *The social component.* Defined most broadly, this category included income and employment differentials between racial and gender groupings as an indicator of discrimination. Cost of living, crime rates, housing quality, and the presence of sports and cultural opportunities were other aspects of this general category.

Liu noted that in 1970 there were 243 metropolitan areas in the United States with populations of 50,000 or more,* in which lived 68.6 percent of the total population. For purposes of comparison he subdivided these into three groupings according to population size: 65 cities of 500,000 or more; 83 cities of between 200,000 and 500,000; and 95 cities of 50,000–200,000. For every city the quantitative indicators used for each component were combined into a single numerical index. The scores on each component were then summarized as "grades" ranging from A (outstanding) to E (sub-standard), and a total score was arrived at by summing a city's five scores. Table 2.1 presents Liu's findings for the 65 largest metropolitan areas, dividing them into five grade levels.

These findings are interesting in a number of ways. For instance, only one urban place in the United States, the greater Portland, Oregon, area, got straight A's. Sacramento, California, in second place, got strong A's on four of the five components but only a C on its economic quality. On the other end of the scale, only one large city, Birmingham, Alabama, got straight failing grades. And even then Jersey City, New Jersey, with some areas of strength but also severe problems in economic, health, and social areas, ranked below it on the overall numerical quality-of-life score.

Some cities, including Cincinnati, Honolulu, and Dallas, had a tremendous variation across their five components, receiving different grades in each rated area. Using a total summed score, Cincinnati fell statistically in the middle

---

* In discussing Liu's research I shall use the terms *city* and *metropolitan area* interchangeably. Technically, however, the unit used was the Standard Metropolitan Statistical Area (SMSA), the one utilized by the U.S. Census Bureau. The SMSA represents an area with a central city of 50,000 or more and is usually geographically larger than the city the name of which is typically used to represent it.

Table 2.1. *Quality-of-life rankings of the sixty-five largest cities of the United States*

Outstanding	Excellent	Good	Adequate	Substandard
1. Portland, Ore./Wash.	14. Anaheim–Santa Ana–Garden Grove, Calif.	26. San Bernadino–Riverside–Ontario, Calif.	38. Newark, N.J.	56. Tampa–St. Petersburg, Fla.
2. Sacramento, Calif.	15. Buffalo, N.Y.	27. Houston, Tex.	39. Patterson–Clifton–Passaic, N.J.	57. Philadelphia, Pa./N.J.
3. Seattle–Everett, Wash.	16. Oklahoma City, Okla.	28. Phoenix, Ariz.	40. Springfield–Chicopee–Holyoke, Mass./Conn.	58. Memphis, Tenn./Ark.
4. San Jose, Calif.	17. Omaha, Nebr./Iowa	29. Akron, Ohio	41. Youngstown–Warren, Ohio	59. Norfolk–Portsmouth, Va.
5. Minneapolis–St. Paul, Minn.	18. Albany–Schenectady–Troy, N.Y.	30. Cincinnati, Ohio/Ky./Ind.	42. Detroit, Mich.	60. Greensboro–Winston-Salem–High Point, N.C.
6. Rochester, N.Y.	19. Syracuse, N.Y.	31. Honolulu, Hawaii	43. Richmond, Va.	61. Jacksonville, Fla.
7. Hartford, Conn.	20. Washington, D.C./Md./Va.	32. Dayton, Ohio	44. Fort Worth, Tex.	62. San Antonio, Tex.
8. Denver, Colo.	21. Los Angeles–Long Beach, Calif.	33. New York, N.Y.	45. Atlanta, Ga.	63. New Orleans, La.
9. San Francisco–Oakland, Calif.	22. Columbus, Ohio	34. Dallas, Tex.	46. Fort Lauderdale–Hollywood, Fla.	64. Birmingham, Ala.
10. San Diego, Calif.	23. Boston, Mass.	35. Kansas City, Mo./Kans.	47. Miami, Fla.	65. Jersey City, N.J.
11. Grand Rapids, Mich.	24. Cleveland, Ohio	36. Indianapolis, Ind.	48. Nashville–Davidson, Tenn.	
12. Milwaukee, Wis.	25. Toledo, Ohio	37. Chicago, Ill.	49. Pittsburgh, Pa.	
13. Salt Lake City, Utah			50. Allentown–Bethlehem–Easton, Pa./N.J.	

51. St. Louis, Mo./Ill.
52. Gary–Hammond–
    East Chicago, Ill.
53. Louisville, Ky./Ind.
54. Providence–Paw-
    tucket–Warwick,
    R.I./Mass.
55. Baltimore, Md.

Source: Adapted from *Quality of Life Indicators in U.S. Metropolitan Areas: A Statistical Analysis* by Ben-Chieh Liu. Copyright © 1976 by Praeger Publishers, Inc. By permission of Praeger Publishers.

(thirtieth of the sixty-five large cities), because of poor health and social ratings in spite of its strong economic and political status. Dallas came out thirty-fourth on its combined score, rating high on its economic and environmental components but low in health and politics. Honolulu, thirty-first overall, was found lacking in its economic and political life even though it received high grades in health and environmental qualities.

In commenting upon these results, the first and most important thing to acknowledge is that quality of life in cities is a *multidimensional* concept and that efforts to reduce it to a single indicator or component are bound to be misleading. Although some few cities were able to maintain constant high (or low) scores across the five components, the components were not found to be strongly correlated in any consistent manner. Economic well-being in a city does not guarantee a strong social quality of life; nor does a positive environmental picture assure a city of a strong health and education outlook. Moreover, for some of the components, especially the health and social areas, scores varied greatly between the best and the worst of the cities. For the political component, on the other hand, there was not a great disparity among cities, a finding that suggests that this component was not good at differentiating one city from the next.

In summarizing his own work, Liu admits quite frankly that he simply added up the five components to reach a composite rating because this method was less complex and therefore less controversial than any more sophisticated one. In fact, the matter of how much each component contributes to the total quality of life, and therefore how much to weight each one statistically, is one of the most controversial questions in this area. It is only slightly less sticky than that of what to include in the first place and that of how to measure those things that are included.

But a more fundamental question seems to underlie the inability of researchers who use objective data to agree on how to generate an index of urban livability: To what extent is this sort of determination a matter of data or objective truth and to what extent is it a matter of opinions, interests, and values? Could it be that livability, like beauty, is in the eyes of the beholder? Liu's data indicate, for instance, that the Minneapolis–St. Paul area is one of the top 5 in the United States. Yet in spite of the numerous positive qualities that earned Minneapolis its high rating, for a person who greatly dislikes severe winters no number of other positive features could possibly provide a sufficient reason to want to live there. Miami came out forty-seventh overall (but was third in environmental quality) and is a city widely known as a retirement haven because of its high livability. The growing metropolis of Atlanta came out forty-fifth overall; nonetheless, many career-oriented people are moving there because of its hearty economic outlook (sixth overall in Liu's data), which makes it for them a highly livable city (Marlin & Gelatt, 1976).

Not only are there problems concerning the relative importance of objective qualities, but often there are also discrepancies between what the *data* tell us and what the *people* tell us about a given city. The Greensboro, North Carolina, area comes out sixtieth of sixty-five large cities, but a study by Richard Lamanna (1964) tells us that the residents of Greensboro are generally quite content with the city and its living conditions. Cleveland comes out as first in the nation in the presence and availability of spectator sports, and although the people of Cleveland may or may not agree with this assessment, there are undoubtedly many people in Boston, New York, Chicago, and Los Angeles who would challenge it.

In 1976 the editors of *Saturday Review* (Marlin & Gelatt, 1976) attempted to choose the 5 most livable cities in the United States. It is informative to compare their *impressions* with Liu's *data*. Like Liu, they selected Seattle, Minneapolis, and San Diego (all fall in his top 10). Yet their choice of Cincinnati is somewhat at odds with Liu's data; and their rating of Savannah, Georgia, is totally counter to the implications of his figures. Savannah came out for Liu in the bottom 10 percent of small cities, receiving a rating of E on all but the environmental component (and only a C there). Then why did these journalists like it so much? They state that it was chosen because of its climate, its ease of pace, its population mix, and its vibrant sense of history. Obviously, it would be difficult to measure, quantify, or standardize many if not most of these qualities. Yet if they are important, should we not make some effort to find how to measure and include them?

Subjective approaches to urban description

Researchers, planners, and policy makers have historically placed their reliance on objective measures of the city and life in general. They have measured things such as housing, health, and income because it appears only natural that these conditions are inherent in the "good life." Also, these kinds of measures are useful because we can tell quite directly whether employment is up or down this year from last, higher or lower for blacks or whites, better or worse in one community than the next. But what these statistics mean and how they relate to subjective experience remain open questions. Angus Campbell, Philip Converse, and Willard Rodgers (1976) have discussed this issue in its general form:

We take a measure of rooms per person as a substitute for the feeling of pleasure and satisfaction a person gets from his housing; we take a measure of occupational status as an indicator of the sense of fulfillment a person gets from his work; we take the crime rate in a neighborhood as a measure of the insecurity the people who live there feel. These translations all appear eminently reasonable but the fact is that we do not know how well objective measures like these represent underlying psychological states or how well social indicators can be taken to represent the quality of life experience . . . The relationship between objective conditions and psychological states is very imperfect and . . . in order to know the quality of life experience it will be necessary to go directly to the individual himself for his description of how his life feels to him. [Pp. 3–4]

Still, it is one matter to assert the imperfect relationship between objective conditions of life in a city and the citizens' subjective experience and quite another to demonstrate it. Campbell and his associates, in a massive national survey of adult Americans, closely investigated the relative contribution of objective environmental attributes and their respondents' reported opinions on living conditions to satisfaction with community, neighborhood, and housing. They found that in each case, although the objective variables had some effect, their ability to account for satisfaction was strongly mediated by people's subjective assessments.

In a similar type of study, Michael Schneider (1975) compared a wide variety of objective and subjective measures that should reflect quality of life in fifteen major American cities. He found that many differences in objective conditions across cities were not reflected in residents' feelings. For instance, the objective likelihood of being robbed was approximately twenty times greater in Washington, D.C., than in Milwaukee, yet residents felt only slightly safer in Milwaukee. Second, he found that the existence of important group differences (e.g., between blacks and whites) makes it misleading to issue a blanket statement about the quality of life for "the people" of a city. As an example, of all fifteen cities studied, Pittsburgh was the one in which black residents were most satisfied, yet whites in Pittsburgh were less satisfied than whites in thirteen of the fifteen cities. In all, Schneider found that of 416 possible intercorrelations between objective and subjective indicators, barely 10 percent reached a statistically significant level – and half of these were in the opposite direction from what would have been expected.

This lack of association between Schneider's objective and subjective measures can be accounted for in a number of ways. The first involves the difficulty of comparing data at the aggregate level (which is the form of many of the objective measures) with data at the individual level (which is the form of most subjective data). Second, it might be argued that each individual's or group's knowledge of the city is idiosyncratic, and therefore each one's judgment is not of the same "object" (e.g., consider black and white residents' ratings of the "same" city). Third, there is the obvious possibility that objective conditions simply do not translate in a one-to-one fashion into people's cognitive judgments.

With the recognition that subjective and objective indicators are not always in agreement and that subjective measures are the more direct way of measuring qualities of the urban environment, there has been a recent upsurge of research that attempts to locate the *perceived* sources of satisfaction in the environment. John Lansing and Robert Marans (1969) measured residents' satisfaction, dividing it into three broad categories: physical appearance (e.g., housing style and condition, landscaping), social conditions (e.g., friendliness of neighborhoods, ethnic composition), and symbolic value (e.g., prestige and status of neighborhood). Frances Carp, Rick Zawadski, and Hassein Shokrkon (1976), in a comprehensive study of the San Francisco-Berkeley area, identified six factors by which people evaluated their residential areas. In addition to the categories proposed by Lansing and Marans, they found degree and source of noise in the area, feelings of safety, and convenience of transportation to be important. In other, more recent studies (e.g., Barrett & Guest, 1983; Brudney & England, 1982; Widgery, 1982), it has been found that community satisfaction can be predicted by looking at concrete matters such as the evaluation of specific municipal services, as well as at more abstractly defined issues, such as optimism about the community.

This kind of research provides a useful alternative to that which uses census, police, or municipal statistics alone by adding the subjective element, but it still falls far short of the sort of subjective notions discussed earlier in this chapter. The desirability of capturing the character or the feel of a city is recognized even by those who use objective data exclusively. Yet despite its potential importance, the issue that most troubles such people involves our ability to assess this essence:

> Of course there is no way to hold a tape measure to every single factor that influences the quality of life in a given locality. For instance the "tone" or the "spirit" of a place makes a lot of difference. The researchers recognized that this exists but *cannot be measured*, so they simply examined the measurable factors. [Liu, 1976, p. 33, italics mine]

But why should it be impossible to measure urban character? Is it a concept like "love" that either cannot or should not be approached with the social scientist's barometer? Although many people would tell us that we might as well keep away from certain realms of social phenomena and human experience, others have tried with reasonable success. Social psychologist Zick Rubin, for instance, has had the audacity to try to measure love (Rubin, 1973); and although his research will never embody the beauty of the poet's sentiments, it has nonetheless provided us with some interesting and important insights into the nature of interpersonal attraction.

In the realm of urban character there are also a few notable, however limited, attempts, with each researcher taking a different approach to the task. Stanley Milgram and his students (Milgram, 1970) placed advertisements in two newspapers asking people to give them accounts of specific incidents in New York, London, and Paris that best illustrated the character of that particular city. They then developed a set of questionnaires about each and gave them to people familiar with at least two of the three cities. They found that distinctive themes emerged that differentiated each from the others.

New York was characterized physically, by its diversity, size, and pace and its cultural and entertainment opportunities. In addition, some had the impression that its people were highly diverse, yet socially isolated from one another (heterogeneous, yet ghettoized). The profile of London was focused on the quality of interaction between residents, with the major themes involving tolerance and courtesy. Paris, on the other hand, elicited responses concerning both its physical and its sensory qualities. Many people claimed that Parisians are unfriendly and cold; others referred mainly to cafés and parks, feeling that it is a city of great amenity.

The feeling that Paris is a city of comfort and amenity is shared by many tourists and visitors and further emphasizes the differences between the way a city is seen subjectively and the nature of objective data. R. C. Fried and P. M. Hohenberg (1974) point out that although many "experts" have rated Paris as among the best in the world in "amenities," this finding is inconsistent with the fact that two-thirds of the dwellings in the city lack baths or showers (this is what they call the "view-from-the-Hilton" syndrome).

Milgram's approach allows us to retain a good deal of the richness of description of various cities, but it is not very systematic. In fact, it is barely one step beyond the approach of the essayist, in that here we rely on a pool of opinion rather than on the views of a single person. A second approach to capturing the character of the urban environment is that of geographers David Lowenthal and Marquita Riel (1972). The generalizability of their conclusions is somewhat limited by the particular technique they chose, but the extent and complexity of their analysis makes it noteworthy nonetheless. Their findings back up impressionistic data with statistical structure.

Lowenthal and Riel recruited observers from a great variety of backgrounds (from nurses to Boy Scouts to architects to senior citizens) in four cities: New York; Boston; Cambridge, Massachusetts; and Columbus, Ohio. Each observer was asked to walk along a set of six to ten different routes in his or her city, routes that had been selected as representative of its environment as a whole. Lowenthal and Riel obtained the impressions and judgments of each observer through a range of methods, including free comments, interviews, and responses concerning fifty environmental qualities on a questionnaire. The researchers carefully compared the data across different modes of response and across different groups of observers for each city. They found that although there were some differences, there was a surprisingly high degree of consensus.

Table 2.2 presents the descriptive terms most often applied to each of the four cities in the free-form descriptions. The portrait of New York City is very much in line with Milgram's descriptions, although as in the comments

Table 2.2. *Descriptive terms most frequently applied to the four cities studied by Lowenthal (1972) (numbers are percentages of all words used to describe the city)*

New York (n = 1,570)		Boston (n = 3,586)		Cambridge (n = 3,678)		Columbus (n = 1,582)	
Busy	3.8	Crowded	4.3	Green	5.1	Green	9.3
Wealthy	2.7	Old, quaint	4.3	Run-down	3.5	Run-down	3.5
Class, fashion	2.7	Busy	3.5	Varied	3.0	Messy	2.8
Alive	2.2	Run-down	2.4	Busy	2.8	Varied	2.5
Crowds	2.2	Different	2.4	Peaceful	2.8	Peaceful	2.3
Depressing	2.2	Peaceful	2.2	Depressing	2.3	Neat	2.0
Varied	1.7	Green	2.0	Mess	2.2	Children	2.0
Colorful	1.5	Shops, stores	1.8	Academic	2.1	Depressing	1.5
Touristy	1.4	Mess, litter	1.6	Residential	1.7	Hilly	1.5
Happy	1.4	Colorful, character	1.6	Old, quaint	1.6	Apartments	1.3
Cheap, vulgar	1.3	Filthy	1.5	Traffic	1.6	Churches	1.3
Run-down	1.3	High-class	1.4	Dull	1.3	Schools	1.0

Source: Environmental Assessment: A Comparative Analysis of Four Cities by D. Lowenthal. Copyright © 1972 by the American Geographic Society. By permission.

cited earlier in the chapter, there are a good number of positive as well as negative reactions. Of the four cities studied, only New York was judged as light and rich. Like Boston, it was seen as moving, vivid, and noisy, but to a much greater degree. Still, the qualities seen as unique to New York were with few exceptions positive.

Boston, a city whose popular impression seems to be generally positive, did not fare as well on the basis of the subjects' walks. It was regarded as uniquely chaotic and dirty and, more than any of the other three cities, dense, old, and bounded. The two smaller cities, Cambridge and Columbus, were judged to have fewer distinctive qualities. Although a city with many contrasts, Cambridge was found dull and average and was the city in which people reported being least aware of their environment. Columbus was characterized as New York's essential opposite: green, natural, quiet, and not vertical, dense, or businesslike – the "perfect suburb," yet a city of over half a million people.

It is difficult to gauge the extent and kinds of biases introduced by basing these city ratings on a set of walks, especially since they were preplanned and made the observer a passive rather than active participant. Still, the Lowenthal-and-Riel study is notable for its attempt to bring some *structure* to the work of subjective environmental and urban description. Rather than merely listing trait after trait and seeing how often each was mentioned in one city or another, their research went on to discover how these traits fit together.

As a first step, they used factor analysis to discover which of the words supplied by the observers in each city were grouped together. Next they looked to see whether the structure of associations varied greatly from city to city. They reported that the rating structures were similar enough to allow a consideration of groupings regardless of the locale being judged. They found four meaningful factors: items referring to evaluative aspects of the environment (e.g., *beautiful*, *rich*), to the presence of activity (e.g., *moving*, *noisy*), to the spatial orientation of the setting (e.g., *horizontal*, *open*), and to general nonevaluative descriptions of the setting (e.g., *uniform*, *dense*).

Since the work of Lowenthal and Riel, others have attempted to develop more systematic and parsimonious ways of capturing urban character (Logan & Collver, 1983; Rietzes, 1983). My own research (Krupat & Guild, 1980a, 1980b) has had this goal as its main focus. The major premise of this work is that whether we want to describe the characteristics of large cities in general and differentiate them from those of smaller cities and towns or whether we want to distinguish the feel of one great city from that of another, there ought to be some finite set of *subjective* dimensions or traits by which we can accomplish the goal.

In considering how to go about this task, William Guild and I came upon the extensive research that Rudolph Moos has performed in assessing the social climate of a number of institutional settings, from college dormitories (Moos, 1979) to prisons (Moos, 1974b) to residential care settings (Moos, 1980). In the very way that Anselm Strauss referred to urban character, Moos has stated that "environments have unique personalities, just as people do" (1974a, p. 1) and has suggested that this perspective, known as the social climate approach, can potentially be applied to any environment. Differing somewhat from Moos in the techniques we used, we set about finding ways of measuring the personalities of *cities* just as others had gone about measuring the personalities of *people*.

Since (1) the quality of a measuring instrument can be only as good as the materials from which it is derived, in this case the questions or items of the scale, and (2) we wanted to get as directly as possible at people's feelings and experiences, we did not choose items from any preexisting scale or theoretical position but rather went directly to the people themselves. We quickly found that when people are asked what makes a city a city, or what makes one good or bad, they rarely give textbook answers. People tend to describe a city in terms of their relationship to it rather than in terms of its objective qualities. Our respondents said things such as "A city is a place that makes you feel ... " or "A city is a place where people are ... " or "A city is a place where you can [or cannot] ... " These responses guided the research, because no matter how accurate or inaccurate, biased or fair, factual or stereotypical they may be, they are still the cognitions and feelings that guide people's behavior in their everyday interactions within the city.

In order to get at this sort of description, Guild and I borrowed a technique used by personality psychologists and adapted it to our own purposes. In the "Who Am I?" test, individuals are typically asked to list the 10 "things" that could best summarize and describe them to a person they had never met before. We changed "Who Am I?" to "What Is One?" and asked 100 undergraduates to list the 10 things that would best describe a big city (or a small town or an ideal place to live) to a mythical person unfamiliar with our civilization. (Actually the scenario went like this: "Suppose a Martian landed and asked you where you live and you said, 'A big city.' But he said, 'We have no such word in our language. Tell me the 10 most important things you can so I can know what one is.' ")

This procedure generated more than 300 different words and phrases. All duplications, synonyms, and idiosyncratic characterizations were deleted, and only a few traits that had not been mentioned but occupied important positions in the theoretical discussions of other researchers were added. The resulting list of 75 terms was presented to an additional group of 154 college students who came from a wide range of small, medium, and large places, and all students rated each of the 75 terms for its applicability to (1) a large metropolis, (2) a mid-sized city, and (3) a small town. The data provided by the students were subjected to statistical analyses in order to determine how they felt about

Table 2.3. *Attributes of big cities (75% or more agreement)*

Population	Atmosphere	People
Characteristic		
Is heterogeneous	Is competitive	Are untrusting
Is dense	Has much entertainment	Are interesting
Is integrated	Has much activity	Are often lonely
Is crowded	Allows choice of friends	Don't intrude on others'
Has many nonnatives	Has atmosphere of	affairs
Is large	culture	Are liberal
	Is fast-paced	
	Makes one feel	
	anonymous	
	Makes one feel isolated	
	Has diverse set of	
	activities	
	Is modern	
	Is impersonal	
	Fosters feeling of	
	confusion	
	Allows lifestyle choice	
Uncharacteristic		
	Is peaceful	
	Is safe	
	Is healthful	
	Is countrylike	
	Is close-knit	
	Is relaxed	
	Has sense of intimacy	
	Is nonpermissive	
	Is quaint	

cities and small towns. We found that for 33 of the city items there was agreement among 75 percent or more of the students that a trait was either characteristic or uncharacteristic of a large metropolis. We divided these items into three categories: those referring to traits of the *people* living there, those referring to the *atmosphere* of that place, and those referring to general *population* characteristics. The results, as indicated in Table 2.3, point to the major characteristics of the urban population as most people know them: large, dense, mixed, and mobile. City people were seen as untrusting but interesting, often lonely and often liberal, and most often not intruding in others' affairs. The ambience of the city was the thing on which the most people could agree. On the positive side, cities provide entertainment and

Table 2.4. *Attributes of small towns (75% or more agreement)*

Population	Atmosphere	People
Characteristic		
	Is peaceful	Have integrity
	Old ways are valued	Are sentimental
	Is safe	Are friendly
	Is laid out in orderly way	Are law-abiding
	Is healthful	Are nosy
	Is countrylike	Gossip a lot
	Is close-knit	Don't like outsiders
	Is relaxed	Are religious
	Has sense of intimacy	Are prejudiced
	Is quaint	Are helpful
	Has sense of roots	Form cliques
Uncharacteristic		
Is dense	Has much entertainment	Are violent
Is crowded	Is dirty	Are liberal
Has many nonnatives	Is fast-paced	
Is large	Is anonymous	
	Is impersonal	
	Fosters feeling of confusion	

activity; they allow a choice of friends and lifestyles; they are modern and permissive. On the other hand, they are competitive and impersonal; make one feel anonymous; and are not peaceful, safe, close-knit, or relaxed.

The picture that was painted of the small town is to some extent a mirror image of that of the city, but it differs in certain interesting ways, as we can see in Table 2.4. Small towns were seen as not large, dense, or crowded; but neither were they seen as necessarily homogeneous. The atmosphere of the small town was pictured as much the reverse of that of the city: People could agree that it is peaceful, safe, and relaxed and that it is not impersonal, does not make a person feel anonymous, and does not provide a great deal of entertainment.

The most interesting difference between the two portraits, though, is in the levels of agreement reached. People were able to reach some consensus about the typical atmosphere of the city (23 instances of agreement) but not about the typical people of the city (5 instances of agreement). Cities were thought to be fast-paced, anonymous, and competitive; but about whether city *people* are unfriendly there was no consensus. Are they helpful, prejudiced, open, enthusiastic, affluent, religious, or aware of things beyond where they live?

Again, there was no consensus. The students were able to agree on 19 descriptions of the small-town atmosphere and were also far more able to come up with a characterization of the small-town person (14 instances of agreement).

What this finding suggests is that differences between the city and the small town cannot be adequately captured on a single dimension. Small towns are just that, small. Our subjects seemed to feel that they knew the people and their manners almost as well as they knew the place and its ways. Big cities are, to make a noncontroversial statement, big. Our subjects indicated that they knew the conditions of big-city living and some of their consequences, but they could not say the same thing concerning the residents. Cities are diverse, and so are their people; both extremes exist, and so does everything in between.

Our goal, however, was not to provide yet another long list of terms but, rather, to see if there were a small number of factors or groupings of terms that could be used to capture the social climate of any community. Through factor analysis we found that 30 of the items could be summarized into six meaningful factors by which the social climate of differing communities could be compared:

1. *Warmth and closeness.* This first and most important factor contains items reflecting the general feeling of security and support that an environment may provide. It has a strongly evaluative tone. Representative items are "is a relaxed place," "is peaceful," "people are friendly," "provides a feeling of intimacy."

2. *Activity and entertainment.* This factor has a flavor of Osgood, Suci, and Tannenbaum's (1957) activity dimension. It contains items such as "has a diverse selection of activities," "has much entertainment," "has an atmosphere of culture." It is interesting that "has a dense population" is included here, since density is most often associated with crowding and considered to have negative outcomes. Here it was characterized as being related to opportunities for enrichment, a positive aspect of urban life.

3. *Alienation and isolation.* This factor contains items such as "people are apathetic," "people are lonely," "people are untrusting," "people are violent," "fosters a feeling of confusion." Whereas these are primarily "people" items, one very different one, "is a dirty place to live," is also included here. Perhaps this condition is seen as a cause or consequence of a breakdown in interpersonal solidarity.

4. *Good life.* This factor consists largely of "people" items, but in this case they are elitist characteristics. Some items included here are "people are intellectual," "people are affluent," "people are not natives," "is a prestigious place to live," "old ways are valued" (negative loading).

5. *Privacy.* This factor contains items such as "people tend to gossip," "people tend to intrude on one another's affairs," "people are petty," "peo-

ple are ignorant.'' Inclusion of these last two items implies that these behaviors carry a strong negative connotation.

6. *Uncaring*. This factor includes ''people are snobbish'' and ''people are insensitive.'' Notably, ''is a depressing place to live'' is associated with this factor rather than loading positively on the Alienation or Privacy factors or negatively on the Warmth, Activity, or Good-life factors.

Having condensed these many items into a manageable number of factors, we compared our subjects' ratings of each of the three types of communities for Factor 1, and then again for each of the other five factors. We found that each of the six factors significantly differentiated the large metropolis from the medium-size city and the medium-size city from the small town. In a related study (Guild & Krupat, 1979) subjects made comparisons among fourteen major American cities, assessing what they would be like to live in. In this study we found that people felt capable of making subjective comparisons among cities and also that these cities could be meaningfully located along a pair of subjective dimensions.

Donald Rietzes (1983) has performed research of a parallel nature but has applied it directly to the evaluations and behaviors of people living in one particular city, Atlanta. In addition to finding a similar set of subjective dimensions, his work demonstrates that blacks and whites share a common set of meanings about the city (at least in Atlanta), even though their evaluations and preferences are different. Most important, he has found that these subjective perceptions and evaluations influence activity patterns, affecting the use of the downtown area in relation to both instrumental and entertainment activities.

Subjective "versus" objective

Classification systems can be based on any number of criteria. Depending on the nature of these criteria, the same object may appear very different. In order to decide which ones are most useful for an urban taxonomy, we must ask about the ends to which the classification will be put. That is, what kinds of outcomes do we want to explain, predict, and possibly even affect? The social-environmental psychologist's interests lie in understanding a broad spectrum of feelings and behaviors associated with the city, ranging from the amount of use urban facilities get (day and night) for such activities as recreation and shopping, to interpersonal orientations and patterns of social interaction, to the desire to leave, come to, or stay in the city. We are also interested in people's overall satisfaction with home, neighborhood, and city as a whole.

Having indicated the kinds of outcomes in which we are interested, we must still ask, Which kind of variables, objective or subjective, are most useful in accounting for them? Traditionally, those in the objective school of thought (e.g., Wicker, 1979; Wirth, 1938) have acted as if subjective impressions did not exist or at least made little difference. They have pointed out that objective conditions operate directly, providing the context for action and placing constraints upon behavior. For instance, it has been argued (by Wicker, 1979) that city size in itself determines so much of the form of urban social interaction that the effects of individual differences, subjective perceptions, and personal beliefs are relatively unimportant. Other objectivists have taken a less extreme approach but have continued to minimize the subjective element, stating either that as a class subjective variables cannot be operationalized and assessed reliably or that even when measured, subjective data represent just another class of outcome as determined by the objective environment.

The subjective school of thought (e.g., Craik, 1971; Rapoport, 1977) argues that if our interest is in how people behave, their perceptions, cognitions, and evaluations are the most direct determinants to consider. These theorists argue that if a person believes a place unsafe, it makes little difference if by all objective indicators there is no danger; the person still will not go there. The subjectivists emphasize that regardless of the nature of the environment as described physically or characterized objectively, people act only after considering and evaluating various alternatives (i.e., by choice). Since different people have differing kinds of information available to them and since they process this information in differing ways, behavior will vary from person to person – not as a result of the environment as it "really" is but as a function of their cognitively mediated appraisals of that environment.

Subjective concepts such as social climate can be systematically studied and measured, and they do critically mediate between environment and action. I suggest, however, (1) that the two kinds of description, subjective and objective, may be most useful in explaining differing kinds of urban outcomes and (2) that the interaction between the two kinds of description (their degree of discrepancy or agreement) may, in fact, provide the most useful form of description. In effect, I propose that these two orientations constitute *complementary* rather than mutually exclusive ways of describing cities.

In order to clarify these points, let us take an example. Consider the desire of a city planner to know whether people will use a newly renovated public facility (e.g., a neighborhood park) at night. Objectively, one can cite crime statistics, count numbers of police present, and measure the amount of light. Subjectively, one can consider the potential users' perception of safety, the perceived visibility of the police, and beliefs about whether they are capable of preventing crime. Whereas quite often both sets of criteria point in the same direction in accounting for use or nonuse, what happens when the two sets are not in agreement?

When statistics show the park to be safe but people see it as unsafe, attempts

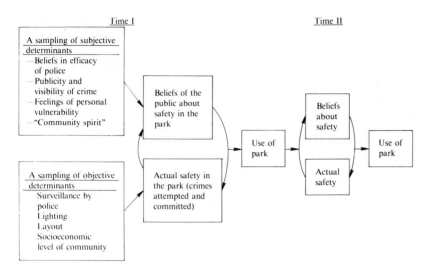

Figure 2.1. Beliefs about crime, rate of crime, and use of an urban park.

to get people to use it are not likely to succeed if they look only to one aspect. That is, attempts to change attitudes and perceptions without carefully looking into their sources in the objective environment and attempts to bring in more police or improve lighting without knowing whether people will notice or care will be less than totally effective. In fact, regardless of which came first, perceptions of safety or the rate of crime, they combine to produce a certain level of use, with level of use then affecting both future crime and future perceptions in an endless feedback loop.

As Figure 2.1 illustrates, the level of crime and public perceptions about the safety of a park both are influenced by any number of other factors. When combined, they affect use in what can be a vicious or benevolent cycle. Greater use is likely to lead people to believe in the park's safety and also to lead to decreased crime opportunities (when there are many people present, it is more difficult to attack isolated individuals). On the other hand, if few people use the area, it is seen as a dangerous place to be; and this view results in even less use and an increased likelihood that those who use it will be attacked.

It is also important to recognize that different outcomes may be sensitive to different classes of predictor variables. Take the case of an urbanite's use of car or subway to get across town. If we are interested in predicting which mode of travel will be chosen, it would be best to know the person's subjective perceptions concerning traffic flow, the perceived likelihood of auto or subway breakdown, and the like. But to predict the degree of success with one mode or the other, it would be better to have objective indicators of the same variables. Similarly, the actual size of a city affects the likelihood that any two given people will meet and may even influence the kinds of settings under which they do encounter each other; yet it is the particular social climate in which they interact, the prevailing norms, and their individual characteristics that will most likely affect whether they remain strangers or develop into friends.

Kinds of human communities

As a demonstration of the complexity of what *city* means to us, I have often asked students in class to name its opposite. Although some terms are suggested more often than others, it is the variety of "opposites" available that is most informative. *Small town* is popular, along with *suburb, village, country, farm*, and *rural*. The fact that city has so many opposites implies that there are many dimensions by which we can define it. If the predominant dimension in a person's mind is size, then big city is most often contrasted with small town. Many other dimensions might be equally salient, however, and could be used to define reality in terms of the urban–nonurban distinction. When we go from city to non-city, is the difference that is noticed most a change in density, lifestyle, economic activity, population mix, or home ownership pattern? The type of community known as a suburb contrasts in many ways with the city. Yet many suburbs that are just beyond major cities grow to be quite large themselves and represent "cities" of considerable size as judged by the census. The place where I live, Newton, Massachusetts, is a suburb of Boston's. According to the 1980 census it has a population of about eighty-five thousand. If that same "suburb" were in Wyoming, Delaware, Maine, West Virginia, Vermont, Montana, New Hampshire, North Dakota, or South Dakota, it would be the single largest city in the state. In the next chapter we will see that the differences between city and non-city begin with size but that other elements have been chosen as key in defining urban life.

Summary and conclusions

In this chapter we reviewed the dimensions and criteria with which people have considered not only cities but communities of all different types. Behind this review is the notion that before we can identify how (and also possibly why) life in one place differs from life in another, we must discover a set of underlying variables to describe and classify communities.

In reviewing the literature on community differences and urban quality we began with the subjective reports of individual commentators, of novelists, essayists, and poets. To take the language of the theater, what does one do when the reviews are mixed? In hearing what a given play (or city) is like, it is difficult to know the extent to which we are finding out about the object itself, rather than simply about the preferences of the reviewer.

Given such a general hesitancy of social scientists to rely upon opinion or hearsay, it is not surprising to find that the bulk of the empirical literature on community or urban differences has relied upon data that are objective – that can be counted and measured untouched by human hands (or human values). In reviewing these data we have noted a number of interesting findings, depending on the method and package used for the data. But we have also been critical of sole reliance on objective information, citing (1) examples of inconsistency between objective indexes and large-scale empirical studies of subjective opinion and (2) instances where useful research on the social climate of communities has been initiated.

Near the end of this chapter we asked which system would be the more useful, but in considering the relative usefulness of different approaches, we found that even on this question the answer cannot be either–or. Objective and subjective descriptions should be thought of as complementary rather than competing systems. Each may be relevant to differing kinds of behaviors and outcomes, and it is the interaction of the two that is most likely to explain the full range of urban behavior.

Suggestions for further reading

Hadden, J. K., & Borgatta, E. F. 1965. *American cities: Their social characteristics*. Chicago: Rand McNally.

Liu, B. C. 1976. *Quality of life indicators in U.S. metropolitan areas: A statistical analysis*. New York: Praeger.

Strauss, A. L. 1976. *Images of the American city*. New Brunswick, N.J.: Transaction Books.

White, M., & White, L. 1962. *The intellectual vs. the city*. Cambridge, Mass.: Harvard University Press.

3
DEFINITIONS AND MODELS OF URBAN LIFE

What absurdity can be imagined greater than the institution of cities. Cities originated not in love but in war. It was war that drove men together in multitudes and compelled them to stand so close and build walls around them.
– Elizabeth Peabody of Brook Farm

Whatever had been my taste for solitude and natural scenery, yet the thick, foggy, stifled elements of cities, the entangled life of so many men together, sordid as it was, and empty of the beautiful, took quite a strenuous hold upon my mind. I felt as if there could never be enough of it.
– Nathaniel Hawthorne, The Blithedale Romance

In Chapter 2 we were concerned with looking at the approaches used to classify cities and to characterize the quality of life in them. In this chapter we move our focus from a description of the characteristics of the *city itself* to a consideration of viewpoints that help explain the *impact* of the city on its people. As is consistent with the position of multiple and contrasting realities, each of the schools of thought and theorists we discuss has chosen a different aspect of the city and has built a model of urban life around it. Each of these perspectives on the city represents a unique and personal construction of urban reality and points to a different element as holding the key to understanding why urbanites behave as they do. The people who have developed each of these models have looked at the city, just as we have done, and have been struck by one or more distinctive features of urban life. We will now consider these distinctive features and see how each defines the city by asserting what it means to live in an urban environment.

The most obvious feature to anyone from a town is the city's size. This, along with the density in which people lived, traveled, and worked and the great variety of people the city had, struck Louis Wirth and his colleagues in the first third of the century in Chicago (McKenzie, 1926; Park, 1926; Wirth, 1938). Comparing the city to the country in caring and closeness of relations, Wirth and his colleagues developed a model of the city in which social and personal disorganization were seen to be inherent aspects of life. In contrast, Claude Fischer (1984) looked at the great numbers of people in the city and equated numbers with similarities, possibilities, and opportunities. Rather than argue unequivocally that the presence of many people drives them apart, Fischer pointed out that the large numbers allow meaningful subcultures to persist and thrive in the city.

Others have looked at the great numbers of people in the city and placed yet a different meaning on them. Whereas Fischer translated numbers into potential connections, Lyn Lofland (1973) saw a different but equally important social consequence of numbers: They made almost all of the people around her strangers. Lofland developed an approach to urban life based on what it means to live in a situation that encourages such a large degree of personal anonymity. Stanley Milgram, another person who developed a model of urban life (Milgram, 1970), was struck by another consequence of size. He argued that size affects relationships through a very different mechanism. Feeling that the presence of so many people, sights, and sounds can overwhelm a person's ability to take it all in, he concluded that size translates into cognitive overload, and he noted that people must make a number of adaptations in order to cope with this stress. Finally, Roger Barker and his colleagues (Barker & Gump, 1964; Barker & Wright, 1955), extrapolating from observations of small-town life to the city, pointed out that the critical determinant of day-to-day urban experiences involves the number of behavior settings available and the number of people available to "man" them.

Each of these positions is the product of an inquiring mind noting something different about the city and building a set of principles, processes, and consequences around a particular distinctive feature. Although some of their conclusions are contradictory, most of their insights complement one another. Most important, *each* of these is a legitimate representation of the city for at least some people at some times. It is a key characteristic of urban life that it is capable of containing within it such multiple and sometimes contrasting elements, and we shall explore each of these in this chapter.

Cities and size

In the search for the characteristics that define a city, many social scientists have used population size as a starting point. This variable is easy to conceptualize and measure since it can be objectively defined, and it *ought* to have relevance to the nature of life in a given place. Claude Fischer (1984) has pointed out that in many ways *city* is but a convenient term for distinguishing high from low population concentration. Demographer Otis Dudley Duncan (1957) has noted that big cities (as defined by size) differ from small towns in that they have a greater percentage of working women, a greater percentage of white-collar workers, more females and young people, a higher median income, and a lower percentage of married people. Clearly, these (objective) population characteristics associated with size should have implications for the style of life and the nature of interactions and opportunities in the city.

Yet although size is undoubtedly the right place to start, it is a necessary but not sufficient condition for understanding the effect of cities on people (Sweetser, 1982). In noting the correlation of size with certain population characteristics or urban phenomena, we should not be lulled into the thought that size is the direct cause of these effects. Suppose for the moment we were to take a small city (or shall we say relatively urban area) just outside Boston and place it in the middle of a large midwestern state three hundred miles from a major urban center. Would there be changes in the way of life, the nature of the people who would come, stay, or leave? There would be – not simply as a result of the relative size but as a result of the relative isolation of the place as well. Sidney Verba and Norman Nie (1972) refer to this proximity-of-location variable as *boundedness* and note significant differences among communities of similar sizes but different degrees of boundedness.

Further, size alone suggests something about the importance of municipal or administrative boundaries, something that can be misleading. Imagine that we took Chicago, with a population of more than 3 million, and divided it into four hundred "small towns," each with a population of fewer than ten thousand. Arbitrarily, we would have created political units that would not enter in most classifications of urban places. But would we have created small towns in any other sense of the word? The reason why very little would have changed is that size alone provides a means of describing an environment. It allows for excellent actuarial predictions, but it does not necessarily help us explain how and why people act. For explanations we must look at a host of other variables and consider how they impact on the individual as well. In short, we must find out what size implies.

The human ecological approach

One of the earliest and still one of the most influential social science models of urban life is that of the human or urban ecologists. It is a conception that begins with size, adds other variables associated with size, and proposes a broad range of effects and consequences that follow. This viewpoint, which can be traced back to the work of Robert Park in the early 1900s and Louis Wirth in the 1930s, attempted to draw upon the principles of plant and animal ecology and give them social equivalents. The urban ecologists approached the study of a distinct environment such as the city just as they might have approached the study of a lake, a mountain, a species of animal, or any other natural unit.

Just as plants compete for light, space, and water, so do people in the city compete for scarce economic and social resources. Just as various species adapt their behavior according to their needs for dominance and survival, so does the human animal adapt its way of life to the requirements of the environment. In taking this perspective, urban ecologists assumed a one-way influence relationship between the structure of the environment and the behavior of the individual. Therefore, they concluded, a person's mode of behavior is *determined* by the environment, and the person either adapts or fails to survive.

The classic statement of this position is contained in Wirth's highly influential essay "Urbanism as a Way of life" (1938). There he pinpoints three features as distinctive of urban life and constructs a model of impact around them. He states that the city can be defined and understood through the use of three characteristics: size, density, and heterogeneity of population. From these three a whole set of consequences can be deduced as necessarily following. He begins by saying that the existence of large numbers of individuals implies the likelihood of a wide range of differentiation among them. With such great variation in racial, ethnic, economic, and class lines, the bonds of kinship and neighborliness and a sense of community are likely to be absent or at least greatly weakened. Without community, consensus is impossible. And without consensus the moral order will be destroyed.

The results of this chaos will be competition, exploitation, and the substitution of formal controls for the bonds of solidarity that otherwise hold people together. According to Wirth, "The clock and the traffic signal are symbolic of the basis of our social order in the urban world" (p. 56). He sees the social and economic conditions of the city as reinforcing this moral disorder, producing competitiveness, indifference, even a predatory orientation toward others. These qualities are, he thinks, necessary for success in the city, a success that is at the expense of others in an environment of limited resources and rewards.

Another consequence of large numbers that Wirth describes is the segmentalization of human relationships. With so many diverse people living together, it is impossible to come to know others as "whole persons." Therefore, relationships with faceless people become superficial, anonymous, and transitory, and city people come to look on others coldly as means to their own ends, rather than as individuals.

Wirth sees density as intensifying all these effects by forcing uninvolved people to rub elbows with one another constantly. Close physical proximity, coupled with great social distance, gives rise to a sense of loneliness, nervous tension, and mutual irritation. For Wirth, the metaphor of the subway, with great numbers of people being "herded" together in "inhuman masses," captures the essence of urban existence.

The fact that heterogeneity comes along with size simply makes the matter more difficult. Because there are so many groups to which the urbanite may hold allegiance, and because much work and play take place outside the home, the effect of heterogeneity is to break down the family unit and segment the person even further. And while Wirth admits that in the city we do gain "a certain degree of emancipation or freedom from the personal and emotional control of intimate groups," we sell this mess of pottage for our birthright, "the spontaneous self-expression, the morale, and the sense of participation that comes with living in an integrated society" (p. 54). Thus not only can Wirth account for personal disorganization and individual pathology, but he can also account for the breakdown of the social order and various forms of social pathology.

What we see, then, is that in a single set of broad strokes Wirth has explained all of city life as the logical extension of a small set of ecological variables. The city is a human settlement type characterized by *large numbers* of *varied* people living in *close proximity* to one another with a *distinctive way of life*:

> The distinctive features of the urban mode of life have often been described sociologically as consisting of the substitution of secondary for primary contacts, the weakening of bonds of kinship, the declining social significance of the family, the disappearance of the neighborhood, and the undermining of the traditional basis of social solidarity. [P. 60]

Thus, as Wirth depicts it, the city offers few advantages in exchange for stress, anonymity, alienation, and personal and social disorganization.

There is a sense of loss in this description – not so much what we lose, as opposed to gain, by living in the city as, rather, a sense of "paradise lost": the simple life that can never be regained. To put Wirth's writings in perspective, it should be noted that his observations on the city were influenced by a sociological tradition that tended to compare the "unnatural" environment (the city) with simpler settings in other, less advanced cultures (see Redfield, 1941). These small, primitive folk societies were endowed with a mystique of goodness and simplicity belonging to Rousseau's noble savage. The city was seen as robbing people of their innocence and spontaneity, leaving them savage but hardly noble.

Another important point to recognize is that much of the human ecologists' writings on "the city," implying *all* cities, were based on observation of Chicago in the 1920s and 1930s. This was a period of unplanned and unchecked growth in which thousands of people came from the farm and country to seek their fortune. The city was not ready to accommodate or acculturate those who migrated to it, nor were many of these new migrants ready or able to adapt to a new pattern of living. The city was larger and more complex than anything they had encountered before; it called for new ways of thinking and seeing the world as well as new ways of acting; and there were few of the current mass media to prepare urban migrants for all they would encounter. Many of these new urban settlers experienced a form of culture shock and became confused and overwhelmed as a result of being set adrift in an alien culture. Assuming that Wirth and his colleagues took the perspective of these new urbanites, it not very difficult to understand the version of urban reality that they constructed.

Critical comments on the human ecological model

More than any other single perspective on urban life, human ecology has exerted a major influence on both social science and popular conceptions of the city. Because its impact has been so strong (and because its position is strongly antiurban), the human ecological approach deserves close critical scrutiny. What is important to note in this analysis is that nowhere do I propose that its conclusions are incorrect – only that what it presents should not be accepted as the only or the complete explanation. In fact, some human ecologists, such as Amos Hawley (1979, 1981), have taken the basic perspective and developed a more positive view of the city from it. Yet because the work of Wirth has been taken as the prototype of ecological thinking, it is necessary to consider in depth the many alternative interpretations of the effects of urban conditions.

An initial problem of an approach such as Wirth's is a strong sense of environmental determinism. This approach assumes that the city dictates a way of life and the individual obeys. This position remains satisfactory as long as we are discussing plants or lower animals that lack the ability to make choices. As stated in Chapter 1, however, the perspective that environmental psychologists currently prefer characterizes the relationship of the individual to the environment as one of *dynamic* and *mutual* influence. To the extent that people must live where and as they are, they will adapt. But people are constantly changing and influencing their environments on a massive scale. They make demands on the environment, and if it is not flexible enough, they may simply choose to leave.

The slogan that is best suited to the ecological model – "Adapt or die" – has its alternative – "Vote with your feet," the idea that people are capable of making choices and moving into or out of environments according to their preferences (Michelson, 1977). As a result, the "necessary" consequences of ecological variables that Wirth envisioned are not as necessary as he depicted. Our image of the individual as an active agent in the environment will not allow us to accept Wirth's characterization of the urbanite as "being reduced to a stage of virtual impotence" (p. 61).

Another set of problems involves both the *descriptive* accuracy and the *explanatory* accuracy of the ecological perspective. First, although there is no doubt that anybody who has ever lived in or even visited a large city recognizes some of the effects Wirth mentions, many of them remain part of the stereotype and folklore of the city rather than the result of empirical documentation. Second, Wirth's characterization, even if we were to accept it as accurate in description, still may be incomplete in description. That is, his version of urban reality is but one view of the city. It emphasizes the negative effects of urban life while almost never mentioning the freedom, the possibility of choice, or the virtues of diversity, density, and size.

Harold Proshansky (1978) has said, for example, that cities make people versatile because of the variety of people and circumstances that they will inevitably encounter. In order to handle the degree of complexity and uncertainty inherent in the urban setting, he believes that city dwellers must learn to approach new situations in a flexible and adaptive manner. Using a different line of reasoning, Jonathan Freedman (1975) points out that the city may have either a positive or a negative effect, depending upon the characteristics of the person or the requirements of the situation. Offering what he calls the density–intensity hypothesis, Freedman has argued that the effect of a variable such as urban density is to intensify or amplify the individual's typical response to a given situation. If this view is correct, then as a result of living in a large city, a lonely person would come to be even lonelier (negative effect), but an active person would come to be even more active (positive effect).

Another issue concerning Wirth's position involves a confusion between the social *outcomes* of urban life and the *mechanisms* that determine them. For instance, the bases for friendship choices in the city and in the country are usually different. In the country proximity is the strongest determinant, whereas in the city common interest plays a greater role and proximity is less important. This finding does not, of course, automatically imply that city dwellers have fewer or less intimate relationships than country residents: That people who live in an apartment building do not know the other people on their floor does not imply that they do not have friends across the river or three bus stops away. This matter serves to point out a second distinction that urban ecologists fail to make, that between behavior in public and behavior in private. Although the city person may be unfriendly toward strangers on the street, there is no reason to believe that the same person is not warm and close to friends in the home (see Chapter 6 for an extended discussion of these issues). Clark McCauley and his associates (McCauley, Coleman, & DeFusco, 1978; McCauley & Taylor, 1976) have demonstrated that although the reactions of city people to strangers in public are clearly indicative of a desire to avoid contact (more so than in small towns), relations among acquaintances and friends are highly similar in city and town.

Subcultural theory

In direct response to the ecological school, Claude Fischer (1984) has developed the subcultural approach. While Wirth believed that the major effect of size, density, and heterogeneity was a breakdown of close social ties, Fischer suggests just the opposite. His view of the urban scene emphasizes the similarities among groups of people rather than their differences. He points out that in the city people with a whole range of characteristics, interests, values, and skills are far more likely than country dwellers to find others who are similar to themselves.

Ethnic and racial communities evolve, neighborhoods based on occupations and social class form, and areas united by lifestyle are generated and emerge as vital subcultures. Cities often become, in Park's (1916) words, "mosaics of little worlds." A tour of greater Boston would include Chinatown, the North End (the Italian section), Southie (the Irish section), Roxbury (the black section), Kenmore Square (the student section), Brookline (the Jewish section), Harvard Square (the intellectual or bohemian section), and Beacon Hill (the ultrafashionable section). These are but some of the larger and more easily identified pockets and subcultures. Many other, smaller subcultures could be defined both physically (by geographical reference) and psychologically (by reference to lifestyles and interests).

A key concept in the subcultural point of view is that of *critical mass*. As an example, Fischer considers the odds that a subculture of people who love modern dance will emerge in communities of different sizes. If on the average one in every thousand people is devoted to modern dance, then in a town of five thousand, about five such people might be found. The five might get together and talk or practice, but it is unlikely that they would become a vital group. Given the same rate of one in a thousand modern-dance lovers, a city of a million would contain about a thousand such people. With this sort of critical mass, they could and likely would open up studios, give public performances, and invite other performers to visit. More than likely the five people from that small town might even come to see the city dancers, and some of the five might decide to move to the city to be close to the action. In short, the group would flourish, and its members would be expected to thrive as individuals. Societies of poisonous-snake lovers, fanciers of fifteenth-century Slovakian literature, and followers of small religious cults all are more likely to find happiness with others of a similar bent in the city than in the small town. The following is a slightly edited version of a notice I found posted on a pole at a busy urban street corner. We can imagine the odds of finding a person to answer this informal ad in a community of five thousand, as compared to one of five hundred thousand:

Are You a Percussionist with Subtlety and Integrity?
Perhaps we could get together. I play string bass meditation music on Cooper Street and am looking for that rhythmic interplay. I usually play for 45 minutes to 1 hour per session, so proximity is favorable. Trap set available (brushes only please!). Tablas welcome. Call John, 555–3939.

Fischer also suggests that when groups form, they are likely to come into contact with other subcultures that are different and even alien to them. At this point sparks fly. Some degree of conflict may result and some mutual influence may take place. (He cites the example of young construction workers' growing beards and long hair even while criticizing "hippies" and "freaks".) But most important, members of subcultures usually recoil from contact with the outside and retreat all the more intensely back into "their own kind." As a result, close and meaningful contacts with one's group intensify and come to play an even larger role in one's self-definition and everyday social participation.

Although Wirth's and Fischer's depictions of urban life point in opposite directions, we can accept them both as having validity if we recognize that each applies to cities at different stages of their development, and to some residents more than others. This applicability will depend on factors such as who the residents are, how long they have been in the city, and where they are coming from (in both the literal and the figurative senses). The urban reality seen by Wirth was of an evolving and chaotic city. Many of its residents were new and disoriented. People who were once both physically and psychologically close to friends and relatives now found themselves physically distant and did not yet know how to compensate. The means for re-creating old relationships were not obvious, and the knack of developing new ones was still not well developed.

Wirth's problem – and the problem of any single viewpoint that attempts to encompass the entire urban experience – was that he focused so closely upon the negative that he left little room to see the positive. There were many important and close ethnic and occupational enclaves in the Chicago of his time. He himself wrote and taught within the tightly knit academic subculture of the University of Chicago. Fischer's contrasting urban reality points in an opposite but equally biased direction. The city can be a lonely place. There are many, many people who fail to become part of any significant community of support. Within the Italian, black, Chinese, Irish, and Jewish sections of Boston, many people (the elderly, poor, and sick) are part of some subculture in name but not in practice. And many others fall through the seams between subcultures. Both realities are "correct," but neither is complete.

The overload model

The overload model proposed by social psychologist Stanley Milgram (1970) is different from both Wirth's and Fischer's ways of looking at urban reality: It is not as optimistic as Fischer's, which sees opportunities for people to become actively involved with others via subcultures, nor is it as pessimistic as Wirth's, which sees people as passive, isolated objects in their environment. What the overload model proposes primarily is that people are active in dealing with their environment and that they develop mechanisms for coping in order to meet the city's demands. The result, according to Milgram, is that urbanites become close to some people and sensitive to some important parts of their environment but at the expense of alienation from other aspects of the city and its people.

Like other theorists before him, Milgram also looked at the size of the city, but rather than simply equating size with *people*, he noticed that size also brings with it an infinite variety of sights, sounds, and smells – huge amounts of physical as well as social stimulation – that can overload the cognitive capacities and strain the urbanite's ability to deal with it all. In a way, this theory is not greatly different from the human ecologist's view of the buzzing confusion of the city until we look at the differing descriptions of the city person's *reaction* to it all. Whereas Wirth saw the individual as being overwhelmed, Milgram saw him or her as merely overloaded. *Overwhelmed* implies an incapacitation by the environment, so that the person cannot overcome its demands and therefore reacts passively. If this is one's version of urban reality, then it is not surprising to see personal and social disorganization resulting. Milgram's concept of overload emphasizes the ability to adapt, to cope with and overcome the environment. And although not all of the outcomes he proposes are positive ones, they still represent forms of personal organization and coping, rather than forms of pathology.

Overload has been defined formally as the inability of a person (or any system) to process a set of inputs that are presented simultaneously or consecutively. Georg Simmel, the noted sociologist, was the first to analyze the city from this perspective when he wrote early in the twentieth century. He believed that since urbanites were constantly being called upon to deal with a barrage of demands, their intellects would predominate at the expense of their feelings and emotions. Stating that "the urban man reacts with his head instead of his heart" (Simmel, 1950, p. 410), Simmel also assumed that city dwellers would become blasé and indifferent to the needs of people around them. Resurrecting this concept three-quarters of a century later, Milgram has refined it and presented specific means by which people adapt to the many demands on their time, interests, and efforts.

One mode of adaptation available to city people is to give less time to each person or each encounter. This reaction would account for the feeling many people get when dealing with urbanites that they are always busy, that there is always something requiring them to cut things short and to move on. But this kind of mechanism is still too gross, too general, to be really adaptive. City people are not *always* busy; they are not in a hurry for everyone. In fact, perhaps the single most important thing that overloaded people do is to set *priorities*. Whether consciously or unconsciously, the urbanite discriminates between those people and activities that are most important and most interesting and those that are less salient. Important people and activities are dealt with first, best, or longest – and those that are unimportant are handled last, least, or not at all.

If such priorities are important to the urbanite, one consequence is that there will be a strong line of cleavage between "friend" and "stranger" in the city. Urbanites can be expected to attend to the needs and come to the aid of those whom they know and care about, while simultaneously disregarding the demands placed upon them by others. This theory has been confirmed in laboratory and field research and observed in real-life instances of altruistic behavior (Krupat & Epstein, 1973; Latané & Darley, 1970).

As a more formalized mechanism of avoiding the need to deal with people they do not care to know or meet, city people may resort to having unlisted numbers or keeping the phone off the hook at certain hours. But more subtle and informal ways can be adopted to keep out unwanted stimulation. One such way involves the taking of an unfriendly pose while navigating one's way through oceans of people. In a small-scale test that I conducted (Krupat, 1984), candid photos of people walking on the sidewalks of New York and Boston were taken for comparison with a similar set of candid shots of people in two small towns. Sampling from these pictures at random, photos from both settings were presented to a group of college students, without any other information, as part of a study of "first impressions." The big-city people pictured were perceived as consistently less friendly, less easygoing, and more tense than the small-towners.

Overload and underload

Although Milgram's explanation of the process by which people react to, and deal with, the city is far different from Wirth's, it is interesting to note that they share the assumption that what the city presents to its residents is a case of "too much." One of Milgram's former students, Daniel Geller, has proposed a very different version of urban reality within this framework (Geller, 1980; Geller, Cook, O'Connor, & Low, 1982). He has suggested that it is equally important to look at people's needs for complexity, novelty, excitement, and exploration when we consider the city. If we emphasize this class of human needs, maybe the city is just right and the small town is a case of "too little." For some people the real problem may be "rural underload" rather than "urban overload." (This matter will be discussed in greater detail in Chapter 5.) Geller implies the existence of multiple and contrasting realities by noting that the environment will be experienced differently by people with differing characteristics. Perceptions of it as complex and stressful or boring and dull will vary from person to person, depending on the individual's needs, cognitive style, information-processing capacities, and prior environmental experiences.

What the overload model offers, then, is a different way of capturing the effects of size, one whose main focus is on intrapersonal cognitive processes rather than on interpersonal social processes. Yet this model clearly makes the link between psychological functioning and social interaction. It absolutely rejects the ecologists' notion of urban pathology, but at the same time it accepts their contention that relations among strangers in urban public settings can be cool and calculating. It implies that although urbanites are often callous to the needs of others in public encounters, this is the price to be paid for maintaining warm, close relations among high-priority people in private. On the individual level, this approach closely parallels Fischer's group-level discussion of the process by which ties are strengthened *within* subcultures through the creation of hostilities *between* subcultures. The end result in both systems is paradoxical. City people must take other people into account in order to avoid them. They maximize involvement with some at the expense of being indifferent to others. They are intimate with a few while being anonymous to most. Therefore dealing with overload brings individuals closer to certain parts of the environment while at the same time estranging them from other parts of it.

The world-of-strangers approach

In their approaches to the city, both Milgram and Fischer make a distinction between relations among friends and those among strangers that Wirth fails to make. For Fischer especially, city life appears generally positive because of a focus on the intimate world of those who share things rather than on the world of strangers who know and care little about each other. Yet when Lyn Lofland took a look at the urban world, the distinctive feature that she saw was that she knew and was known by such a minute percentage of the population. She felt that the key to understanding the urban experience is an acknowledgment that to live in the city is to live in a world of strangers. Rather than labeling this as a negative aspect of urban life and going no further, however, she suggested that perhaps urbanites adapt to this by learning how to develop satisfying fleeting relationships as well as more long-lasting and deeper ones.

In order to get a sense of the sheer numbers of people in the city, let us consider statistics of the Regional Plan Association: "In Nassau County, a suburb of New York City, an individual can meet 11,000 others within a 10-minute radius of his office by foot or car. In Newark he can meet more than 20,000 persons within this radius. But in midtown Manhattan he can meet fully 220,000" (cited in Milgram, 1970, p. 1461). The numbers are impressive, but there is a subtle flaw in the language that conveys more than the numbers do. In Nassau County we might *encounter* 11,000 people and know or meet some reasonable proportion of them. But one does not *meet* 220,000 people. Quantitative differences in the numbers of people around oneself imply qualitative differences in the nature of one's relationships to them. In midtown one might pass by a great blur of humanity, but the odds of knowing even a single person in the stream are quite low. Jane Jacobs (1961) has summarized this distinction quite pointedly: "Great cities are not like towns, only larger. They are not like suburbs, only denser. They differ from towns and suburbs in basic ways, and one of these is that cities are, by definition, full of strangers" (p. 30).

Once stated, this point may seem so self-evident and straightforward as to be useless. For urbanites it may seem to be so much a given in the facts of life that it is no more enlightening than to tell a fish that it lives in "a world of water." Yet for those of us who live in or near a large urban center it is important to realize that life in a world of strangers is a very recent historical development. In the lengthy history of civilization, people in most times and most places lived among people they knew by face or name. Even the great cities of ancient history would be dwarfed in population size by the urban centers of today.

If and when strangers were encountered, they might be interrogated, feared, celebrated, or possibly eaten. In most times and in most places they were the subject of fear, suspicion, or at least curiosity. Today in cities we have so adapted to living under present conditions that we move among masses of strangers with perfect ease and express surprise when we meet a familiar face rather than a strange one. City people expect and tolerate strangers, and many prefer their public relations to remain on that basis. Even those people whom we encounter each day while waiting for a bus or an elevator rarely become more than, as Milgram (1977) has called them, "familiar strangers."

For Lofland, then, to live in a city is not so much to deal with the issue of overload as to deal with the crucial problem of *anonymity*. A pointed demonstration of urban anonymity is represented in an example filmed by Stanley Milgram on the streets of New York. A man stands on a street corner in midtown Manhattan. He is holding a large placard with a giant photograph of a New Yorker – not a famous person, not a politician, just a New Yorker. Ten dollars is offered to anyone who can identify the man in the picture by name. Thousands of people stop, look intently at the photo, throw up their arms in frustration or make wild guesses. Hours later the ten dollars has not been given away. Is the mystery man a misanthrope, is he friendless? No, he is just another anonymous urban face.

Once anonymity is considered carefully, one comes to the realization that it can be thought of in two different ways. The first is the unknown quality *of others*, of the nameless, faceless nature of the strangers around us (as in the filmed example). The second involves being anonymous *to others*, of being nameless to, or not cared about by, the people around us. The one involves not knowing, the other involves not being known. As for this first aspect, it is suggested that we come to know how to relate to strangers by an "ordering" of the populace on either of two dimensions. That is, we gain clues about what people are like and how we should treat them as a function of either appearances (e.g., dress, personal manners) or locations (the places and circumstances in which we encounter them). By developing a keen sense for such cues, the urbanite can anticipate the actions of others and offer the appropriate degree of respect, formality, or interest in any given interaction.

As for the sense of personal anonymity, Lofland indicates that although people can accept a limited dose of it, total anonymity would be intolerable. Therefore, the urbanite makes use of public settings in such a way as to develop varying degrees of personal or private relationships within them. The analogy used to illustrate differing levels of urban intimacy involves the relationships of customers, patrons, and residents.

In a relationship in which your role resembles that of a customer, you simply come and go. Others may take note of you, but there is no more chance that you will return than that you will never be seen again. The relationship is transient, people are strangers, and knowledge of one another is at best casual. Such fleeting encounters abound in the city. As a patron, however, you are not just a customer, you are a regular customer. You are still passing through, but you are coming to be known and recognized by your fellow travelers. Personal knowledge in such a case remains largely superficial, but the relationship at least reaches a state of familiarity, with a small but potentially growing commitment between people. Finally, by forming a relationship in which you are a resident, you have turned public territory into a "home territory." Residents know not only the features of a place but also its people and patterns of use. Their relationships develop to the point of intimacy and caring, and they feel at home there among other residents. Only residents know which other people are customers, which are patrons, and which are fellow residents.

What Lofland means to convey by this analogy is that urbanites learn to adapt to living among great numbers of others by knowing how and when to anticipate and develop differing kinds of relationships. Urban concentration has not created a race of people who have lost the capacity for close, caring relationships; rather, it offers people the skills for having satisfying fleeting relationships. The urban experience is neither singular nor unvarying. Sometimes people are known and sometimes they are unknown, sometimes they know and sometimes they are unknowing – depending on the time and place. That anonymous face on the placard that passersby could not recognize is probably known as "Daddy" to one or more young urbanites and loved or hated by his colleagues at work. Many kinds of relationships abound for the urbanite, from anonymous to fleeting to deep; and each fits into a larger whole of urban experience. Having many kinds of relationships can often be satisfying and can sometimes be frustrating, but according to Lofland it makes the experience of city living both interesting and unique.

The behavior-setting approach

Whereas others have anchored their versions of urban reality in the numbers of people (Wirth), the numbers of unfamiliar faces (Lofland), the numbers of subcultures (Fischer), or the amount of stimulation (Milgram), Roger Barker and his colleagues (Barker & Gump, 1964; Barker & Wright, 1955) have taken a very different approach in dealing with the meaning of size. Whether Barker was looking at a city, a small town, or any of a number of organizational settings (e.g., a school), he looked first at its facilities, its behavioral resources, and its activities – its *behavior settings*. He looked at the people in relation to their activities and involvements within these settings, and as a result he looked at their activities and involvements with one another. Although most of this research and theory has been generated in settings other than the city, it provides a unique if not contrasting perspective on urban life and, therefore, is worthy of attention (see Wicker, 1979, for a thorough and concise review of Barker's general approach).

To summarize briefly the relevant aspects of the theory, a behavior setting is a discrete physical setting (e.g., a restaurant, a classroom) in which a standing pattern of behavior takes place (e.g., eating, lecturing). The density of an environment is not calculated by the people per unit of land but rather is represented by the number of people available to populate (or "man," in Barker's terms) each of the behavior settings. As population increases, the number of settings also increases, but at a slower rate than the number of people. The larger the environment (big school, big city), the more people there are available to be involved in each setting, with the result that any given large setting is likely to be overmanned. At the opposite end of the population scale (small school, small town), environments are more often undermanned: They have fewer people than necessary to maintain them and handle all of their necessary activities.

Research in a number of organizational environments has shown that people's experiences and behaviors in undermanned environments contrast with those in optimally manned or overmanned environments. Occupants of undermanned settings more often serve in positions of responsibility, engage in activities important for the setting's proper functioning, perform a wide range of activities, work harder and feel more responsible for the fate of the setting. People in overmanned settings are more likely to report satisfaction from vicarious identification with the setting and its occupants than from direct participation.

Even though only limited research in this tradition has been done within the urban context itself, the possibilities for drawing analogies are still great. For instance, one could argue that as an overmanned environment the city allows its residents few opportunities for direct involvement in its communal and organizational life. A person cannot become involved with a group just because he or she wants to help. There are too many others who also want to be involved – "put your name on the waiting list." Therefore, when involvement and responsibility become honors bestowed on very few rather than obligations jointly shared by all the members of a group, there is a possibility of the kind of alienation and anomie to which Wirth refers.

Clearly, much of the reasoning and evidence offered by Barker and his colleagues points to the value of smallness. Yet whereas counting and classifying behavior settings may be appropriate for a formal organization or even a small community, there is also the possibility that the analogy may break down at certain points when considering cities. First, the mere number of behavior settings in a city is so large that although it might be overmanned on the whole there is still a strong likelihood that a given person will find a niche among them. This suggestion is consistent with the subcultural approach. There is a trade-off between having a large number of activities and groups available in absolute terms and the likelihood that a person can have a relatively deep involvement in any one of them. It is not accurate, therefore, to say that urbanites are any more or less versatile than small-town people overall. Rather, it is probably the case that they are more versatile across settings and less versatile within them.

Second, in many types of activities and many public areas, the changing relationship of behavior and place does not allow for a simple classification in the behavior-setting scheme. We should not limit the operational definition of satisfaction to the sense of obligation and participation in a specific setting. Just as Lofland points out that relations between person and person can be expected to be different in city and in town, relations between person and place or person and activity are also likely to differ. Whereas one measure of satisfaction involves having a choice among many roles in a theater company putting on a production, a very different type of satisfaction comes from having the choice of attending any number of different plays being produced by skilled professionals on a given evening. Cities provide many more such person–activity combinations where the relationship is asymmetric – opportunity without obligation. Also, cities provide more vicarious identifications and involvements. To be an avid fan of the Yankees, the Celtics, or the Steelers, all professional athletic teams, may provide a great deal of satisfaction or involve much of a person's time and self-image, even though these may be judged passive involvements in the behavior-setting scheme.

The compositional approach

All of the versions of urban reality presented so far in this chapter, however different their consideration of process and outcome, have had one element in common: They are all models of *urban impact*. They look at the city and note how the conditions of urban life have had an effect on people's lives.

As Milgram (1970) has stated: "I suggest that contrasts between city and rural behavior probably reflect the responses of similar people to very different situations, rather than intrinsic differences in the personalities of rural and city dwellers" (p. 1465).

Herbert Gans's (1962a) view of urban–nonurban differences is just the opposite. He and others (i.e., Oscar Lewis, 1965) believe that the critical factors that distinguish urban from rural life can be attributed to differences in the *populations* inhabiting these different settings. The differences between the "urban way of life" and the "rural way of life" are not as great as the differences that distinguish the typical behavior patterns and preferences of people of various races, ethnic groups, social classes, and ages. This compositional approach, as Fischer (1984) has called it, emphasizes that there is a self-selection of people into cities and out of them and that people exercise choices and move on when they want different environments. According to Gans, cities are reflections of their people; people are not reflections of their cities.

In order to make this point, Gans has compared the city to the modern suburb, listing some of the most important differences cited as distinguishing urban and suburban lifestyles. He points out, however, that once we control for the personal characteristics of the residents in the two places, few differences remain. Ktsanes and Reissman (1959–60) have proposed that those people who move to suburbs from the city are *already* different in their values and orientations from those who do not. The suburbs, they suggest, rather than being places that take similar people and require them to adopt a new or different way of life, are simply "new homes for old values." Gans has stated:

Concepts such as "city" and "suburb" allow us to distinguish settlement types from each other physically and demographically but the ecological processes and conditions which they synthesize have no direct or invariate consequences for ways of life. The sociologist cannot, therefore, speak of an urban or suburban way of life. [P. 47]

I began this discussion of varying versions of urban reality with the deterministic position of the human ecologists and then introduced other theories that specify how people adapt to, and deal with, the city. In the last position to be discussed, Gans brings the pendulum from one extreme of its swing to the other: He discounts the physical and ecological impact of cities, accounting for differences between urban and rural locales by the differences in their people. One problem with this extreme is that it denies both the structural and the psychological constraints of size and density, as well as their enabling qualities. Cities may differ very much from one another because of their differing population characteristics, yet they still hold key ecological similarities. The predominant population characteristics might lead Detroit to be termed a blue-collar city, Miami to be called a tourist or old-age city, and Boston to be labeled a highly Catholic city. Still, there seems no doubt that each of these places resembles the others in many ways – far more than any one of them resembles a small town. Gans is correct: Different kinds of people structure and act upon the environment according to their unique values and preferences. But the other positions are equally correct because we cannot deny the basic physical context within which people live. This is a fundamental part of seeing the city as a place of multiple and contrasting realities and merely reiterates the basic Lewinian position that behavior – in this case urban behavior – must be explained as a *joint function* of the person *and* the environment.

Summary

In our quest to discover the effects of living in a city, we have begun with the most obvious fact available to us: Cities have larger populations than other places. The most direct manner of measuring size and its impact is to count heads and look at the demographic correlates of a large population. Another way to look at size is from the point of view of the anonymity it brings. In this approach we would count not heads but familiar faces. At an abstract level, we can consider size as a matter of the demands for processing stimulation, the need to pay attention to and deal with the sights, sounds, and demands of the city. On a more concrete level, we can look at size as a matter of urban subcultures or the number of discrete behavior settings in a city that engage people and direct their activities. Or we may even decide that size is largely irrelevant and look at "who" populates the city rather than "how many."

Reviewing each of these perspectives reminds us that the point of view from which the city is considered determines the questions that are asked, the ways in which the questions are studied, and the answers that come about as a result. It is equally important to recognize that the interpretations of these answers and the conclusions that are reached also derive from the idiosyncrasies and limitations of one's starting point. The fact that the city is large may lead us in any number of directions, depending on how its size impinges upon us. According to the distinctive features we see, it may appear to bring opportunities and alternatives or it may seem to bring mostly strain and discomfort. City life carries both these advantages and these disadvantages, and therein lies its hot–cold nature.

Suggestions for further reading

Fischer, C. 1984. *The urban experience* (2nd ed.). New York: Harcourt Brace Jovanovich.

Gans, H. J. 1962a. Urbanism and suburbanism as ways of life: A reevaluation of definitions. In A. M. Rose (Ed.), *Human behavior and social processes*. Boston: Houghton Mifflin.

Lofland, L. 1973. *A world of strangers*. New York: Basic Books.

Milgram, S. 1970. The experience of living in cities. *Science, 167*, 1461–1468.

Wirth, L. 1938. Urbanism as a way of life. *American Journal of Sociology, 44*, 1–24.

4
THE CITY AS I SEE IT: IMAGE AND ACTIVITY

...consider the cases of men who, through brain injury, have lost the ability to organize their surroundings. They may be able to speak and think rationally, even to recognize objects without difficulty, but they cannot structure their images into any connected system. These men cannot find their own rooms again after leaving them, and must wander helplessly until conducted home, or until by chance they stumble upon some familiar detail ... The whole situation parallels, in a curious fashion, the way in which we proceed in an unfamiliar city.
– Kevin Lynch, 1960, p. 125

Part I of this book has been involved in laying the groundwork concerning the many ways in which we can conceive of cities and their effects on people. Chapter 1 set out the general orientation to be taken, and Chapter 2 addressed itself to the search for relevant dimensions of urban description and classification. In Chapter 3 we explored a set of more fully developed models of city life, discovering that the basis for each was the set of characteristics that each theorist has seen as critical or at least distinctive. I believe, however, that the defining feature of city life is not the existence of any one element but the fact that the city has so many apparently distinctive aspects. Whereas one person may note the existence of crowds and strangers, another will find the existence of small subcultures most salient. Although they are differing and sometimes directly contrasting views of the city, each is correct – for some people and at some times.

The focus of this chapter is on the *image* of the city that people develop. There are as many different images as there are people. Each is unique, some are directly contrasting, and all serve as guides to people's thoughts about, and behavior within, the cities they encounter. Here, therefore, we move from the perspective of the social scientist to that of the urban resident, from the position of the outside observer to that of the person in the city.

As W. H. Ittelson (1978) points out, we tend to talk about "the city" as if it were a giant, monolithic structure. Actually, each of us only knows parts of it and experiences only bits and pieces of it at any one time. It is much like the contrast between someone sitting in a concert hall and experiencing a large and complex piece of music as a whole, because he or she is an outside observer, and the members of the orchestra, all playing their own parts and getting very different and highly selective or idiosyncratic impressions of the total work. In this chapter, then, I ask the following questions: How is the city seen? How is it known? In what ways do people build up images of the city, and of what use are these images? We will be exploring what Steven Carr (1970) has referred to as the "city of the mind."

Let us take an example that should illustrate the importance of these issues. Though the exact scenario may vary, some version of this experience should be familiar to anyone who has ever moved to a new environment. A young couple with two children is planning a move to a large midwestern city as the result of a job transfer. They have never before visited the city, and they have no friends living there. They have heard many good things and some bad things about it, and now (with the children being cared for at home) they have arrived on a house-hunting trip. Armed with nothing more than their wits and the maps and tour books from their local AAA, they are about to plunge feet first into the highly exciting and sometimes threatening process of urban knowing.

The ride in a cab from the airport seems an inordinately long one. From their viewpoint in the back seat, the highways they are traveling look like highways anywhere else. As they go along, however, the texture of the scene outside changes little by little from trees and open fields to people and concrete towers. As the cab turns up a series of wide avenues and down a number of narrow side streets, all sorts of thoughts go through their minds: "Is it much further?" "Who knows?" "Are we being taken for an expensive, roundabout ride by a cabbie who has spotted two newcomers as fair game?" "It's impossible to tell." The point is that these people could be taken by almost any route because they have no spatial sense of where they are going or how to get there. They have no significant means by which to orient themselves to their surroundings. In short, they have no image of the city.

Within a year or two they will be able to state without blinking an eyelash how to get from home to work, how to get to their children's schools, to the doctor's office, and to the movie theater that plays only classics. They will be able to tell you why and when to visit each of the three local shopping centers, what areas of the city to avoid at night, how to find parking downtown, and which routes of public transportation are most reliable. They will have invested their environment with order and meaning; and in the process they will have been transformed from people carrying maps in their hands to people carrying maps in their heads (see Kaplan, 1973; Kaplan & Kaplan, 1982).

Some basic terminology

Before going any farther, it would be best to define certain critical terms such as *perception* and *cognition* as they apply to our urban concerns. Although these words have been used interchangeably by many urban researchers, there are some subtle and not so subtle distinctions between them that are important to make (Rapoport, 1977). *Perception* denotes the direct sensory experience of a stimulus or an environment. It refers to the immediate imposition of some form of energy on the individual sensory receptors. Thus via perception an individual *gathers* or *obtains information* about the environment.

When we use the term *cognition*, we imply more. The word refers to the process by which gathered information is *organized* and *structured*. Via cognition, existing information is categorized, sorted, and placed in meaningful groupings. All future information is dealt with according to these categories and either is modified itself or, in certain cases, modifies the very system into which it was placed. A third term, *evaluation*, is relevant here as well. This process is one step beyond cognition and refers to the addition of *values* and *preferences* to structured cognitions. What may be seen as an undesirable slum neighborhood by one group of observers may be seen as a pleasant and reasonable place to live by others (Fried & Gleicher, 1961). Thus urban behavior, whether it follows a small decision, such as the choice of a route to take to work, or a major one, such as the choice to stay or to move, is the end product of all three processes. People act on the basis of information that is collected (perception), encoded (cognition), and judged (evaluation).

In reference to the contents of this chapter, when we speak of the city of the mind, we are most directly dealing with the realm of cognition. Cities are large and complex. They cannot be perceived as a whole. Rather, we have cognitions about the whole. These cognitions – or, to use a more popular term, *impressions* – may be linguistically encoded, as dealt with in Chapter 2, or spatially encoded. These spatial encodings, images of the city, form the focus of this chapter. That is, when we refer to the formation of cognitive maps of the city, we are referring to a process by which people acquire, store, recall, decode, and use information about their spatial environment, about structure, location, direction, and distance in the cities in which they live.

The functions of urban cognitive images

First of all, we should ask why the individual needs a cognitive map of his or her city. What purpose does it serve? What is the difference between a person who has a good one and a person who does not? Steven Carr (1970) begins to answer these questions by using the analogy of the infant trying to make sense of the world. Just as the young child must create a stable and meaningful environment out of a blooming, buzzing confusion of disconnected events, so must individuals entering a novel environment build up a model of that world to simplify and connect events for them. If I recall my own first, brief trip to Boston (which was as an adult), I can distinctly remember being driven along some large streets (the names of which I did not remember at the time), past Boston University and Boston College, and spending some time downtown along the Freedom Trail; but I can just as distinctly recall having no sense of if or how these things were related to one another. I had a sense of whether I liked the things I saw at each discrete stopping point, but had I somehow been separated from my hosts, I would have been as successful at re-creating the trip or retracing my steps as Hansel and Gretel without their bread crumbs. What I was missing and what each person needs to develop, according to T. R. Lee (1969), is a sense of *whatness*, the qualities of objects and places and their value to us, and of *whereness*, the location of objects in space and their relationship to one another. Having developed such a sense of orientation, we can turn random behavior into "planful" behavior (Carr, 1970).

Kevin Lynch, the noted urban planner whose book *The Image of the City* (1960) is credited with having generated the current interest in this field, has suggested that the image of the city serves a number of important functions. The first and most basic is what we might call its *mobility* function. That is, a clear image of the city allows people to move around quickly and easily from one place to another. It also allows them to analyze contingencies and formulate plans for alternative routes to a given destination. When a person with a good image of the city sees a traffic jam ahead on the road, he or she can get off, go through a series of side streets, and end up in the right place without losing much time. The person without a clear image, however, is left with the choice of sitting in the car and enduring the wait or taking a chance and running the risk of getting hopelessly lost.

More than simply facilitating strategic interactions with the environment, the cognitive image serves a more general purpose that we may label its *organizing* function. The image serves as a broad frame of reference, as a means of structuring beliefs and knowledge about the city as well as activity in it. As stated in Chapter 3, the environment provides a surfeit of cues, more than any one person could ever pay attention to. Norbert Weiner (in Carr, 1970, p. 520) has suggested that each of these may be seen as a "to whom it may concern" message that people with differing needs, interests, and purposes may choose to deal with or not. Once people have developed a set of cognitive-spatial categories by which to code and store information, they can begin to be effective in selecting certain messages while disregarding others. As a result, what might seem a hopelessly busy and chaotic city to a newcomer becomes a manageable and livable place to the possessor of a clear image.

These first two functions complement each other in several ways. For instance, while the mobility function increases the person's freedom of choice and opens up options for behavior, the organizational function decreases the need for making choices by providing a set of guidelines that allow the person to move through the city as if on automatic pilot. In addition, whereas the image's organizational aspects allow people to deal with an overload of cues, the mobility function allows them to make their way through the city with what might otherwise seem like a lack of cues.

A third aspect of the cognitive image mentioned by Lynch is what we shall call its *emotional* function. By this we mean that having a map of the city in one's head allows a sense of comfort, ease, and emotional security in movement that one cannot feel without a clear image. Visitors to Boston or Rome may see their crooked and narrow streets as a labyrinth of mirrors and wonder how and when they will ever get out; yet longtime residents are likely to take pleasure in exploring them and appreciating their complexity, knowing how to "escape" if they should ever begin feeling lost.

A recent experience of my own with the New York City subway system provides a case in point. Not having lived in New York for almost twenty years, I am a bit weak on the current details of the subway system. But because I lived there from birth through college, my general feel for the city and its public transportation system is still quite strong. On a visit a year ago, I was faced with having to decide on the spot whether a certain train would get me to my destination or not. Had I been a newcomer, for fear of getting lost I would have waited and checked the subway map. But having one neatly tucked under my hat, I got on the train, knowing that although I might go wrong, I need not have any *fear* of getting lost. Why? First, I could recognize if I were going in the wrong direction; second, I knew how to correct this error; and third, I would know – even if my choice proved wrong – where I was, whether the place was safe or not, and how to get help in finding my way if I needed it. Thus we can see that mobility and security go hand in hand.

Finally, Lynch mentions the *symbolic* function of the urban image. He says that images provide symbols and strong associations with a place that facilitate communication between people who share a common environment. Collective memories of hometowns and shared images of current places of residence provide strong bonds between people. The instance of two strangers meeting in a foreign country and saying, "Are you really from Fort Worth? That's where I was born," will often lead to a long and pleasant conversation. The fact that mental representations of certain landmarks, meeting places, or special neighborhoods can be shared suggests, therefore, not only that cognitive maps serve a purpose on the individual level but also that they are capable of playing an important social or interpersonal role.

The image itself

Given that cognitive maps serve a number of functions, the next set of issues we shall pursue involves their nature and characteristics. How do we know what a person's map looks like, and what can we say about a city on the basis of these maps? To talk about the "how" of obtaining cognitive maps it is best to start with Lynch's work and then note how others have refined it, changed it, and derived new means from it.

Map making and analysis

Lynch chose three cities that appeared to be very different and recruited thirty residents in Boston and fifteen each in Jersey City, New Jersey, and Los Angeles. He asked these people first of all to draw maps of their own cities as if they were making a rapid description for a stranger. He also asked them to list the elements of the city that were most distinctive; to provide detailed descriptions of their trips through the city, including areas passed through and their reactions to them; and to describe any strong emotions toward specific features of the city. Using the map drawings as his primary source of data, Lynch sought out areas of consensus in order to form what he called "public images" of each city.

In analyzing the maps, he was concerned with two desirable urban qualities, *imageability* and *legibility*. By imageability, he was referring to the ability of objects to evoke strong associations and emotions – images – in any given observer. By legibility, he referred to the pattern or organization of the elements of the city that allows them to be seen as a coherent whole. Thus a city that was highly legible and imageable would contain individual structures and whole areas that were both distinctive individually and clearly interconnected in a way that the people of the city could appreciate. Such a place "would seem well formed, distinct, remarkable; it would invite the eye and ear to greater attention and participation" (Lynch, 1960, p. 10). In short, the more imageable the city, the more pleasing it would be to live in.

In order to study these public images and construct aggregate maps from individual maps, Lynch classified their contents into five elements: paths, nodes, districts, landmarks, and edges. *Paths*, which often serve as the basic element of a mental map, are represented by any channel of movement – streets, highways, bus or train lines. They are the routes by which people move from one place to another. To the extent that people travel by any means through the city, they know the environment as a set of paths. On a map a path is what the eye follows, and on the ground it is what feet and tires follow.

Not all paths run parallel to one another. They must meet or intersect at certain critical points. These points are known as *nodes*. A major square in a city, a subway station, or any strategic or distinctive point can serve as a node. Activities and events are often concentrated there, and people usually arrange to meet one another there, saying, for instance, "I'll meet you at the corner of Broadway and Forty-second Street." A node also often serves as a focus or symbol of another map element, the *district*. A district is a region or section of the city that is recognized as having a common character. Although it is not necessarily marked off physically, people recognize that they have entered a given district by any number of means. It may simply have a peculiar or unique flavor (Greenwich Village, the Left Bank), it may be ethnically distinctive (Chinatown, Harlem), or it may be functionally distinctive (Wall Street, the red-light district).

If districts are distinctively large physical regions that are memorable in certain ways, on a smaller scale a critical element in imageability involves a city's *landmarks*. These are specific and discrete physical objects such as buildings, monuments, or fountains that are especially distinguishable or notable. They are often found at important nodes, and they also may serve as points of reference to indicate distance and direction (e.g., "Go to the Sears Tower and turn left for two blocks"). In addition, a landmark may itself serve as an element that symbolizes a city as a whole – the Eiffel Tower in Paris, the Empire State Building in New York, the Golden Arch in St. Louis.

Finally, *edges* are elements that are linear like paths but that are not thought of primarily as paths. They may outline an area the way the shoreline does in Chicago; they may be physical barriers separating districts or may act as something that psychologically makes two areas distinct. The classic instance is the case of coming "from the wrong side of the tracks." The railroad in this case serves as a marker of discontinuity between two separate urban elements. Although an edge may sometimes serve as a path, the major distinction between these two is that paths are thought to serve as *connectors* whereas edges are considered elements that *separate*. All five of these elements are neatly capsuled in Figure 4.1.

Lynch and many other urban planners have used these elements to describe and analyze a number of cities throughout the United States and the world. For instance, Lynch found Boston to be a highly imageable city. Its public image proved to be well defined, consisting primarily of many loosely connected districts in addition to notable landmarks and an edge (the Charles River) that defined the city as funnel-shaped. Although residents were often confused about the pattern of streets, the major paths were well known and clearly distinct. Los Angeles (whose downtown only was studied and mapped) was found to have fewer distinctive features and was seen as less differentiated and lacking a clearly defined center. Still, while its image was less vivid, the fact that the downtown area was laid out in a clear, gridlike system did allow for mobility and a good sense of orientation. At the opposite extreme from Boston, Jersey City provided a low degree of imageability. Residents did not have a comprehensive view of the city, nor were there many distinctive elements in it. In fact, the things that people noted most were often edges

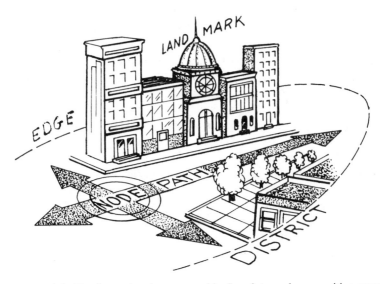

Figure 4.1. The five major elements used by Lynch to analyze cognitive maps. After Lynch, 1960.

that served as boundaries or barriers. Another major aspect of the image was not of Jersey City itself but of the view of the New York skyline lying beyond the city. The composite images of these three cities are shown in Figure 4.2.

Although we could spend a good deal of time comparing Lynch's techniques with those of others, or looking at images of cities in the Netherlands (see de Jonge, 1962), Italy (see Francescato & Mebane, 1973), or Venezuela (see Appleyard, 1976), our interest is not in the cognitive representation as an end in itself. Rather, we want to look at how environment, image, and behavior mutually affect one another. Specifically, we want to know how images are formed and how they are related to urban experience and behavior. Figure 4.3 shows a simple model of this interaction, emphasizing (1) that the environment provides the basic material in the form of distinctions and relations, (2) that the individual selects, organizes, and gives meaning to these in creating an image, (3) that activity and mobility are based upon each person's own cognitive representation of the environment, and (4) that each activity and experience of the individual is capable of providing modification in the image itself, which in turn affects future behavior. Thus there is a dynamic and reciprocal relationship between image and activity.

Different maps in different minds

If we are to consider the mental map from the perspective of the way it affects an individual's patterns of behavior, we must go back to the *personal* rather

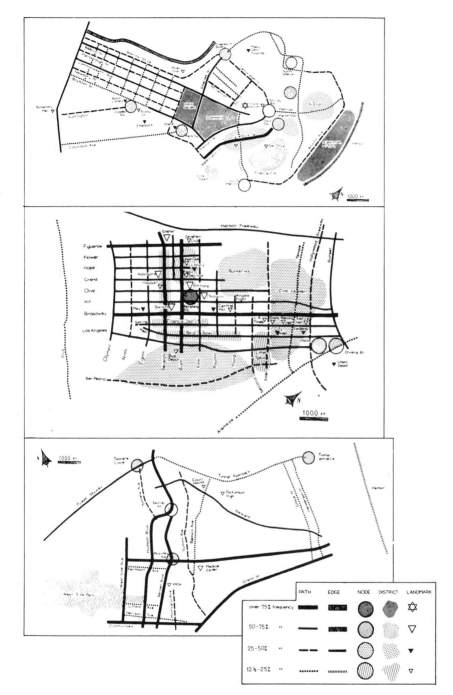

Figure 4.2. Composite images of Boston (top), Los Angeles (middle), and Jersey City (bottom). From *The Image of the City* by K. Lynch. Copyright 1960 by MIT. Published by the MIT Press. Reprinted by permission.

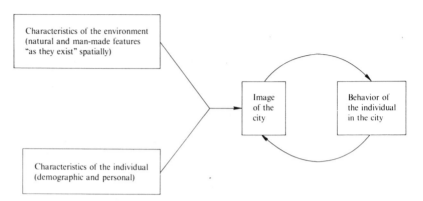

Figure 4.3. Relationships among person, environment, image, and activity.

than the public image of cities. Whenever we look at a given person's mental map we know that it differs in certain critical ways from the cartographer's map. First of all, it is selective in what it includes, almost as if it were a projective test of the environment. It is incomplete and sketchy. It does not include every path, district, and landmark; nor would we expect it to. What will be of particular interest in this section, however, is the question what it does include and what it does not, and why.

A second major characteristic to be considered is that the mental map contains many inaccuracies. Still, because we would not expect a freehand map to provide a perfect picture, perhaps a word more appropriate than *inaccurate* would be *distorted*. Distances and sizes are often grossly over- or underestimated; and the relationships between objects may be depicted in a way that bears no particular relationship to reality (Kuipers, 1982). Although they are images not of the city but of the country or the world, Figures 4.4–4.6 graphically capture these characteristics of selectivity and distortion. The size and importance of the things that are known or deemed significant grow to huge proportions in each of the caricatures, but in a basic sense they are not greatly different from actual maps drawn by real people.

Forming the image: modes of travel

Since the manner in which we know the city depends in large part on our interactions with it, it follows that the means by which we encounter and experience it should make a difference in what is actually seen and what is thought of as important (i.e., in the information that is received and also in how it is coded and stored). In this section I shall review a series of studies and generate some conclusions about the different amounts and kinds of information that drivers, passengers, and pedestrians receive about the city.

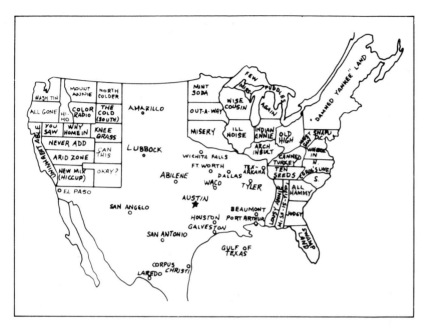

Figure 4.4. A Texan's map of the United States. From *Maps in Minds: Reflections on Cognitive Mapping* by R. M. Downs and D. Stea. Copyright 1977 by Curteich and Company. Reprinted by permission.

Since people are not drivers *or* passengers *or* pedestrians exclusively, however, my purpose will be to demonstrate how each of these modes contributes unique forms of information. Together they transform an image that is vague and disconnected (and therefore of little use) to one that serves the various functions described in the previous section.

A number of studies have suggested, for instance, that the activity or passivity of one's "navigational experience" is a critical determinant of how one knows the city (Moore, 1979). The more active one's commerce with the city, the better one should know it. Thus walkers (followed by bicyclists, then car drivers, and then passengers) ought to have the most ability to change routes, control pace, and direct their experience according to their interests.

In a study that predated *The Image of the City* by a year, Kevin Lynch and Malcom Rivkin (1959) asked people to take a walk around a particular block of downtown Boston to get the point of view of the urban pedestrian. These walkers were asked to report on what they saw and how they felt about the "trip." The researchers found that the walkers reported most on the spatial form of the environment: open spaces and particular structures that were dominant by virtue of their uses or associations. Of particular interest, Lynch

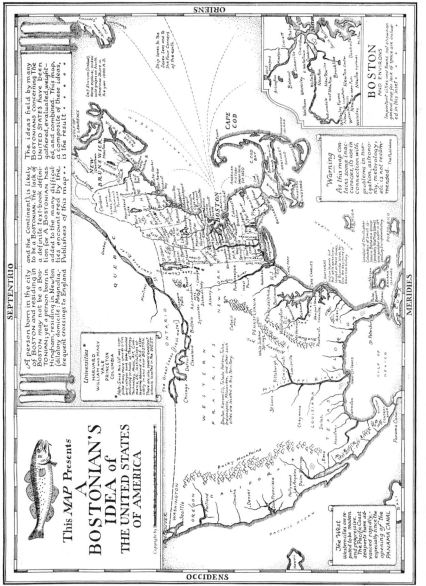

Figure 4.5. A Bostonian's map of the United States. Courtesy of Mrs. Florence V. Thierfeldt.

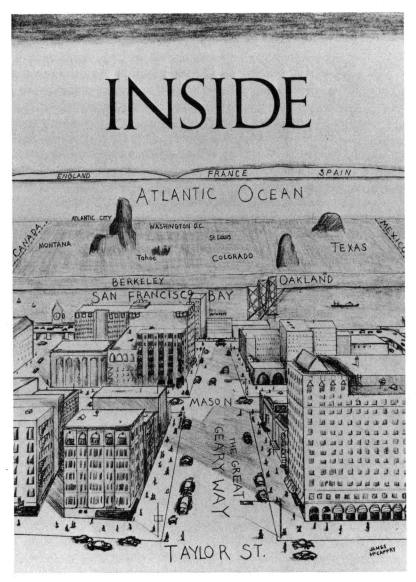

Figure 4.6. A San Franciscan's view of the world. Courtesy of Arts and Leisure Publications.

and Rivkin noted that subjects also made many reports about the texture, color, and state of repair of the sidewalk pavement. That is, the walker in the city is capable of noticing things about it at two extremes of scale. On the one hand, he or she is free to pay attention to the large-scale ordering of open and closed spaces to get a sense of the general form of the surroundings. On the other hand, the walker can notice things on the smallest of scales, finding cracks in the pavement or the difference between cobblestone and tarred streets to be of great enough significance to note and remember.

The size of modern cities and the need to travel greater distances than can be handled by foot have made the city as seen from the automobile an important topic. In their book *The View from the Road*, Donald Appleyard, Kevin Lynch, and John Meyer (1964) characterize the city as seen from behind the wheel in a way that clearly differentiates it from the pedestrian's perspective. The driver's view of the city is "a sequence played to the eyes of a captive, somewhat fearful, but particularly inattentive audience whose vision is filtered and directed forward" (p. 5).

In *The City as a Trip*, Steven Carr and Dale Schissler (1969) performed a careful and systematic study of the ways in which people form cognitive representations of the city while driving. Subjects in this study were pretested about their prior conceptions of the city and the roads that they were about to travel. Then they served as either passengers or drivers in a car on the Northeast Expressway in Boston. Their eye movements were recorded, and their memories of the trip were tested immediately, one day later, and again one week later. What the researchers found is that memory for differing elements of the trip was a function of the time an object was in view, the ease with which it could be labeled linguistically, how much it dominated or stood out from the existing context, and the subject's degree of general familiarity with it. Elements directly on the route (e.g., bridges, overpasses, and toll booths) were remembered most often; the next category was objects in the nearby perceptual environment (e.g., houses and billboards). Distinctive buildings in the distance and the general skyline were also noticed, though to a lesser degree.

Another interesting finding was that passengers and drivers generally tended to remember the same things in the same order of importance, but that drivers tended to have less detail in their recollections and descriptions. This finding is at variance with the principle stated before, that people in more active commerce with the environment should have better or more complete images than those whose roles are more passive. It also disagrees with the findings of Donald Appleyard (1970), who found in a study of drivers and commuters in Ciudad Guayana, that drivers had more complete mental maps than commuters.

These conflicting findings may be due to an artifact introduced into the Boston situation. That is, in Ciudad Guayana passengers were not aware that

3. In drawing their maps, wives used the home as the basic reference point, whereas husbands used more abstract coordinates

These results can be explained, much as the social class findings just given can be, under the assumption that women typically have a functional relationship to the environment different from men's. The women in these studies probably spent more time inside the home, organized their activity around it, and had a narrower range of environmental experience than their husbands. Although I am not aware of any available data relevant to this question, we could certainly hyothesize that in a situation where the wife worked outside the home, these differences would be erased, or that in a case where the husband stayed at home and the wife worked outside, these findings would be reversed. Once again, the argument is that what we have are not so much sex differences as differences in functional orientation and environmental experience affecting the nature of the urban image.

Changing images over time

Perhaps the single most striking factor affecting the cognitive image, aside from the *nature* of experience with the city, is the absolute *degree* of experience one has with the environment. For instance, there is a striking resemblance between the maps drawn by newcomers to a city and those created by young residents. Lynch (1960) found that people who knew Boston the least well oriented themselves by its topography, its larger districts, its generalized characteristics, and broadly defined directional relationships. Those who knew it better referred to specific paths and interrelationships and relied upon smaller landmarks rather than particular regions or paths. A study comparing the environmental images and behavior of experienced and novice cabdrivers in Paris (Pailhous, 1970) found that the two groups could not be distinguished by the extent to which they knew and used the primary path structure, nor were there differences in their familiarity with or use of smaller secondary paths: Neither group used them very often. What distinguished the novices from the old pros was that the experienced drivers had more complete and extensive images of the network of primary paths, and as a result this group were more efficient in finding their way back to the beaten path quickly and easily.

Relatively few studies have actually followed people over time rather than simply comparing newcomers and old-timers. Ann Devlin (1976) studied the wives of navy officers all of whom had recently moved to Idaho Falls, Idaho (population forty thousand). Devlin had these women draw maps after two and a half weeks in town and then three months later. She found that the initial maps most often showed the major arteries in town and were clear only in the path structure around the house, as Orleans and Schmidt had found.

Three months later, the maps contained more information (more streets, more landmarks), and the home territory was much less prominent than in the first maps. What gained greater prominence was the downtown, now that it had been explored. Other functionally relevant landmarks, such as parks, hospitals, and golf courses, also grew in prominence. In short, the image was sharpened and extended with a great deal more elaboration.

Research by Gary Evans and his colleagues (Evans, Marrero, & Butler, 1981) in two very different cities, Irvine, California, and Bordeaux, France, allows us to see whether the changes found by Devlin are common to many settings or unique to the place she studied. Irvine is a small city in southern California that is dominated by large, modern buildings and a state university that was barely fifteen years old at the time; Bordeaux, in the wine country of France, has its architectural and environmental roots firmly planted in the medieval era. Evans and his colleagues had their research subjects draw maps of their cities during their first week and after their first year in residence. In spite of the differences in the cities themselves, the pattern of environmental knowing developed in the same manner in both places. Landmarks served as the initial anchor points, with path structures elaborated around them. Over time, path structures between key locations became more elaborate, and as a result locations became better linked and distances more accurately defined.

Ittelson (1978) has proposed a series of steps by which such changes take place. First the resident must develop a sense of orientation. He or she must have a base of operations, a place from which relationships can start. Then exploration itself takes place. As a result of this exploration, categories for analysis of the city are developed, categories governed by the resident's goals, predispositions, and expectations. Having formed these categories, the person can then analyze all sorts of environmental contingencies and can take purposeful action. The subsequent interaction of the person and the environment are seen as a testing of categories and contingencies and as a further development and refinement of them.

To generalize from these studies, we find that the person unfamiliar with the city most often sees it in either of two ways: as a series of scattered spatial elements or as a sequence of main routes that are disconnected and fragmentary. As familiarity and sophistication increase, these maps shift from sequential or partially coordinated structuring with fixed reference points to spatially abstract structures with a great sense of coherence. With greater familiarity, people continue to rely on the same paths and landmarks; the difference is that these are now embedded in a highly developed network or pattern of elements (Appleyard, 1970).

Gary T. Moore (1974, 1979) has proposed and tested a model of developmental stages or levels of cognitive maps in children. This three-stage model provides an interesting analog between the way children learn to form more complex images of the world as they develop over time and the way adult newcomers develop their representations at a more accelerated pace. The three levels of representation in children differ according to the frame of reference through which the child sees the environment. As shown in Figure 4.7, the sequence of development goes in the following order:

1. *Egocentric*. At this stage the child's image is based on his or her own body and place in space. Images include personally significant streets and bear little resemblance to any geographic relationships.
2. *Fixed*. At this stage, the child uses a fixed frame of reference. The elements of the map are organized around known areas and key landmarks, but there is little overall coordination of elements.
3. *Coordinated*. At this stage, the child's images resemble the adult's. Here the images have the characteristics of associability (i.e., a given place can be reached by different routes) and reversibility (i.e., a route can be retraced).

Cognitive distance

Throughout this chapter I have taken the position that the image of the city is not important to us in and of itself. Rather, we need to be interested in how it reflects the multiple realities of the city that people construct cognitively and how it contributes to the varying behavior patterns that city people exhibit. Consider how people go about finding material objects and needed services in the city. It is possible that they are aware of and able to consider the full range of available options that exist throughout the city, but it is far more likely they know only certain areas well and have major blind spots in their images of the city as a whole. Obviously, the images of those sections of the city that are used most and are most familiar are more complete and fine-grained; people may be barely aware of the existence of other sections. As suggested by the research on class and sex differences, when people have more restricted images, it is also not surprising to find that their range of movement and activity is also limited. Quite simply, if a spot "doesn't exist" in our personal image, it is unlikely that we will ever go there, and vice versa. The image, then, provides people with the basic input that they need to *make a decision* to go from one place to another, and also with the information necessary to *execute that decision*.

One aspect of people's cognitive representations of the city that has attracted particular interest among psychologists, planners, and geographers has to do with the accuracy of distance estimations. Many researchers have been interested in this matter as a means of quantifying cognitive images, but for our purposes the concept of cognitive distance is important because it relates directly to decisions about movement. If the image and the environment are in close correspondence, there is good input with which to make an efficient

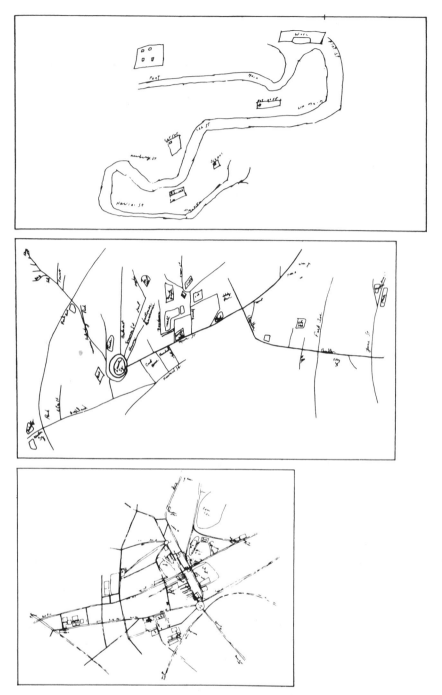

Figure 4.7. Sketch maps by children at three levels of development: egocentric (top), fixed (middle), and coordinated (bottom). From ''Developmental variations between and within individuals in the cognitive representation of large-scale spatial environments,'' by G. T. Moore. In *Man–Environment Systems,* 1974, *4*, 55–57. Copyright 1974 by the Association for Man-Environment Relations. Reprinted by permission.

decision. But if a place is cognitively (subjectively) distant, though objectively close, we will probably not go there even though the place is accessible to us. Conversely, if a place is cognitively close but objectively far, we will be late, frustrated, or confused in our attempts to get there. The following excerpt from a letter to the editors of *Newsweek* should offer (on a global rather than an urban scale) a sense of how distance may be cognitively distorted:

In its foreign policy cover story, *Newsweek* (December 14, 1970) reports that "a Marxist has taken over on the USA's doorstep in Chile." Have any of your comrades ever looked at an air distance chart lately? Santiago is over 5,100 miles from New York. Or, if you prefer, Moscow is over 400 miles *closer* to New York than Santiago. Ultimately, we may have reason to be bugged by developments in Chile, but proximity surely won't be one of them. [Donald Kline, January 18, 1971]

Concerning judgments of distance in the city, a number of studies (e.g., see Lowrey, 1970), have demonstrated that people in general are quite accurate in their estimates of distance between places. However, an interesting debate has arisen concerning the manner in which *direction* may distort accuracy in judgment. On one side of this issue is the research of T. R. Lee (1970). Lee performed a study in Dundee, Scotland, in which people estimated a number of distances that were either inward, toward the center of the city, or in the opposite direction, going away from the city. He found that there was a consistent underestimation of distances going inward and a similar overestimation of distances going outward. This finding was consistent with a long-existent but never carefully tested retailing principle, Brennan's Law (see Porteous, 1977). According to this law, an urban store does not draw its customers equally from all directions around it (as would be the case in Figure 4.8A); instead, the majority of customers will be found in a semicircle on the side away from town, as in Figure 4.8B. If this is true, we would expect the person depicted in 4.8C to be more likely to frequent store X than store Y because the influence of direction exceeds that of proximity.

In the case of the result depicted in 4.8C, Brennan argued that shopping at the inbound though farther store is not a violation of the principle of least effort, because it is reasonable to assume that people are likely to be on their way inbound anyway: The visit to store X will be just another stop. In his own research, Lee found empirical support for Brennan's Law. Of his subjects, 67 percent said that they would choose the nearest shopping center when it was inbound, but only 25 percent said they would do so when it was outbound. He found, further, that the inbound stores were preferred not because of their incidental convenience but because of his subjects' cognitive images. He proposed that a positive orientation toward the center of town shortens the distance in that direction. Just as "time flies when you are having

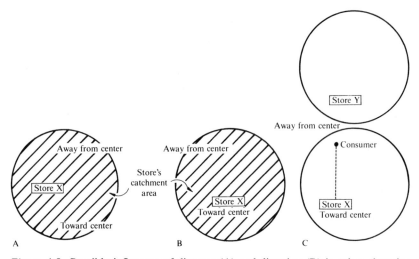

Figure 4.8. Possible influences of distance (A) and direction (B) in urban shopping behavior, and prediction according to Brennan's Law (C).

fun," "distance flies when you are thinking about places you would like to be." In other terms, there is something cognitively accurate as well as linguistically appropriate when we refer to having a "close friend" or a "distant relation."

These findings concerning Brennan's Law would be far simpler to deal with without the reverse findings of Ronald Briggs (1973) and Ronald Golledge and Georgia Zannaras (1973). Golledge and Zannaras had students make a series of distance judgments between the Ohio State University campus and a number of places located along a major highway. They found that distances into town were judged as relatively longer than distances out of it. Although one obvious possibility is that these particular intown locations were seen as unpleasant, Golledge and Zannaras suggest that when a trip leads people to encounter more traffic, is broken up into more small elements, and is more complex (as is a journey toward the center of town), people will experience it as longer.

It may seem that there is a direct conflict between Lee's findings, explained as a matter of positive and negative affect, and Golledge and Zannaras's findings, explained as a matter of cognitive complexity. Yet others have pointed out that these findings might be accounted for by a much simpler third factor, namely, that Lee was dealing with estimates along a generally featureless countryside, whereas Golledge and Zannaras's subjects were making estimates along a major path. Edward Sadalla and his colleagues (Sadalla & Magel, 1980; Sadalla & Staplin, 1980) have demonstrated, using both laboratory and field methods, that the greater the number of turns and intersections encountered, the greater the distance is judged to be.

From this discussion of cognitive distance we can see once again that what was phrased initially as a simple inbound/outbound difference is really potentially more complex. A number of factors influence the way in which relations (e.g., distances) between places are cognized. As stated by David Stea (1969), these include not only actual geographic distance but also

1. The relative attractiveness of origins and goals
2. The kinds and numbers of barriers between places
3. Familiarity with the area and connecting paths
4. Attractiveness and complexity of the connecting paths
5. Mode of travel
6. Whether the estimate assumes a straight-line path – ''as the crow flies'' – or considers the number of corners to be turned

As for this last point, to take one example, in order to get from my home to Tufts University – just a few miles in a straight line – I have the choice of going far west along a major route and then taking a high-speed, great-circle expressway or going on a seemingly endless number of small streets through three other towns to reach the same place. Although the direct-line distance is not great, the cognitive distance is immense, and not surprisingly I rarely find myself visiting the Tufts campus.

Going even one step farther in considering the cognitive relationship between places in and around a city, we might even ask about the *metric* by which distance is judged. Whereas some people cannot even imagine what one might substitute for miles, meters, or even blocks, ask a native New Yorker how *far* it is to get across town during rush hour. The answer will probably sound like, ''Traffic looks pretty bad today; it will probably take about an *hour*.'' Thus the very conception of distance may vary depending on travel mode and kinds of barriers – and with it so may our mental images and patterns of behavior.

Image and design

We have considered components of and differences in personal images of the city because of their importance to the individual, but it should be remembered that others, particularly urban planners, have studied these images with a different purpose in mind. Given the set of assumptions about the functions of mental maps stated in the beginning of this chapter, it could be reasoned that a city with a clear public image will allow for greater mobility, a heightened sense of security, and a greater aesthetic enjoyment than one that does not. It follows from this conclusion that if cities can be planned and designed so as to maximize imageability, the result ought to be maximization of the relationship between the person and the environment.

As Lynch found in a number of studies, the highly imageable city of Boston received positive ratings from his walkers, drivers, and map makers. At the other extreme, Jersey City, which was not very imageable, was rated quite low in satisfaction. Concerning distance, David Canter and Steven Tagg (1975) found that in Tokyo, a city with a confusing image, distances were generally overestimated, a finding that suggests that objects and areas were seen as far apart symbolically. On the other hand, in more highly imageable cities such as Glasgow and Heidelberg, distortions of distance were in the opposite direction.

Planning the city

With the knowledge gleaned from research like that presented in this chapter, planners and designers have gone about building new cities and remaking old ones. They tell us that if we want to make the structures and places in the city more distinctive, and therefore more imageable, a number of components need to be considered (Harrison & Howard, 1972). The first of these is physical appearance. In order to be recognized and remembered, a building should provide some visual appeal in its style, color, and design. Most important, it should also stand out from those around it. Second, its location should be considered. Ideally, it should be near a center of activities and either offer a view or serve as a reference point for other buildings and landmarks, so that it will become cognitively as well as physically accessible. Third, it should contain symbolic links to the cultural associations of the people of the city, whether these be historical, religious, or political. Stanley Milgram and his associates (Milgram, Greenwald, Kessler, McKenna, & Waters, 1972) have taken into account both physical design and social factors and have summarized these in a simple formula: Recognition $= f$ (centrality to population flow $\times$ architectural and/or social distinctiveness). Although these things are hardly subject to simple quantification, this formula should help estimate the general imageability of any given scene in the city.

More than with the imageability of any particular object, designers have been concerned with the ability of the city as a whole to present a clear-cut, coherent image (the quality of legibility) as well as to be striking and capture the eye and the imagination (imageability). Discussing a factor that is not subject to design, Douglas Porteous (1977) has suggested that when an urban area includes a hilltop from which the city can be seen as a whole by residents, this view creates a cohesive image. Derk de Jonge (1962) has suggested that an image is easier to form if the street pattern creates regular and dominant paths.

Yet although we must be able to make sense of the city, to find order in it and uncover relationships, many planners have pointed out that we do not want to make the city *too* legible. The environment should permit choice. It should contain novelty, challenge, and some degree of uncertainty. It should be open-ended and flexible, thereby leaving room for individuals to make themselves an active part of it. A. E. Parr (1973) has stated this perspective in relationship to individual buildings and whole cities in saying that "just as our bodies need food and exercise to grow strong and healthy so does our brain need an adequate sensory intake for its optimum development" (p. 32). He refers to the environment in which complexity and detail have been eliminated as being "pure as laundered sheets drying in the sun, but less lively" (p. 30); and he tells of the behavioral and symbolic effects of the bland environment: "In this stern environment, we walk when we feel in need of exercise or when the dog has to go, but we do not promenade for the visual pleasures of varied experience" (p. 30). Good design, then, satisfies two conflicting needs. It provides enough order to facilitate comprehension, movement, and security, and at the same time it offers enough complexity and change to stimulate curiosity and exploration.

Summary

In this chapter we reviewed a number of issues concerning the image of the city to find out how images differ among people and why they are important to all people. First, we found that the image serves four functions: It allows for mobility; it provides a general framework in which to organize activities; it allows the resident to feel emotionally secure; and it permits symbolic communication between people who share a common setting. Second, we briefly analyzed the maps people have provided of different cities, emphasizing the elements by which we can analyze them more than their content per se. Third, we considered how maps are developed and how they differ, discovering that people with differing social characteristics and varied travel modes come to generate images of the city that are somewhat idiosyncratic. Fourth, we considered cognitive distance as a means of studying urban images and discussed the factors that may affect estimations of closeness or distance. Finally, we looked at ways in which the designer can use this sort of information and take into account the cognitive abilities and needs of people in planning the city.

This chapter concludes Part I. In it we have looked at a number of multiple and contrasting ways of viewing the city: through the eyes of the social critic, the novelist, the social scientist, and the resident. We have compared verbal descriptions and cognitive images, objective modes and subjective descriptions. In Part II the focus will change from what the city is and how it *looks* to us to how the city feels and what it *does* to us. We will consider the effects of crowds, noise, and other stressful elements of city life, as well as friends, family, and other supportive elements of the city. Then we will follow up the discussion near the end of this chapter and note how design and planning can help create cities that satisfy the cognitive and emotional needs of their residents.

Suggestions for further reading

Downs, R. M., & Stea, D. 1977. *Maps in minds: Reflections on cognitive mapping*. New York: Harper & Row.

Evans, G. W. 1980. Environmental cognition. *Psychological Bulletin, 88,* 259–287.

Kaplan, S., & Kaplan, R. 1982. *Cognition and environment*. New York: Praeger.

Lynch, K. 1960. *The image of the city*. Cambridge, Mass.: MIT Press.

Moore, G. T. 1979. Knowing about environmental knowing: The current state of theory and research on environmental cognition. *Environment and Behavior, 11,* 33–70.

PART II
LIVING IN THE CITY

In Part I we considered various ways in which social scientists describe the city and also the ways in which the city is seen by its residents. In Part II we will get more directly into the experience of living in the city, by considering the conditions of urban life and the effects they have on people.

In Chapter 5 we will consider and analyze an approach toward urban living that focuses particularly on the stressful elements of the city, such as noise, crowding, commuting, and pollution. Then we will look at the effects of these conditions on a variety of outcomes. In Chapter 6 we will focus more on people in the urban environment, asking whether the city tends to encourage or prevent the development of close and caring relationships. We will be particularly interested in the concept of community and the role of the urban neighborhood in the development of urban friendships. In Chapter 7 we will look at the role of the physical environment in supporting or discouraging coping, friendship formation, crime, and fear. We will conclude in Chapter 8 by considering alternatives to the city and looking at ways of making city life better.

The approaches reviewed in the first two chapters of this part are very different in the ways they depict urban residents and the environment in which they live. In Chapter 5 we will consider the individual as an information processor and the environment as one that is potentially difficult to cope with – one that is stressful. The individual makes attempts at managing the environment and, depending on the success of these attempts, experiences positive or negative outcomes. In Chapter 6 the individual will be seen through a thick social fabric, as Fischer (1984) has put it. The person is more of a support seeker than an information processor, and happiness is measured by whether he or she becomes involved in networks of others who can provide support and comfort. Although the two perspectives differ quite a bit in emphasis and focus, there is nothing within either that is inconsistent with the other. Rather, each is an accurate but only partial description of the urban dweller.

In Chapter 7 we will add a third element, noting how the processes discussed in the two preceding chapters can be affected for better or for worse by the actual physical design of the city. Here we will find that although no form of design can create friendships or totally overcome the effects of overload, careful and informed urban planning can help insulate people from unwanted intrusion and disruption and can facilitate social interaction and social cohesion. That is, although the city will always contain some good as well as some bad, good design can accentuate the positive and go a long way toward eliminating the negative. In Chapter 8 we will weigh both the good and the bad, not only of the city but of other types of community as well. We will then conclude by looking at various means – interpersonal, architectural, and political, among others – of deemphasizing the negative aspects of urban life while maintaining the best of its positive qualities.

5

THE CITY AS TOO MUCH: CROWDING, NOISE, AND ALL THAT STRESS

It was 6:00 a.m. on a balmy April day in 1964. The place was a six-block stretch of Manhattan's Sixth Avenue between Radio City Music Hall and Central Park, in the heart of New York City. . . . Suddenly all hell broke loose. What someone later termed a "symphony of insanity" had begun. The overture to a three year concert combined the sounds of air compressors, jackhammers, rock drills, chain saws and dynamite blasts.
– Robert Baron, 1970, pp. 3–4, describing workers beginning a subway-extension project

New York is great. I've got so much noise. Subways. Horns. I can't stand nothing quiet, I go nuts.
– Jazz musician Miles Davis in the San Francisco Chronicle Review, *1981*

For a great many people the city is a place where they would *not* want to live: too many people, too much noise, too much dirt, too much pollution. Also, it sometimes seems as if people in the city do not care about one another. A person lying on the street might just as likely be stepped over as be helped. Some people are greatly bothered by these things, whereas others feel that they are a small price to pay for the advantages the city has to offer. But whether or not one is disturbed by the presence of noise or crowds, there is no denying their existence as part of everyday city life.

The task before us, then, is to consider the conditions of urban living and to see what the effects of these conditions are. We will review those aspects of urban life that have received the greatest attention in social scientific research – density, crowding, noise, commuting, and pollution – as major examples of the kinds of stressful elements people encounter daily. Having considered these things, we will attempt to go beyond mere description to consider *why* they are stressful at some times and not at other times.

The concept of stress

Although we shall be covering a great many different variables, both as causes and as effects, this approach to the city has one common theme: the city as an environment that is stress-producing. A basic model is shown in Figure 5.1. This model proposes that the experience of the city is a joint function

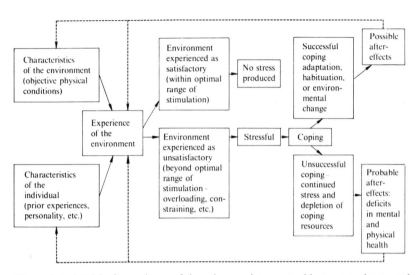

Figure 5.1. Model of experience of the urban environment with stress as the central concept. Adapted from *Environmental Psychology* (2nd ed.) by J. Fisher, P. Bell, and A. Baum. Copyright © 1984 by Holt, Rinehart, and Winston. Reprinted by permission of CBS-College Publishing.

of the objective characteristics of the environment and the individual characteristics of the person (e.g., how long the person has been in the city and what he or she was used to previously). Although it points out that the city may be experienced as satisfactory (i.e., as nontaxing or nonthreatening), the emphasis of the model is mainly on what occurs when the environment exceeds the individual's optimal level of stimulation (Wohlwill, 1966) or proves to be too constraining – that is, what happens when excessive demands are made on people's time and attention: when a person gets endlessly jostled trying to get from one end of a department store to another, for example, or when the noise from traffic or airplanes is so loud as to be totally distracting and interfere with work.

At this point the individual is said to experience stress, and he or she employs various strategies to cope with it. These may be personally functional or dysfunctional and may have various societal effects that are positive or negative. In addition, even when they are successful, they may result in various aftereffects. Throughout this chapter we will consider this urban-stress perspective. In doing so, we will try to take equal note of two contrasting aspects of urban stress: the ability of stressors to disturb and overwhelm the city dweller and also the urbanite's ability to adapt and thrive in spite of it all. These multiple and contrasting perspectives are captured by David Glass and Jerome Singer (1972) in the following statement:

Life in the city is an endless round of obstacles, conflict, inconveniences and bureaucratic routine. The urban dweller is confronted daily with noise, litter, air pollution and overcrowding. Some of these conditions are pervasive. Others occur only at home or at work or at transit. Their incidence is profoundly disturbing . . . yet observation of urban life cannot but lead to the conclusion that despite the unpleasantness of stressful conditions life goes on. Families are raised, jobs are accomplished and even social graces and amenities are preserved in some quarters. Either the stressors are not as potent as popularly believed or else man has the capacity to adapt and even shrug off the stress. [Pp. 5–6]

Basic processes

Stress, especially as it derives from environmental interactions and as it affects health and well-being, is a topic that has undergone much analysis in recent years (see Cohen, Krantz, Stokols, & Evans, in press; and Evans, 1982, for excellent discussions of this issue). There are many specific definitions of stress, almost all of them referring to an event or force (a stressor) that is unpleasant and, therefore, threatens the well-being and existence of the individual affected. Once they become aware of such threats, people react in some way (make a stress response) in an attempt to reduce or eliminate them. According to the classic model of Hans Selye (1956, 1976), which is based on the physiological response of the body, three stages of response can occur. The first is an *alarm reaction*, which mobilizes the body's resources and prepares it for resistance. Next is the stage of *resistance*, in which various attempts at coping are employed. These coping mechanisms continue until the stress has been successfully eliminated or until the body's resources have been used up and active coping can no longer be continued. This is the stage of *exhaustion*, when the body is likely to be highly susceptible to physiopathology such as invasion by germs and disease. This model can be adapted to a broader, nonphysiological approach: We can look at people's attempts to cope with events around them and can consider the possibility that unsuccessful or prolonged coping may result in the development of psycho- or sociopathologies.

Kinds of stress

Stressful events come in many different shapes, sizes, and forms. Richard Lazarus and Judith Cohen (1978) have identified three major classes of stress, varying in intensity (from strong to weak), duration (from long term to short term), and impact (from many people affected to only one or a few). *Cataclysmic phenomena* (e.g., floods, earthquakes, and other natural disasters) are sudden and extremely powerful events that affect large numbers of people.

Such a specific event may occur once and then disappear quickly, but still it tests the adaptive capacities of people to recover over a long period of time.

A second kind of stressor that Lazarus and Cohen have identified may be sudden or not and can be equally powerful, but it is focused on a single individual or small set of people. Examples of this class might involve the loss of one's job, a death in the family, divorce, or separation. Since fewer people are involved, and the stress cannot be as widely shared and supported, this situation also puts a severe test on the individual's coping resources.

Although some urbanites do lose their jobs, get divorced, or get uprooted by some natural (or perhaps bureaucratic) disaster, the kind of stress most relevant to our discussion is Lazarus and Cohen's third category, which they call *daily hassles*. These are the minor or semiminor annoyances that seem to crop up forever (as noted earlier by Glass and Singer). Individually considered, or taken as once-occurring events, no single daily hassle would tax the city dweller's ability to cope. Unlike the acute events included in the first two classes, however, these stressors tend to be multiple, chronic, and repetitive. A recent study by Lazarus and his colleagues (DeLongis, Coyne, Dakof, Folkman, & Lazarus, 1982), for instance, found that the number and rate of hassles experienced was an excellent predictor of overall health status and individuals' perceived level of energy.

These characteristics of urban stress act as a double-edged sword. On the one hand, any situation or stimulus that is chronic or repeated should make for greater ease of adaptation or habituation. That is, when first presented with a potentially threatening situation, an individual responds with great alertness and vigilance. Take, for example, one's first look at the downtown Los Angeles freeways at rush hour, with its resulting alarm. After driving home on the same route month after month without any great harm occurring, however, one discovers that the situation is relatively benign (i.e., that there was no reason for feeling threatened in the first place or that one is capable of coping with the threat anyway).

On the other hand, Glass and Singer (1972) point out that urbanites may pay a price for adapting, in the form of "psychic costs." Since much of human adaptation involves cognitive rather than physical work, adaptive efforts may begin to use up the available psychic resources over time, and urbanites may find that they are less able to cope with other kinds of demands and frustrations that occur subsequently. In addition, adaptation often involves a form of insulation from events and other people (as noted in the discussion of Milgram's overload theory in Chapter 3), so that a mode of coping that is functional on the level of the individual may prove to have very negative effects on a community-wide or societal level.

Having considered stress as a general concept we can now begin to understand how and why any particular stressor may affect people in cities. In the next section we will turn to an analysis of some of the major forms of urban stress.

Crowding

In 1962 John Calhoun published the results of a series of rather dramatic studies he had performed with rats. He started with a group of rats that were housed in four pens in a ten- by fourteen-foot observation room. The rats were supplied with all the food and water they needed and were provided with comfortable housing. Naturally, given such surroundings the rats multiplied greatly, eventually reaching densities far beyond what their person-built environment was meant to hold. By closing the partitions betweens pens one and four and using the elevation of the ramps between pens to vary the difficulty of getting from pen to pen, Calhoun encouraged an unequal distribution of the rats such that the two center pens had the major proportion of the rat population. Eating in the central areas became a social event, and many rats came there to eat and remained (often because a dominant rat kept them from going back to their original areas by blocking the ramp to the pen from which they came).

These overpopulated central areas Calhoun labeled a "behavioral sink," because in them there was a general breakdown of individual, social, and sexual patterns. Throughout the population, but far more in these two tightly packed areas, all sorts of pathology began to emerge. Elaborate courting, nursing, and nest-building patterns deteriorated severely. Some rats totally withdrew from interaction, some became extremely aggressive, and some became hyperactive and sexually deviant, mounting males and females in an indiscriminate fashion. Rates of miscarriage grew, and infant mortality reached as high as 96 percent in the sink area.

Calhoun's work, combined with the results of previous animal research (e.g., Christian, 1975), led some researchers to anthropomorphize and cite the evils of overpopulation for humans. Others, although they did not look from these results to the coming of Armaggedon, did think they warranted making human comparisons to the "inner urban core" of rat-dom (i.e., the middle pens), where the greatest problems occurred, and to the less densely populated and less affected "suburban" end pens. Still others denied the relevance of animal studies totally, pointing out that humans are the products of culture rather than instincts. They argued that we are so much more socially and cognitively complex (and therefore adaptable) that we need not take any caution whatsoever from the behavior of rats. The most useful response to this research, not surprisingly, has come from those social scientists who said "maybe" and went to work empirically observing and testing the effects of high population density on humans.

Defining the concept

The first and most basic task in dealing with crowding and its effects on city dwellers is to define just what it is. Daniel Stokols (1972) points out that when dealing with humans it is important to maintain a distinction between density and crowding. Density is a *physical* description of people in relationship to amount of space, a necessary but not sufficient condition for crowding. Crowding is the *psychological* or *subjective* experience that results from a recognition that one has less space than one desires. Crowding can occur when an increased number of people occupy a space formerly occupied by fewer, as when a commuter train fills up on its way into work (social crowding, in Stokols's terms), or when a constant number of people come to share a smaller area, as when a hallway full of people tries to fit into the same elevator (spatial crowding, according to Stokols). The key to all of this is (1) a matching of available space against ideal or desired levels of space for accomplishing one's goals or against social norms and (2) a resulting feeling of unpleasantness or dissatisfaction owing to infringement, constraint, or interference when there is not enough space.

The psychological or subjective nature of crowding becomes evident when we ask what is "enough" space and recognize that there is a wide range of variation among people (Taylor, 1980, 1981). As an example of the personal and cultural determinants of the experience of crowding, Amos Rapoport (1977) points out that 340 square feet per person is a recommended minimum for housing in the United States, whereas in Europe the figure is 170 square feet. In Hong Kong 43 square feet per person does not seem to be an unreasonable figure (i.e., one that leads people to feel crowded). Therefore, in a technical sense, in most cases we will be reviewing studies of high-density living, and all we can do is to try to *infer* from these studies whether people actually experience a feeling of crowding.

Another issue to be recognized is that even when we are speaking of density alone, there are many ways of defining people in relation to space. Consider two high-density automobile situations that are very different in certain ways and yet are similar in that they are both likely to lead to a feeling of crowding:

1. You are in a Volkswagen Rabbit driving along an empty expressway doing the speed limit. There are five passengers in the car, you being the middle one in the rear seat.

2. You are the only occupant of the same automobile, but the traffic outside is packed bumper-to-bumper and you have moved about a mile in the last half hour.

Obviously, both situations are likely to be experienced as crowded and unpleasant. Still, depending on whether we measure the amount of space and

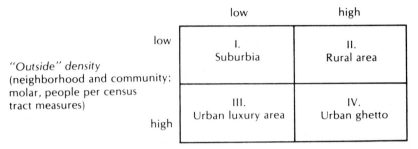

Figure 5.2. High-density situations of four differing types. From "Crowding and human behavior" by S. Zlutnick and I. Altman. In J. F. Wohlwill and D. H. Carson (Eds.), *Environment and the Social Sciences: Perspectives and Applications.* Copyright 1972 by the American Psychological Association. Reprinted by permission of the authors.

number of people inside or outside the car, we are likely to get very different readings of density. Using this reasoning, we can see that it is important to pay careful attention to the ways in which density is measured (Zlutnick & Altman, 1972).

Figure 5.2 demonstrates that urban density may be measured from either a *molar* or a *molecular* point of view. The first refers to crowding on a large scale, crowding on the outside. The second is just the opposite, referring to crowding on the inside or crowding defined from a small-scale point of view. Cell 3, labeled *urban luxury area*, is a situation in which density within the residential unit, the apartment, is low. Rooms are likely to be spacious, and the number of people per room, especially the number of people sharing sleeping quarters or bathing facilities, is low. Yet the building is likely to be many stories high and located next to another such building packed in beside it. Therefore, while the measure of people per room tells us one thing about the density of conditions under which such people live, if we compute the number of persons per acre (or, as is often done, per census tract) we will get a directly contrasting impression of how crowded these living conditions are.

Just the reverse picture describes cell 2, labeled *rural area.* In the case of the rural poor, especially when families are large, people may be forced to share a small set of rooms and may come to feel crowded in one another's presence. Yet if we look at the outside spacing of homes and people in relationship to one another, densities are extremely low. To complete the picture: In suburban areas, inside and outside densities are both low, whereas in urban ghettos, the number of persons per unit space is high whether we look inside or out.

Therefore, as we consider (1) research that measures density and then looks for the effect of crowding on people and (2) the theories suggesting why high-density living may be disturbing to urbanites, we must be aware in each case of how density and crowding have been conceptualized and measured. We will also note that whereas many of the earlier studies relied on a single definition (inside or outside) and just one measurement approach (subjective or objective), as studies have become more sophisticated they have included multiple perspectives. Table 5.1 shows how Sandra Newman (1981) used thirty-one different measures of crowding and density, including objective and subjective, interior (residential) and exterior (areal) measures.

Crowding research

Research on the effects of crowding on humans comes from two very different traditions, the experimental orientation of the laboratory and the demographic-correlational field approach. While lab-experimental research has much to recommend it, it is less relevant than field research to understanding urban crowding and, therefore, will not be dealt with in great detail (the interested reader should consult Baum & Epstein, 1978, and Fisher, Bell & Baum, 1984, for excellent treatments and reviews of this approach).

As for the demographic studies, it should be said at the outset that their results are highly inconsistent. For almost every researcher who claims a significant finding, there is another who has criticized his or her sampling, methods, or statistical techniques. And for every study in which gross area measures of density show a strong relationship with indicators of social disorganization, there is at least one that shows micro-level measures of crowding to be more important, and two others that show no significant or consistent relationship between crowding and pathology regardless of how each is measured (Choldin, 1978; Freedman, Heshka & Levy, 1975; Loftin & Ward, 1983). In addition, there are even reports indicating that for certain variables high density is associated with positive effects (Taylor & Verbrugge, 1980) and *lower* rates of pathology (Freedman, Levy, Buchanan, & Price, 1972; Webb & Collette, 1975; Winsborough, 1965). We shall review some of the major studies, propose reasons for the overall inconclusiveness of this literature, and then consider why, when, and for whom crowding might be most disturbing.

One of the earliest studies of note dealing with urban crowding was done by Robert Schmitt and was based on the 1950 Honolulu census (Schmitt, 1957). Schmitt considered a number of measures of density, ranging from the macro level (number of people per acre) to the micro level (number of

Table 5.1. *Measures of density and crowding used by Newman (1981)*

I. Objective residential crowding

   1. Household size
   2. Number of rooms
   3. Persons per room
   4. Required minus actual number of rooms
   5. Persons per bedroom
   6. Persons per bathroom
   7. Required minus actual number of bedrooms
   8. Pass through bedroom
   9. Pass through bathroom

II. Objective areal crowding

   10. Population per square mile
   11. Number of stories in structure
   12. Neighborhood single-family homes
   13. Number of dwellings in structure
   14. Dwellings per acre in development or parcel
   15. Average square feet per dwelling in development or parcel
   16. Feet to adjacent structure
   17. Park or vacant land on block
   18. Population per square mile (residential)
   19. Number of housing units per square mile

III. Subjective residential crowding

   20. Dislike dwelling size
   21. Dislike dwelling layout
   22. Dislike insufficient closets
   23. Dislike insufficient storage
   24. Lack of privacy or space
   25. Insufficient rooms problems
   26. Insufficient space problems
   27. Insufficient closets problems
   28. Insufficient storage problems
   29. Room size evaluation
   30. Dwelling space evaluation

IV. Subjective areal crowding

   31. Crowded area

Source: Residential Crowding: A Study of Definitions by Sandra J. Newman. Copyright © 1981 by the Institute for Social Research. Reprinted by permission.

dwelling units with 1.01 or more people per room), in relationship to a number of measures of social pathology, including rates of infant mortality, suicide, juvenile delinquency, and tuberculosis. He found a set of strong relationships between these indicators of pathology and density as measured by people per acre. After controlling for the education and income of residents, he found the relationship of persons per acre reduced somewhat but still significant. But the relationship between percentage of units with more than 1.01 persons per room and these measures of pathology proved to be insignificant.

Although the population and setting were completely different, similar results were found in a study of the Netherlands (Levy & Herzog, 1974). The researchers concluded that the number of persons per square kilometer accounted for more than 30 percent of the variance in juvenile delinquency, property crimes, and births to single women, even after socioeconomic status, religion, and number of persons per room were controlled for.

In contrast to the Schmitt and the Levy and Herzog studies, much other research has found that when density effects can be detected they are most often sensitive to measures that consider number of persons and amount of space ''in dwelling'' (i.e., micro-level measures). These studies propose that this is the level where feelings of crowding are most likely to occur from a disruption of social interaction. One piece of research that has attracted much interest is that of R. E. Mitchell (1971) in Hong Kong, an area known for very high densities both internally and externally. Among Mitchell's sample, for instance, 28 percent slept three or more to a bed and 13 percent four or more to a bed, and almost 40 percent shared their dwelling units with people to whom they were not related. Using personal interviews rather than simply relying on local records, Mitchell found that people who lived in high-density dwellings rated themselves as less happy and more worried than those whose dwellings were (by Western standards) less ''packed.'' However, there were no general differences in emotional health that could be attributed to density, and density effects in general were quite small. Most notable in Mitchell's findings were the effects of two other variables on emotional problems. People who lived with others who were unrelated to them and families living on the sixth or higher story of their apartment buildings were found to have the most hostility and the most significant signs of emotional illness.

An important series of studies that considers both the different types of crowding and the effects of other variables is the work conducted by Omer Galle, Walter Gove, and their colleagues, using data covering a period of forty years in Chicago. In one of their most widely cited studies, Galle, Gove, and J. Miller McPherson (1972) measured density as defined in each of four ways: number of persons per room, number of rooms per housing unit, number of housing units per structure, and number of residential structures per acre. They related these measures to five measures of social pathology. Using careful controls for social status and ethnic background, they found that people per room was the only density variable capable of accounting for a significant proportion of the indexes they measured. In order to test the stability of these findings over time, Galle and Gove (1979) further refined their statistical analysis and applied the same questions to census data collected every ten years from 1940 to 1970. They found that each set of data revealed similar outcomes.

As a result of their extensive research, Galle and Gove have generated a set of propositions regarding density and crowding. First, they find that there is a small but significant amount of variance that can be explained by density that is *statistically* independent of social structural variables such as race, income, education, and occupation. More important, they suggest that regardless of our ability to tease apart the effects of crowding and of demographic variables via complex statistical procedures, the effects of density and social structure are so highly intertwined that we should not discuss them as if they had independent effects. For a number of the measures, over 90 percent of the total variance explained by density and social structure could not be attributed separately to either one. As a result, they argue that we cannot, in attempting to explain various urban problems, look to density independent of social structure, nor can we blame urban ills on social structural variables independent of density. They suggest in this way that another yes–no, either–or debate needs to be looked at from a more complex point of view:

After all, it is a fairly reasonable statement that poor people, who cannot afford better housing arrangements, are much more likely to be found in crowded housing conditions. This statement appears trivially obvious to many, but the strength of this finding over alternatives – density as a major cause of pathological behavior or social structure as a major cause – needs to be stressed. Even though those who wish to shape public policy may desire strong and simplistic statements, these data do not lend themselves to that task. [Galle & Gove, 1979, pp. 26–27]

Dealing with the hodgepodge of findings

It is clear from this review of the literature that research on the effects of high-density living has been a good deal less than definitive concerning its impact on urban behavior. The reasons for this inconsistency and an eventual explanation detailing why and when density does have an impact can be traced via two routes: first, a consideration of methodological problems and differences among the various studies cited; and second, a conceptual discussion of density and crowding in light of the empirical literature.

Methodological issues

One major problem with sustaining any conclusion about the effects of density from one study to another is that the populations from which samples are drawn are extremely dissimilar. In addition, the specific operationalizations of crowding often differ from study to study. As noted by Sandra Kirmeyer (1978), characteristics of urban areas chosen for study vary widely. The region of the Netherlands studied by Levy and Herzog had high external densities and very low internal densities, whereas Mitchell's Hong Kong sample was among the highest in the world in both. In addition, characteristics of the specific groups have varied greatly from one study to the next. Education, income, occupation, cultural diversity, residential stability, and average age are all critical variables that not only may have independent effects but also may interact with density to create varying results. The Hong Kong sample studied by Mitchell was extremely poor on the average and had inadequate health services available. By contrast, Levy and Herzog's Dutch sample was affluent and well cared for. Cultural differences in modes of adaptation are another set of factors rarely considered in cross-study comparisons. Even heat and climate may play a role (imagine comparing Hong Kong and Chicago or New York and Hawaii on any behavioral outcome without taking climate into consideration).

Household composition is also of critical importance when considering density. In the United States the most important reason for high density within the home is the presence of many children. (In other cultures, the presence of extended family members may be the major reason for high densities.) When inside density is created by the presence of young children, we must consider how (1) problems of privacy among adults and (2) problems in socialization of children will be affected. Galle and his associates (1972) note that children in high-density homes are likely to be seen as a nuisance. Parents are happier when outside, because the demands on them are reduced; and the children actually prefer to be outside as well (i.e., to use physical withdrawal as a means of coping). Once outside, however, they are no longer under direct parental control. They are more likely to be influenced by peers and may become oriented toward or involved in criminal activities.

Another important issue that is rarely recognized or addressed is that when considering high and low inside densities many studies fail to take into account the percentage of people living *alone*. In one of their recent Chicago studies Gove and Galle (1979) found that 28 percent of their respondents were living alone. In a number of studies (Gove et al., 1979; Levy & Herzog, 1974; Webb & Collette, 1975) living alone has been related to higher rates of suicide, of admission to mental hospitals, and of use of stress-relieving drugs. Obviously, there is the possibility that too little contact is just as harmful as too much; but, once again, this idea is rarely discussed or acknowledged in the literature.

Another major problem with just about all of the studies of this type is that they rely on *aggregate* rather than on *individual* data. Aggregate data tell us important things about characteristics of a group (e.g., percentage of people living alone, rate of felonies per hundred thousand population), yet they leave out some important information if we want to draw conclusions about how density affects behavior. First, these are measures that present averages or rates over a wide area or group of people. They tell us little about the variation of density or variation of crime within an area. Two neighborhoods, one with a residential district that has a high proportion of single-family homes and the other with some apartment buildings and much heavy industry, will appear to have equally low density on the aggregate even though they represent very different living circumstances.

Second, it is impossible (or perhaps we should say improper, since it is sometimes done although it should not be) to conclude anything about individual feelings, reactions, or behaviors from these data. What we have is a gross rate of density related to gross rates of pathology. The data do not tell us *how* they are related, that is, how one factor actually impacts on another for the individual living under a given set of circumstances. Therefore, the discussion of psychological processes and intervening variables must be approached with great caution in the context of such studies.

A second characteristic of these data is that they are correlational. This means that whatever the relationship between density and X, density cannot be taken to be *the cause* of X. It may be that other factors related to both (e.g., social class) may cause some form of pathology or even that the direction of causation is just the reverse (i.e., that people who are antisocial or aggressive may prefer or be forced by conditions to move to areas that are high in density). Interestingly, for those people who see increasing rates of crime in the city as due to the increasing density of the city, it should be pointed out that the percentage of high-density dwelling units (those with more than one person per room) has consistently declined since 1940, and that this percentage is higher in rural areas than in metropolitan areas or central cities. Moreover, the number of persons per room is no higher in cities than it is for the nation as a whole (Carnahan, Guest, & Galle, 1974).

Conceptual issues

The association between high-density living and personal or social problems is not an automatic one. In order for crowding to have negative effects, the presence of others must somehow disrupt the development, maintenance, and regulation of typical or desired patterns of behavior. This claim is consistent with one finding that is seen throughout most of the literature: Density within the home is a more critical determinant than density in the immediately surrounding area.

Some of the major explanations offered for the effects of crowding involve excessive stimulation or overload (Milgram, 1970), behavioral constraint or interference (Schopler & Stockdale, 1977), and lack of privacy (Altman, 1975). I believe that when each of these explanations is examined more closely, one common element, the loss of control, is seen to flow through them all. That is, when an individual feels that he or she has lost the freedom to choose or the ability to exercise control over the environment, crowding causes problems. In the next few pages we will consider the relevance of each of these specific explanations to the concept of control in order to determine when and why high density leads to crowding and when and why crowding leads to personal and social problems.

Crowding as an instance of overload can be understood in any number of ways. One form is information overload, in which the amount of stimulation is so great that the individual has to adapt so as not to be overwhelmed. In a series of studies, Susan Saegert and her colleagues (Saegert, 1978; Saegert, Mackintosh, & West, 1975) sent subjects into various public settings (e.g., department stores) in New York City to accomplish a set of tasks. The tasks were carried out during times when the settings were either densely packed or relatively empty. During the busiest times people were still capable of dealing efficiently with the information needed for the main task at hand, but they were not very good at remembering and describing other aspects of the environment. They had narrowed their attention, limited their options, and failed to develop a clear overall image of their environment, in order to focus on its most important and relevant aspects. Charles Korte and his colleagues (Korte & Grant, 1980; Korte, Ypma, & Toppen, 1975) found in addition that people in the city narrow their attention when the input level of their surroundings is high, and as a result they are less helpful to others.

Although overload in public situations such as those studied by Saegert and Korte can be important, overload in one's immediate living situation can and should have even stronger and more direct effects. Although it did not test this issue in an urban setting, the research of Andrew Baum and Stuart Valins (1977) is highly relevant here. Baum and Valins compared the reactions of students living in two differently designed dormitories at the State University of New York at Stony Brook. The first dormitory situation was a typical corridor design in which a number of two-person rooms all opened up onto a long hallway. All the students on the corridor shared a common bathroom and lounge. In the other, suite arrangement, rooms were set up in pairs so that only about six students shared a common area including bathroom and lounge (see Figure 5.3). The actual density of both arrangements was identical in space per person and number of persons per floor, but the ar-

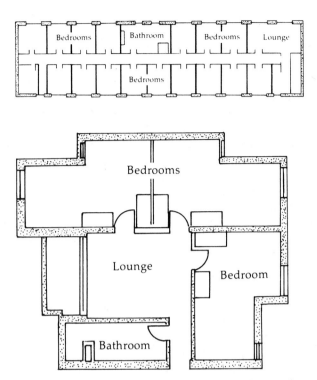

Figure 5.3. Floor plan of the corridor (top) and suite-type (bottom) dormitories studied by Baum and Valins. From their *Architecture and Social Behavior: Psychological Studies in Social Density.* Copyright 1977 by Lawrence Erlbaum Associates. Reprinted by permission.

rangement of space made the corridor residents report far greater feelings of crowding than the suite residents.

In analyzing the feelings and responses of the dorm residents, Baum and Valins noted in particular that the corridor students reported being overloaded with social contacts. The noise was great, the level of activity was frenetic, and people were afraid to poke their heads out of their rooms or walk down the hall for fear of being drawn into a whole set of unwanted interactions. Their most common response was withdrawal, both physical and emotional. Corridor students were less sociable than suite students with people on their floor and made more of their friends elsewhere. Not only did they prefer to stay away from the others on their floor, but even when they were waiting for an experiment in another campus building they sat farther away from a stranger who was already seated on the only available bench.

More than the overload itself, what upset students most was their inability to exert control over the social contacts they had. They complained that they were most frustrated not by the *number* of people to be met, talked to, or dealt with but by not being able *to set the terms* of their dealings with others. They felt that luck (most often, bad luck) seemed to determine when, where, and with whom they interacted.

These results with college students are corroborated by large-scale studies in Chicago (Gove, Hughes, & Galle, 1979) and Baltimore (Taylor & Verbrugge, 1980). In one of the few full-scale urban studies that can truly be called "crowding research" rather than "density research," Gove and his colleagues attempted to assess the ways in which urban density is perceived and experienced. Almost two thousand interviews were conducted with both black and white residents of Chicago in eighty selected census tracts. There were twenty tracts of each of four kinds: low density, low social class; low density, high social class; high density, low social class; and high density, high social class. Using factor analysis the researchers found that two sets of items were strongly related to internal density (number of persons per room) and tapped perceived crowding: (1) lack of privacy and (2) overload of disruptive demands. By combining the objective and subjective measures of density, crowding, privacy, and demand, Gove and his associates found that a substantial amount of variance in their measures of mental health, satisfaction, self-esteem, and alienation could be accounted for.

In Baltimore, Taylor and Verbrugge noted that residents' beliefs that an area is overpopulated produced frustrations. On the positive side, however, they found that some individuals continued to maintain a sense of personal control in spite of high population size and density, and that this sense of control acted as a buffer and minimized the effects of living among many others.

Still, more often than not, crowding, privacy, and control not only are interrelated but also combine to produce negative effects. People who live in close proximity within the home often find it difficult to find enough space for themselves. Oscar Lewis (1976), in his description of a poor family living in crowded poverty, has offered this account of a young girl:

Dressing and undressing without being seen was a problem. At night, we had to wait until the light was out or undress under the blanket or go to sleep in our clothing. Antonia cared least about being seen in her slip, but Paula, Marta and I were very modest. Roberto, too, would get up in the morning wrapped in his blanket and go to the kitchen to dress. . . . But these annoyances were insignificant compared to that of being scolded in the presence of everyone else. I often thought that if my father had berated me in private, I would not have minded so much. But everyone heard the awful things he said to me, even though they pretended not to, and it hurt and shamed me more. [Pp. 241–243]

Here we see that privacy is not merely a matter of being alone but also involves an issue of control, of being able to determine when to be with others and when to be away from their presence. Many current definitions of privacy emphasize this notion of control (Altman, 1975; Rapoport, 1972). Privacy involves "the right of the individual to decide what information about himself should be communicated to others and under what circumstances," according to Alan Westin (1970, quoted in Altman, 1975, p. 17). When this process of maintaining boundaries between oneself and others is beyond one's control, crowding is experienced and negative effects may result.

The notion of behavioral interference is much like the notions of overload and lack of privacy, but it emphasizes the manner in which the physical presence of others blocks individuals from their goals and from access to resources. From this point of view, crowding is bad when it is difficult to get from one point to another or when it means that there are not enough toys, pencils, blankets, or whatever to go around. Daniel Stokols (1976) has pointed to the ways in which the presence of others can cause "thwartings." He notes that these are more disturbing in primary (i.e., private or home) territories than in secondary (i.e., public) territories and when seen as personal (directed at oneself) rather than neutral (not deliberate). However, in Stokols's analysis as well, what is being most greatly constrained by others is the *ability to choose*. The presence of others serves as a threat to behavioral freedom, and people react to crowding by trying to reassert their belief in personal control or by becoming resigned to a feeling of impotence in relation to the environment.

Further support for the crowding–control connection comes from the research on learned helplessness. Martin Seligman (1974, 1975) has suggested that when people live under circumstances where they cannot control outcomes, the environment communicates a message: Events around you are out of your control no matter what you do. This perception leads people to give up trying in general, whether or not efforts at control might prove successful. In one test of this theory, Judith Rodin (1976) took children from high- and low-density homes and exposed them to a frustrating task (an insoluble puzzle). Afterward they were given a puzzle that could be solved. High-density children quickly "learned their lesson" and did not try hard on the second puzzle. Low-density children continued to work hard rather than give up so easily. Similarly, when Andrew Baum, John Aiello, and L. E. Calesnick (1978) studied dormitory residents, they found that those who reported feeling crowded also displayed symptoms of learned helplessness and acquiesced more fully to their environment the longer they lived in the dormitories.

This explanation of crowding effects also throws additional light on the findings of Mitchell in Hong Kong reported earlier in this chapter. As noted, the results of high-density living were most negative (1) when people lived with others not related to them and (2) when they lived on the upper floors of tall apartment buildings. When unrelated families are required to share one roof, problems of coordination and control would seem to be greatly increased. Retreat to the outside might be one alternative, especially for children. When people live high up, however, the ability of parents to monitor their children's behavior outside is greatly reduced, so that learned feelings of helplessness are further exaggerated.

Some conclusions about density and crowding

Having reviewed the literature on density and crowding, we can ask once again the question that people have asked ever since Calhoun's rats started overrunning their own little Garden of Eden: Does high-density living in cities "cause" social pathology? The answer offered is no, with four major explanatory or qualifying statements:

1. High-density living definitely has the *capacity* to be stressful. It creates problems of coordination among people, can reduce people's ability to control their environment, and requires active coping. Yet it is at this point that the "people are not rats" critique must be remembered. People are capable of developing complex individual and collective modes of adaptation by which these problems can in many instances be overcome. In Japan, for instance, cultural norms and internal design allow many people to live in one space without notable problems. Physical and social solutions have been worked out to distinguish between public and private space and therefore to allow people a maximum of privacy even when they are among many others (Michelson, 1976). In dealing with crowding in public spaces, however, we must also recall that certain coping mechanisms may entail various costs to individuals and those around them (e.g., the development of norms of non-involvement or a disregard for the needs of strangers). Thus, although many urbanites may be "rough around the edges," this seems to be more a cost of avoiding true pathology than a form of pathology itself.

2. When we consider that rates of crime and mental problems are higher in the central city than in suburbs or small towns, we have to ask what factors besides density differ among these settings. The most obvious answer involves poverty. As pointed out by Galle and Gove (1979), most people of means do not live more than one per room. Researchers who have attempted statistically to separate the effects of density and social class have consistently found the latter to be more influential; others have suggested that pulling these two factors apart statistically is not meaningful because they simply cannot be pulled apart in reality: The effects of crowding and poverty are not independent and should not be treated as such.

3. The foregoing does not mean that poverty, rather than (or even in addition to) density, is the "cause" of X. It means that more can be learned

about the nature of crowding by looking at it from the point of view of *impact* and *process* than from the point of view of *outcome*. What causes urban pathology – or rural pathology or suburban pathology or pathology wherever it is observed – is a set of stressful conditions that cannot be coped with successfully. Poverty is one such circumstance, but there are many other environmental conditions that may lead people to feel deprived of control or frustrated or constrained. Therefore, density when experienced as crowding can act as a cause of urban pathology. Still, it is only one cause among many; and it need not lead to pathology at all, because people may be able to cope with it successfully.

4. As a result, it is dangerous to think of the presence of other people in too simple a way. Their presence (whether in internal or in external spaces) is not necessarily stressful or even potentially crowding. In fact, one of the most stressful living conditions is isolation, whether the unit is one individual living alone in an apartment or one family living alone in a rural area. Mark Baldassare (1977, 1979) suggests that the presence of others presents potential opportunity as well as potential constraints. Barker (1968) has pointed out that problems of undermanned as well as overmanned environments can be many. The presence of others can be good, bad, or irrelevant depending upon the nature of the person, the others present, the duration of their presence, and the tasks to be accomplished, as well as numerous other factors.

Jonathan Freedman's (1975) density–intensity perspective displays elements of the multiple- and contrasting-realities approach in pointing out that density can have either of two different and opposite consequences. He states that increasing the density of a situation is like turning up the volume of music: Whereas it was once background, now it is more difficult to ignore; if it is music you dislike or if the sound keeps you from hearing something else you want to listen to, then it will be experienced as stressful. But it is equally possible that for some people, under some circumstances, the presence of others will be music to their ears.

Noise and its effects

Urban stresses come in many forms, shapes, and sizes. Although crowding has received the most attention from social scientists, another typical element of urban life that can tax our coping abilities is noise. By definition, noise is *unwanted* sound. It is something that is annoying, can interfere with ongoing activities, and may even be physiologically harmful (Evans & Jacobs, 1982). In a survey of well over a thousand people in London, A. C. McKennell and E. A. Hunt (1966) found that 20 percent of their sample spontaneously mentioned noise as one of the things they disliked most about where they lived. Somewhat more than 30 percent said that noise got in the way of their rest and relaxation; 24 percent said that it interfered with television or radio; and 26 percent said that noises sometimes disturbed their sleep.

The most frequent complaint had to do with noise from nearby traffic. In a study of this form of disturbance that produced similar results, Donald Appleyard and Mark Lintell (1972) compared three San Francisco streets that were similar in many ways but varied in the amount of traffic traveling along them. Appleyard and Lintell found that on the street that had only light traffic, there was an active street life; people used the sidewalks and the corner drugstore as places to meet and initiate interaction. On the heavily trafficked street, in contrast, people tended to use the sidewalk only as a pathway between home and their final destinations; correspondingly, people saw the high-volume street as a less friendly and more lonely place to live than the lightly traveled street.

The most obvious characteristic of noise that can be disturbing is volume or loudness. As in Freedman's density-intensity analogy, when we turn the volume up, sound that is unwanted is difficult to ignore and likely to interfere with ongoing activities. Yet perhaps the most interesting aspects of research on the psychological and behavioral effects of urban noise involve the following findings:

1. It is not the physical characteristics of noise but the social and cognitive contexts in which noise occurs that play the greatest role in determining whether noise has any effect.

2. The effects of noise are not caused by an inability of people to adapt to it. Rather, aftereffects in the form of psychic costs are the major source of noise-induced problems (Glass & Singer, 1972).

Concerning those factors that influence the amount of annoyance from noise, it has been noted that the actual level of noise is capable of accounting for only one-third or less of the variance in reported annoyance (Griffiths & Langdon, 1968). The addition of attitudinal variables raises the predictability of reported disturbance to as high as 65 percent. Tracor, Inc. (1970), found that the best single predictor of reported annoyance from airport noise was perceived danger. Subjective disturbance can also be affected by manipulating residents' orientations (Jonsson & Sorensen, 1973). When told that local officials were concerned about airport noise, residents were significantly less likely to feel disturbed by it than when they were told that the officials did not consider noise to be a problem. Also, the same level of sound was rated noisier if research subjects thought that it came from a teenager's hot rod than if they attributed it to a taxi (Cederlöf, Friberg, Hammarfors, Holmquist, & Kajland, 1961).

Laboratory research

The literature on noise has benefited not only from these generally consistent field research findings but also from research that has gone back and forth between laboratory and field to strengthen findings and test those in one setting against those in the other. Most notable on the experimental side is a series of comprehensive and integrated experiments on the effects of noise by David Glass and Jerome Singer (1972). In their first series of experiments, Glass and Singer questioned whether noise presented to experimental subjects while they were working on various cognitive tasks would affect their physiological reactions or disrupt their ability to perform the tasks accurately. They found that regardless of whether the noise was presented at extremely high volume, at unpredictable and irregular intervals, or under circumstances where subjects had no control over its presence or presentation, there were still few effects on task performance or psychophysiological reactivity. Subjects quickly adapted behaviorally and autonomically. The only evidence for any impairment was on highly complex tasks, and then only when the noise was uncontrollable or unpredictable.

Glass and Singer followed these experiments with others, in which they were more concerned with subjects' responses to frustration *after* exposure to noise than with their performance *during* noise. Using persistence at an insoluble puzzle as their measure of frustration tolerance, their findings indicated that subjects persisted for the shortest time following exposure to loud unpredictable noises, and also that unpredictability was far more important than intensity in producing these effects (i.e., subjects persisted longer after loud predictable noise than after soft unpredictable noise). They explained the great importance of predictability by reference to Seligman's model of learned helplessness, covered earlier in the discussion of crowding.

Glass and Singer reasoned that when noise (as well as other stressors that they tested) is inescapable or unavoidable, it makes people feel as if they are at the mercy of the environment. If and when people feel that they cannot control outcomes, they are less likely to make subsequent attempts at doing so. Thus, Glass and Singer argued it is not the stressful event itself that causes problems for the urbanite but, rather, the message of helplessness that it brings with it. This explanation is supported by the work of Drury Sherrod and his colleagues (Sherrod & Downs, 1974; Sherrod, Hage, Halpern, & Moore, 1977). These researchers gave some subjects control over starting the noise in a study, others control over stopping it, a third group control over both starting and stopping it, and a fourth control over neither. As would be expected from a learned helplessness perspective, the greater control the subjects felt they possessed, the longer they worked at insoluble puzzles after the noise had stopped.

Although the sort of artificial and short-term exposure to noise given to laboratory subjects in research like that done by Glass and Singer may limit our confidence in generalizing to the real world, other studies done in the field support their findings and point to the kinds of feelings that long-term exposure may bring about for urban dwellers. Lawrence Ward and Peter Suedfeld (1973) performed an extremely innovative and informative study by making the real world their laboratory for research. Having heard of a plan to route a major highway very near classrooms and dorms at Rutgers University, they recorded actual traffic sounds on existing highways during various times of the day and exposed students to these realistic sounds through large speakers.

Not only did students feel that it was harder to hear lectures and harder to take notes in the classroom under these circumstances, but observers of the noise-exposed classrooms reported them to have less participation and less attentiveness than no-noise classrooms. Students who were exposed to loud noise in the dormitories reported problems in sleeping and studying and increased levels of nervousness, and there was greater evidence of tension and disagreement among students exposed to the noise than among control subjects.

The Ward and Suedfeld study takes us halfway from the laboratory to real life in the city. One reported sidelight of this study, however, indicates the extent of the reality of this situation, as well as its unreality. Ward and Suedfeld report that twice during the course of their study the electrical cables for their sound equipment were cut, and students actually threatened to destroy the equipment that they were using. Although this reaction demonstrates that the noise was realistic and disturbing, we can only wonder whether the people who cut the power cables of the researchers would have attempted to exercise the same degree of control over the highway traffic or the building of the highway in the first place (Moos, 1976).

The fact that some students mentioned having expected the noise to be even worse and that some others thought they could get used to it if they had to demonstrates the motto of learned helplessness that is so pervasive in urban life: "You can't fight city hall." In commenting on these results, Moos (1976) points out that had the highway been built, residents would probably have learned to put up with the noise as do residents who live near airports.

Aircraft and train noise

A number of studies of naturally occurring noise have shown that residents who live near airports suffer in various ways. For instance, psychiatric-hospital admission rates were found to be slightly higher for those living near London's Heathrow Airport or Los Angeles International Airport than for people not near these or similar locations (Meecham & Smith, 1977). Another study found that men living near Amsterdam's Schiphol Airport were more likely to be under treatment for cardiovascular problems and to have high blood pressure than others living farther away (Knipschild, 1977). Many of these studies, however, failed to control carefully for social class variables.

More closely controlled research that follows up on laboratory findings in actual situations has been done by Sheldon Cohen and his colleagues (Cohen, Evans, Krantz, & Stokols, 1980; Cohen, Evans, Krantz, Stokols, & Kelly, 1981), who studied third- and fourth-grade children attending the noisiest elementary schools in the air corridor of Los Angeles International Airport. These children were matched with others in quiet schools for age, social class, and race, and both groups were intensively studied and tested. The findings point to the effects of noise on a number of variables. Children from noisy schools, for instance, had higher diastolic and systolic blood pressures. Air corridor children were more likely to fail on a cognitive task and were likely to give up more often before the full time to finish the task had elapsed. This result is consistent with the findings of another study, which carefully matched children near Orly Airport in Paris with others and found that the ones who attend school near the airport showed less frustration tolerance than children from quiet schools (cited in Cohen & Weinstein, 1982).

Although a noisy airport is perhaps the most dramatic constant source of urban noise, two well-controlled studies have demonstrated noise effects in other kinds of urban settings. Cohen, Glass, and Singer (1973) studied children who lived in a high-rise apartment building located directly above a busy New York City highway. Controlling for all the usual factors, they found that children who lived on the noisier lower floors had poorer hearing discrimination and lower reading ability on the average than those who lived on the quieter upper floors. Similarly, A. L. Bronzaft and D. P. McCarthy (1975) found differences in the reading achievement scores of two groups of children attending the same school. The only other difference between the two groups, of course, was that the better readers were located on the side of the school that was away from the elevated railway tracks; the poorer readers were located on the noisier side, directly across from the elevated railway – literally on the wrong side of the tracks.

Other forms of urban stress: air pollution and the daily commute

Although crowding and noise have received the greatest amount of research attention, the list of urban stressors hardly stops here. Foul air is another element of urban life that seemingly cannot be avoided. Using air-quality data from 1976, the President's Council on Environmental Quality (1978) determined that forty-three major cities, containing half of the American population, had unhealthy air quality. The U.S. Public Health Service has estimated that air pollution costs $6 billion a year for the treatment of diseases such as bronchitis, lung cancer, pneumonia, and tuberculosis; and it has been suggested that merely breathing the air in New York City is equivalent to smoking about two packs of cigarettes per day (Rotton, 1978).

Air pollution has a number of characteristics in common with crowding and noise. Just as we can see and sense the presence of others and hear loud sounds, when air quality is poor enough we can also detect it with our senses. We can see, smell, and almost taste the smog of Los Angeles and the smoke of Pittsburgh. (Parents in such places have to contend with questions from their children such as "Mommy, where did I come from?" and "Daddy, why is the sky pink?")

Although noises and crowds may have indirect health effects, bad air can have direct and sometimes immediate effects on physical health and well-being. Dizziness, headaches, burning eyes, and a hacking cough can result when downtown air is badly polluted. There are days in many cities when the elderly are warned to stay indoors because attempting to breathe the air would be hazardous to their health. Even more serious than the problem of obvious pollution, however, is the fact that many potentially harmful or even deadly components of air pollution cannot be detected. Carbon monoxide and other toxic gases are odorless and colorless, and people are not aware of their presence. In fact, much of the public's awareness of and concern about air pollution is more directly attributable to media publicity than to absolute levels or relative changes in air quality (Lipsey, 1977; McEvoy, 1972).

There is considerably less research on the psychological and behavioral effects of air pollution than of noise or crowding. One line of research takes an epidemiological approach in looking at the relationship between pollution indexes and mental-health problems. For instance, levels of air pollution and psychiatric admissions in St. Louis are consistently correlated (Strahilevitz, Strahilevitz, & Miller, 1979). James Rotton and James Frey (1982) used records from a two-year period in Dayton, Ohio, and applied a series of sophisticated statistical analyses to their data. They found that even after weather conditions and seasonal trends were controlled for, calls for assistance in psychiatric emergencies were significantly related to the presence of photochemical oxidants (e.g., smog) in the air.

Hans Ury (1968) reported a relationship between traffic accidents and pollution levels in Los Angeles. He proposed that high pollution reduces mental efficiency, impairing the ability to drive and leading to accidents. Rotton (1978), however, noted that the measure of pollution most closely associated with accidents was the level of oxidants rather than carbon monoxide. Carbon monoxide is damaging to the nervous system and can impair mental functioning, whereas oxidants are a source of physical and psychological annoyance. Rotton suggested that pollution works by distracting drivers and making them more irritable. Therefore, the driver is not only less alert but also more aggressive, a combination that is at the root of many auto accidents.

Rotton and his colleagues (Rotton, 1983; Rotton, Frey, Barry, Milligan, & Fitzpatrick, 1979) have followed up on much of the archival and field research on pollution with controlled testing in the laboratory. For practical and ethical reasons this work has emphasized the effects of unpleasant but nontoxic odors in the air and has been set up in many cases to parallel the experimental research on crowding and noise. In these studies, students are brought to a room and asked to perform various tasks under neutral or oops-I'm-sorry-I-spilled-that-awful-smelling-stuff circumstances.

Compared to the neutral (control) groups, students in the bad-odor groups reported feeling more aggressive, anxious, and fatigued and less able to concentrate. People in the rooms that smelled bad found the rooms themselves less visually pleasant and were less attracted to hypothetical partners, no matter how similar to the experimental subjects they were. Rotton (1983) tested the effects of bad odor on the ability to perform mental tasks and on behavioral aftereffects as a function of whether the subjects could exert control over the presence of the odor (i.e., whether they were allowed to remove or avoid the odor). Just as in the research on noise, two results were found: (1) odors impaired performance on complex but not simple tasks; (2) aftereffects, in the form of lack of persistence at an insoluble puzzle, were noted for those subjects who had been deprived of control. In addition, the longer subjects were exposed to the odor, the briefer the time they persisted in working on the puzzle.

Each of the previously discussed stressors impinges on the lives of urbanites with varying degrees of frequency and intensity. Some days the air is more polluted than others. At times one's surroundings are calm and quiet; at others the environment is noisy and hectic. A different kind of potentially stressful situation, one that is a classic example of Lazarus and Cohen's (1977) "daily hassle" category, is urban commuting. In modern cities most people do not live close to their places of employment and must get to work by car, bus, or train. Five days a week the urban commuter leaves the house early in the morning in the hope that this day the trip to work will involve a minimum of complications.

The difference between wanting to get to work with few hassles and actually doing so may be great. Today is a perfect example. As I write, there is a nationwide rail strike and thousands upon thousands of Boston commuters are scrambling to make alternate arrangements individually in cars, via carpool, or by local public transportation (which is not affected). Unfortunately, it is also raining, and owing to the additional highway traffic and a few weather-related accidents, most of the bridges and tunnels are backed up for miles. Luckily, the trolley I normally take was not much more crowded than usual (then again, how could it be?), but coming home I never know how long the wait will be. When a trolley does arrive, will I be one of the lucky ones swept up in the surge of those who make it in, happy to be sandwiched between the door and a number of other straining bodies, or will I be left in the rain to hope for better luck the next time around? It is not very surprising that in a national survey, Robert Quinn and Graham Staines (1979) found that 38 percent of the commuters they questioned reported transportation-related problems – congestion and inconvenience – as among their greatest problems. And in Salt Lake City, 18 percent of the female drivers and 12 percent of the males reported that at times they "could gladly kill another driver" (Turner, Layton, & Simons, 1975, p. 1100).

As with pollution research, there is far more known about the physiological and physical health effects of commuting than there is about its psychological and behavioral impact. A number of studies have demonstrated that people who travel to work in their cars during rush hour each day are more likely than others to have health problems such as chest pains and cardiac arrhythmias (Aronow, Harris, Isbell, Rokaw, & Imparato, 1972); and those urban commuters whose trip is particularly long (e.g., two hours) are subject to a variety of stress-related physiological imbalances (Bellet, Roman, & Kostis, 1969).

Leaving the car at home and using public transportation hardly guarantees a person better health. Jerome Singer and his colleagues (Singer, Lundberg, & Frankenhaeuser, 1978) studied a group of thirty rail commuters in Stockholm. The commuters provided self-reports as well as urine samples taken before leaving for work and just after arriving at their stations. The researchers found that levels of adrenalin and noradrenalin (indicators of emotional or stressful response) were higher after the ride than before it and that people who found their railway cars crowded and were not able to choose a seat were greatly affected even if the commute was short.

The most comprehensive research on the behavioral effects of commuting, from both a theoretical and an empirical perspective, has been performed by Daniel Stokols, Raymond Novaco, and their colleagues (Novaco, Stokols, Campbell, & Stokols, 1979; Stokols & Novaco, 1981) at the University of California at Irvine. Their research group studied one hundred employees of two industrial firms in the Irvine area. Using the concept of *impedance* to indicate the degree to which commuters encountered situations that slowed or constrained the trip to work, they chose three groups that varied in the commuting distance and time involved. For instance, all low-impedance employees traveled fewer than 7.5 miles to work and spent fewer than 12.5 minutes en route in either direction; high-impedance employees traveled between 18 and 50 miles in a commute that lasted 30–75 minutes each way. Participants kept travel logs, underwent physiological testing upon arrival at work, completed a battery of attitude and personality measures, and took many of the stress–frustration tests used in the original Glass and Singer (1972) noise research.

Both distance and time turned out to be good indexes of the behavioral constraints that commuters experienced. The greater the impedance as measured objectively by distance and time, the more the commute was seen as inconvenient and congested, the less the employees were satisfied with their commutes, and the more tense and nervous they reported feeling upon arrival at work. One of the most consistent findings, however, was that impedance interacted with personality variables to determine the perceived stressfulness of the commute and employees' response to that stress. In particular, high-impedance participants who had a strong belief in their own personal control over events (referred to as "internals" on the basis of their score on Rotter's Internal–External scale) experienced greater physiological, stress-related arousal as a result of their lengthy commutes than those who felt little personal control ("externals"). Yet on a set of subsequent task-performance tests, internals were found to perform better in an effort to reassert control and cope with their stressful feelings. This finding strongly suggests that although commuting, or a whole range of urban stressors, may be unavoidable, the way the stress is perceived and reacted to may vary greatly, depending on individual coping styles and coping resources (Lazarus, 1966).

Stress and the city: comment and critique

The research cited throughout this chapter suggests that many of the conditions of urban life – crowding, noise, pollution, commuting, and a host of un-mentioned others – have the capacity to be stressful. We can understand the most about urban stress not by considering each stressor independently but by exploring the common mechanisms by which they all operate.

The physical presence of most of these stimuli or conditions is a source of annoyance because they interfere with or disrupt ongoing behavior. The female rats in Calhoun's animal studies were poor nest builders and infant transporters because they constantly bumped into or were distracted by other rats. A child who grows up sharing a room or even a bed with many others is equally distracted and overloaded and lacks a sense of privacy. Bronzaft and Mc-Carthy, in their research on schools near the elevated trains, found that 11 percent of teaching time was lost waiting until the noise abated and voices could be heard. And commuter traffic jams are perfect examples of the presence of others keeping a person from getting from one place to another.

But just as we discussed in relationship to crowding, each of these stressors has its greatest impact through the message it conveys about ability to exercise control over the environment. It is not the traffic or the noise or the stink per se, but more the feeling people eventually get that they are helpless in the presence of these things. R. E. Rankin (1969), in a survey about air pollution, asked people who admitted concern about the problem why they had never complained or taken action. Almost half responded that they had done nothing because they were sure it would do no good. It is interesting to note that it is the urban poor who are most concerned about pollution (Cutter, 1981), although those higher in status are more likely to complain (McKennell, 1973). This apparent paradox disappears quickly when we realize that the poor are likely to be concerned because they feel they can do little about the situation; the rich complain because they believe they will be listened to (Cohen & Weinstein, 1982).

Glass and Singer (1972) have demonstrated the importance of the loss of control using other forms of stressors as well. In one study in which electric shock was used, they found once again that predictability and controllability were more critical determinants of people's reactions than the actual intensity of the shock. More interesting was an attempt to create a very different but highly typical form of urban stress, the bureaucratic hassle. In this experiment one group of subjects encountered a clerk who was petty and rigid and demanded that the subjects fill out a form over again. A second group was told to redo the forms, but the reason given was that the repeat was required by official regulations. A third group was not hassled at all. The idea was for the first group to attribute their problems to an individual over whom some control was conceivable, but for the second group to feel that little control was possible in dealing with a system that was impersonal and unalterable.

Glass and Singer found that both bureaucratically irritated groups performed less well on a subsequent proofreading task than the controls. However, on other tasks, such as a bargaining game involving active versus passive responses, subjects who were annoyed by a person over whom they might feel control reacted strongly, whereas those who felt they had little control because of "the system" were generally docile and compliant.

This research further corroborates the point that urban stressors can teach us lessons that are maladaptive, that they can lead us to give up without even trying when trying would be just the thing to do. Although they do not share the same root or have the accent on the same syllable, the structural resemblance between the words *impedance* and *impotence* seems a strange coincidence.

Balancing the picture: stress in the eye of the beholder

The urban-stress approach is a useful one and meets certain of the problems of city life head on. Yet in another way it presents the city from a biased viewpoint that if accepted as a complete description would give a misleading account of what urban life is like. How we phrase a question often determines the range of answers that can be expected. When we look only at those aspects of the urban environment that are presumed to lead to negative outcomes and hypothesize that certain conditions lead to certain types of problems, we load the dice against the city in either of two ways. Either we come up with a confirmation of the hypothesis and demonstrate the stressful effects of the environment; or at best we end up with a statement of no difference between lives under conditions *A* and *B*. What this approach largely precludes is the possibility of demonstrating the positive aspects of city life.

The question is rarely if ever phrased to ask whether too little stimulation – the absence of others, silence, a lack of opportunities, or not enough activity – can be equally disturbing. Richard Ashmore and John McConahay (1975), in a fine review chapter on urban stress, have characterized this research focus by using as their title "The City Has Too Much." Had researchers approached their questions from the reverse point of view, the chapter might have been labeled "The Non-City Has Too Little" and might have contained very different implications about the nature of urban life. One personal and positive statement about the high input and activity levels of the city is the following comment:

New York has taught me the solace of walls. I feel more comfortable in a subway than a field, more willing to concentrate on something with momentum than on a landscape that will not flicker or revolve. . . . In people too I demand a cinematic pace the absence of which I am likely to take for distinterest or contempt. That I have come to admire social tension or even require it in my friends makes it that much more difficult to feel at home in Connecticut where the pace is not only slower but less evident and the stress in people mirrored not in their witticisms but in their eyes. [Goldstein, 1972, p. 82]

One approach to balancing the stress perspective uses some very basic principles from the areas of perception and cognition. Daniel Geller (1980), addressing the overload question in particular, has asked: At what point is overload exprienced? That is, how can we distinguish between a person or a system under a heavy, although manageable, load and one whose load has exceeded the person's or the system's capacity? Does the amount of information necessary to produce overload vary from person to person, and can it even vary for a given person over time?

A second issue that Geller raises, and that has already been implied here, is the question of whether there cannot be positive aspects or consequences of a high sensory load. Is it not possible that environments filled with many sounds, sights, and smells excite and please rather than distress and disturb? Or, more generally, just when do environments with high sensory input produce positive effects and when are the effects negative?

In addressing these questions, Geller uses the concepts "optimal level of stimulation" (Wohlwill, 1966) and "adaptation level" (Helson, 1964). Optimal level of stimulation refers to the level of arousal or the amount of sensory information that is evaluated by the perceiver as most pleasant or most satisfying. Figure 5.4 presents an inverted U-shaped (Wundt) curve (see Berlyne, 1970). The abscissa represents a dimension of "arousal potential," including qualities such as novelty and complexity. The figure suggests that

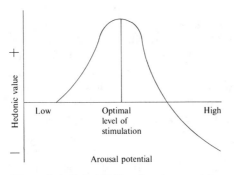

Figure 5.4. Relationship of environmental arousal level to judged pleasantness.

both very low and very high levels of stimulation or arousal can be experienced as unpleasant. Typically the stress-overload approach to the city looks at only half of the curve and assumes that the urban experience falls somewhere far over to the right. Yet a number of noted researchers on basic human cognitive processes (e.g., Berlyne, 1970) suggest that people actively value novelty and surprise and that they are at least as interested in seeking out new positive stimulation as in reducing or avoiding strong or unpleasant stimulation. Therefore, even though there are many extreme negative circumstances (sleeping four to a bed, or trying to listen to a teacher as a train roars by), to assume either that these are typical of urban life or that what is typical must fall to the far right of the optimal-level-of-stimulation curve is inappropriate.

When we speak of the optimal-level-of-stimulation concept alone, however, we run into a different problem. What is optimal for you may be overloading for me or vice versa. Having grown up in New York City, I personally would not want to live there again. I once enjoyed it, but now I find it a bit too hectic. As noted previously, however, my brother (we slept 2.0 to a room), who still lives in New York City, tells me that whenever he is away from the city too long he has to return to savor its pace and craziness. We can see from this that the optimal level of stimulation (1) varies from person to person and (2) may also vary for a given individual as he or she experiences the city over time. Joachim Wohlwill and Imre Kohn (1976) noted that migrants to Harrisburg, Pennsylvania, from small towns and large cities differed in their perceptions of the crowding, noise, and pollution levels of Harrisburg, with the small-town migrants consistently rating the environment as more stressful. In a study of similar intent, I found that students at two universities had highly divergent perceptions of the campuses as a function of the kind of place (city versus town) where they had lived previously (Krupat, 1972).

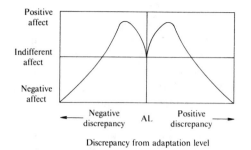

Figure 5.5. Relationship of affective response to deviation from adaptation level. Redrawn from "Discrepancy from adaptation-level as a source of affect" by R. Haber. In the *Journal of Experimental Psychology*, 1958, *56*, 370–375. Copyright 1958 by the American Psychological Association. Used by permission of the author.

By combining this discussion with the concept of adaptation level, however, we can better understand the issue. Adaptation level is the level of stimulation or arousal that is perceived as neutral (i.e., not too hot, not too cold; not too empty, not too crowded). The butterfly curve in Figure 5.5 suggests that individuals at any given adaptation level evaluate the environment as a function of how much it deviates from neutral. Small deviations in either direction (a bit more or a bit less noisy, for example) are experienced as pleasant, whereas extreme deviations are felt to be unpleasant or stressful.

By offering this approach, Geller provides an alternative to the characterization of the city as a stressful setting and makes way for seeing it as a place of multiple and contrasting realities. His approach helps to explain (1) why, as a function of different individuals' adaptation levels, contrasting evaluations are made of the same urban environment; (2) why certain extreme conditions are experienced universally as unpleasant and stressful; and (3) how it is that perceptions and evaluations of the city may change over time. As Geller points out, most personal accounts of first-time encounters with the city show that people do feel overwhelmed and have a preference for relatively simple stimuli and low levels of stimulation. With increased familiarity, however, more complexity may be not only tolerated but sought out. Monotony, whether in the form of dull urban design or of rural isolation, can be just as stressful as any excess of stimulation.

A personality-oriented approach leads us to the same conclusions concerning the variability of response to stressors. This approach emphasizes that according to their personalities, coping resources, and coping styles, people experience and deal with stressful conditions very differently. Stokols and Novaco (1981), for instance, noted that internals and externals did not react to commuting problems similarly. The internals were more aroused but also worked harder to maintain a feeling of control than the externals. Gary Evans, Steven Jacobs, and Neal Frager (1982) have reported differing reactions to pollution among newcomers to and long-term residents of a city grouped according to locus of control (high or low), with newcomer-internals being the one group to alter behavior to adapt to the smog. Other researchers have developed measures of environmental sensitivity (Guild, 1981) and sensation seeking (Zuckerman, 1971), and these variables should also interact with environmental conditions to produce unique response patterns. Therefore, it is correct and important to note physical conditions that are associated with urban living and to consider their *potential* to cause stress or harm, but we should be careful to remember that stressors are perceived and handled in diverse ways by the many inhabitants of a city.

Summary

In this chapter we looked at the city as a place where people, noise, smells, and social demands may overload and overwhelm the individual's capacity to cope successfully with the environment. As noted in Chapter 2, this is a common theme, one that best summarizes the general stereotype of urban living today. Therefore, it deserves not only a detailed look but critical consideration as well. We looked at four kinds of urban stress in varying degrees of detail: crowding and density, noise, pollution, and commuting. In focusing on crowding, the research area that has received most attention, we noted that the differences in populations, methodologies, and definitions used have produced a highly inconsistent picture of when or even whether high-density living is "bad."

In considering each of these forms of stress, we came across a basic theme that pervades the findings. Each individual stressor presents a slightly different problem in everyday living: Privacy is a key issue for people who live in crowded poverty; difficulties in concentrating and listening plague individuals who live or work near train tracks or along airport approach routes; coughing, sneezing, and wheezing trouble the residents of a city that is badly polluted. But each of these conditions causes its greatest problems when it communicates a certain message. When people feel that the environment cannot be controlled no matter how hard they try or what they do, then they will stop trying, and their coping will be less successful.

In addition to noting how urban stressors work, we also asked whether this perspective may not subtly bias our image of the city. We noted that high input levels may be accepted or preferred by some, rather than universally experienced as overload, and that people with certain personalities and coping styles may successfully avoid the message that the city is beyond their control.

This critique of the urban-stress approach is not meant to imply that there is anything unsound about it – only that it is one outlook of many with which to describe the urban experience. People engage the environment not only as *individuals* who experience crowds, noise, and so on but also as *members of social networks* – as friends, relatives, and neighbors. It is to this complementary approach that we shall turn in Chapter 6.

Suggestions for further reading

Altman, I., Wohlwill, J., & Everett, P. (Eds.). 1980. *Human behavior and environment: Advances in theory and research.* Vol. 5: *Transportation environments.* New York: Plenum.

Baum, A., & Epstein, Y. M. (Eds.). 1978. *Human response to crowding.* Hillsdale, N.J.: Erlbaum.

Evans, G. W. (Ed.). 1982. *Environmental stress.* Cambridge: Cambridge University Press.

Geller, D. M. 1980. Responses to urban stimuli: A balanced approach. *Journal of Social Issues, 36*, 86–100.

Glass, D. C., & Singer, J. E. 1972. *Urban stress: Experiments on noise and social stressors.* New York: Academic Press.

6

ISOLATION AND INTEGRATION: SOCIAL RELATIONS IN THE CITY

A specter is haunting the rise of modern mass society, the specter of the isolated alienated urbanite, uprooted, roaming unattached through the streets of the city, a perpetual stranger fearful but free . . . The specter may be likened to a cloud: in part it is a wispy light entity full of holes through which rays of sunlight and blue sky pour, while in part it is what the observer chooses to make of it, an imaginary beast of a benevolent or malevolent mein.
– Albert Hunter, 1978, p. 134

The focus of the preceding chapter was on whether city living can be stressful because of the many demands made on the urbanite. One question in particular was whether the presence of too many others could be bad for one's mental and physical health. In this chapter I take the reverse approach and ask about isolation, especially psychic isolation, and its effects on city residents.

The quotation from Albert Hunter given as epigraph to this chapter raises in rather dramatic fashion the central issue concerning the nature of social relations in the city: To what extent is the stereotype of the lonely, isolated urbanite a myth, and to what extent is it accurate? We will address this question by evaluating a wide array of theoretical and popular positions in light of the available research evidence. Then we will look at the conditions of urban living to discover the ways in which it may place constraints on the formation of close and caring relationships and also the manner in which it may provide resources and opportunities for the development and maintenance of close personal attachments.

It should be said at the outset that the answers will not be simple. Rather, they will point out that urban life contains within it the possibility for *both* isolation and integration. The position taken here is that cities have the potential to pull people apart, and they have equal potential to bring them together. Rather than being better or worse than social relations in other places, urban social relations are simply different. With an analysis that is finer grained than the typical, we can recognize these differences and see how they account for the existence of the city as a place where both isolation and integration can exist.

In this process there are important issues to be raised and distinctions to be made. First, there is the matter of comparing relations in *public* with those

128

in *private*, comparing the differences between interactions with family, friends, neighbors, or co-workers with those with strangers. Second, it is important to look at both the *quality* and the *quantity* of urban relations and also at the *meaning* and *function* for the urbanite of various types of social relations. Third, we must be aware that the *form* and *distribution* of interpersonal relations in the city may be different from what they would be in non-city areas. This matter, in turn, raises important questions about concepts such as "community" and "neighborhood." Finally, we will consider how urban conditions may affect the *process* of friendship formation, a consideration that will lead us toward a more dynamic conception of the matter of urban social relations.

Some key issues: an example

The tragic and now infamous murder of Katherine Genovese on March 13, 1964, in New York City provides us with the backdrop against which we can highlight some crucial issues concerning relations among urbanites. Ms. Genovese, returning to her apartment late at night in a middle-class, tree-lined section of Queens, was attacked three separate times over a period of thirty-five minutes. The first two attacks occurred on the street and attracted the attention of a number of people in the building facing the scene, waking them and causing them to look out their windows. The third attack, in the hallway of her building, proved fatal. What makes this event a sad part of urban life is not the audacity or the brutality of the criminal but, rather, the apparent apathy of the onlookers. Thirty-eight respectable, law-abiding citizens witnessed all or part of this event, but not a single one helped, either directly by coming to her aid or indirectly by calling the police (Rosenthal, 1964).

A sizable research literature on helping has been generated by this event (see Latané & Darley, 1970), but our interest here is not in considering factors affecting urban helping. Rather, we will analyze the popular explanations offered after the fact to account for the lack of aid, seeing how each one represents a position about the quality of urban relationships.

A first general theme uses the following reasoning: A person's friends, even in a big city, will help in a dire emergency. Then why did Ms. Genovese not receive help from her friends? It must be that she did not have any; it must be that in the city people do not form the sort of close, caring relationships in which one person is willing to risk his or her neck for the other. "The city had robbed Katherine Genovese of friends" was a phrase that appeared in editorials and conversations after this event.

This is a theme that derives directly from the human ecological position. It proposes that urbanites' relationships are casual, transitory, and superficial, that "true" friendships are not to be found in the city. In dealing with the evidence relative to this position, we will find that it reflects reality only to a small extent. That is, it overemphasizes the significance of life in public circumstances (e.g., among strangers) and assumes that all interactions among urbanites are colored by the mode of adaptation used with strangers.

Although it would seem bad enough not to have any friends, a second theme on urban alienation is even more damning in certain ways. This argument suggests that people in the city are so indifferent and so uncaring that they would not help even if they recognized or knew the woman being attacked. That is, Kitty Genovese probably did have friends – and is it not all the more shameful that even *they* would not come to her aid?

Although it is not likely that the author of the *New York Times* account of the incident (Gansberg, 1964) intended any such inference to be drawn, the particular language used implies this sort of indifference. The article describes the victim as "Katherine Genovese, known as Kitty to *everyone* in the neighborhood" (italics mine). In suggesting that she was *known* and still not helped, it misleads. It should have read, "called Kitty *by those who knew her* in the neighborhood." Then we could ask, Was she known by the onlookers? The answer to this question is contained in further information in the article. She was young and single, worked nights in a bar, and lived in the only apartment building on a block of expensive single-family homes owned by older, more established people with children. Therefore, it is unlikely that her friends were so callous as to ignore her when she was in need of help, nor is it likely that she did not have any friends. Then where were Kitty Genovese's friends when she needed them? The answer is that they were elsewhere – in other parts of Queens, in Brooklyn, in Manhattan, perhaps.

The second focus of this chapter, then, will be on the different ways in which urban friendships are distributed and the different roles that spatial proximity plays in the development of friendships in cities and towns. We will consider how these differences affect the significance of the neighborhood for urban and nonurban dwellers and what the concepts of "community" and "neighborhood" mean in the context of urban living.

Friends and strangers

As Lyn Lofland (1973) has pointed out, the urban world is full of strangers. Almost all of the people we pass every day on the street are not known to us, and generally we make no effort to enter into relationships with them or even to acknowledge them as people rather than objects. In addition, as correctly noted by the human ecologists, the major proportion of our daily encounters are brief and highly formalized and do not require or encourage us to deal with others as whole people. Most of our dealings with store clerks, bus drivers, and assorted co-workers do not call upon us to share feelings, disclose inner thoughts, or offer support to others. Moreover, given the many demands and varying pulls of city life, Milgram (1970) has suggested that if we wanted to acknowledge each one, it would prove to be impossible or maladaptive at the very least to do so. Yet this is the stuff of everyday urban living.

A reasonable derivation from this picture is the idea that the city dweller is caught in a web of highly segmented roles and strictly functional relationships that either call for little allegiance in the first place or split personal commitments so greatly that little investment can be given to any single one. Urbanites, Georg Simmel (1950) has said, adopt a mode of relating to others in general that is characterized by a tone of reserve and a holding back that makes the formation of primary (total and close) relations difficult and unlikely. In this situation few relationships are begun in the first place, and those that exist are likely to be shallow and weak. At its extreme we have a picture of the urbanite as a person who is *physically* embedded in a tight web of others yet feels *psychologically* almost totally isolated.

Recently an alternative view, as expressed by a number of urban theorists (Fischer, 1982; Franck, 1980; Korte, 1980), has begun to emerge and gain attention. These theorists argue that the compelling presence of masses of strangers in the city has led observers mistakenly to treat the "stranger" as the central character in urban life while neglecting the existence and importance of friends and family. As stated by Franck (1980), "The distinction between the private world of people one knows personally and the public world of strangers has been lost in many theories of urban life [but it] is essential for a full understanding of the nature of the urban social experience" (p. 53).

This position questions the assumption that *all* relationships among urbanites are characterized by the same tone and demeanor as those that we witness among strangers in public. It suggests that the same store clerk who refused to change a ten-dollar bill for me this afternoon would, upon being introduced by a mutual acquaintance, apologize, share a drink, and offer to lend me those same $10 if I ever needed them. It suggests that although the nature of public life among strangers has a tendency to be cool and uninvolved, there is no reason why private life among friends cannot be animated, intimate, and satisfying. Some have even suggested that because of the impersonal and superficial conditions of urban life, the development and maintenance of a network of close contacts is a *more necessary* and potentially even more common occurrence in cities than elsewhere. It is interesting to note that Everitt Hughes, a respected sociologist and colleague of Louis Wirth's at the University of Chicago, has commented in referring to his associate: "Louis used to say all those things about how the city is impersonal – while living with a whole clan of kin and friends on a very personal basis" (quoted in Kasarda & Janowitz, 1974, p. 338).

Urban contacts: the research evidence

Given the controversy about the nature of urban contacts, the only reasonable way to attempt to resolve the issue is by resort to the empirical research in the area. One problem is that very often we accept the general conclusions of research without a critical examination of the methods of the study itself to see if its conclusions are warranted. This is a particular problem with the literature in this area. I would suggest that in order to constitute a complete and vigorous test of the urban contact issue, any given piece of research ought to satisfy four major criteria:

1. The research ought to include comparative data on both urban and nonurban samples. Whereas the language of much of the discussion here focuses on the nature of urban relationships, in all cases there is an implicit understanding that any findings about relationships in the city are meaningful only in comparison with findings in communities of other types and sizes. This first requirement is considered important enough so that we shall be considering here only studies that present urban–nonurban comparisons.

2. Research ought to consider both the qualitative and the quantitative aspects of social interactions. That is, although we may know that contacts are more or less numerous in one setting than in another, in order to present interpretations we need to know also whether they are superficial or deep and whether they serve important functions and needs (i.e., by providing individuals with the support and feeling of intimate association that people require). Because of the difficulty of assessing the qualitative aspects of relationships, much of the research has referred exclusively to quantity. Even to consider quantity alone is not a simple matter. Quantity may be measured by the total number of interactions, the number of interactions with different people, or the number of different persons with whom one interacts. Also, quantity may be measured by the duration of typical interactions with another person or equally by the frequency of contact with that person. Finally, with the availability of the telephone, there is even a problem of knowing just how to define what a contact is (i.e., does it have to be face to face, or can a phone call be considered its equivalent?).

3. The research ought to address itself to the total range of contacts – with friends, family, neighbors, acquaintances, co-workers, and so on. This stricture is important because research that is directed toward only one form of contact may be misleading in that it reveals only one part of a total picture. Such research overlooks the possibility that a lack of contacts in one area may be due to an abundance of contacts in another (e.g., a person does not try to seek X form of contact because he or she is already satisfied with Y) or may be compensated for by contacts in another (e.g., although a person

might have liked X sort of contact, the person's contacts with Y more than made up for the lack).

4. The research ought to control for other critical variables in order to avoid concluding that the results are caused by the effects of place of residence as opposed to other potential covariants, such as length of residence, marital status, social class, age, or sex.

In this section I will attempt to review and highlight some of the many research studies most often cited over the last twenty years that purport to test the urban social isolation question. It will be noted that even those studies most often cited as providing evidence tend not to meet all of the requirements just set out. Yet because of the wide variety of survey questions and techniques used and the large number of different research samples (both in the United States and in other countries), it should be possible to abstract out of this body of research a set of conclusions about urban relationships based more on data than on conjecture.

An early study by William Key (1968) is typical of much of the research in the area in that it does not meet all of the criteria that would allow for an unequivocal interpretation of the findings, but nonetheless it offers a set of rich and complex findings. On the one hand, it considers only the quantitative aspect of urban relations (as defined by the frequency of meaningful contacts) and it does not pay careful attention to eliminating alternative explanations by controlling for personal or demographic characteristics of the respondents in the different settings. On the other hand, it demonstrates that differing kinds of relationships may demonstrate contrasting patterns according to the type of community studied. Key's sample was drawn from five midwestern localities ranging in type from truly rural areas to a city of more than one hundred thousand people (Indianapolis). Separate measures of quantity of interactions (presented as ''social participation'' scores) were collected for immediate family, extended family, neighbors, informal groups, formal groups, and work groups.

Key's findings indicate that there is a consistent and significant decrease in contact with neighbors and a similar increase in contact with people at work as community size increases. For contact with the immediate and extended family, however, the trend is not linear: There is a greater number of such contacts in both rural and larger urban communities than in middle-sized towns. For contact with formal and informal groups, the reverse pattern holds: There is less contact in both urban and rural communities than in middle-sized towns. Most notable in Key's findings are the following:

1. There is no evidence for the disintegration of family in the city, as suggested by some.

2. In overall frequency, residents of different-sized communities have equal numbers of contacts.

3. Differing kinds of relationships take up a greater part of one's life space in different settings. Just as the second law of thermodynamics points to a conservation of energy, perhaps the first law of urban relations might be that contacts are constant and substitutable. Contacts with family and contacts with friends are inversely related; contacts at work are exchanged for contacts within the locality as one goes from rural area to metropolitan.

Other tests of the frequency-of-socializing hypothesis have also failed to show consistent patterns of rural–urban differences. Norval Glenn and Lester Hill (1977) reanalyzed data collected in a 1974 nationwide survey by the National Opinion Research Center. They carefully considered other variables such as community of origin, age, and social class in comparing contacts with relatives, neighbors, and nonlocal friends. They found that for each of these contact types, there were no significant relationships with size of community. Moreover, age, education, and size of community of *origin* tended to be (especially for females) slightly better predictors than size of current community of *residence* for all the contact types analyzed.

More evidence on the quantity of urban contacts is supplied by the research of John Kasarda and Morris Janowitz (1974) in their reanalysis of a survey sample of over two hundred thousand adults in Great Britain. Rather than being asked *how often* they met with others, respondents in this study were asked *how many* friends, relatives, and acquaintances they knew and how many formal and informal local community activities they participated in. Once again, Kasarda and Janowitz found no pattern of differences that would indicate a lack of ties in the city. In fact, they found that urban friendships were somewhat more extensive and that urbanites' memberships in formal organizations seemed to foster greater numbers of friends and acquaintances. Most important of all, they reported that in a majority of the relationships they explored, length of residence *alone* accounted for a greater amount of variance than the *combined* effects of population size, density, social class, and age.

Finally, Albert Reiss's (1959) research is notable in that it relies upon a different form of data collection, the time budget. Reiss solicited subjects in both rural Tennessee and Nashville and asked them to keep a careful record of how much time they spent with whom during a single day from waking to sleeping. The contacts were coded into seven categories: intimate kin, close friend, close associate or client, good friend, distant associate or casual acquaintance, pure client, and "cordial recognition" (just someone to whom one says hello). As in the other studies, Reiss found no overall pattern of differences between his rural and urban samples. He reports that the urban subjects spent more time in primary-level (i.e., close) relationships, but only because of the inclusion of close work associates in this category. In addition, his results are similar for people of higher and lower social class categories.

Although Reiss's research methodology has been cited widely as an innovative alternative to the standard survey, and his results have been used to substantiate claims that urbanites' relationships are equally as strong as rural dwellers', a closer look makes us a bit wary. Since this research is based on the amount of time spent during a single working day, his results reflect largely the structure of work requirements for urban and rural people; and time spent with others during this period does not necessarily tell us much about the significance of the ties. In this way it is similar to much of the other survey research on number of friends or frequency of contacts, telling us little about the depth of relationships and whether they provide people with a sense of support or integration.

There is far less research that attempts to compare the quality of relationships in city and non-city. A study by J. P. Sutcliffe and B. Crabbe (1963), though primarily concerned with number of contacts, defined the various kinds of relationships in such a way as to give some hint of their meaning and function. Sutcliffe and Crabbe used students who lived in urban, suburban, or rural fringe areas in and around Sydney, Australia, and who were matched on a set of relevant personality characteristics. Each person in the sample was asked to name up to forty-four persons whom he or she knew well. After each name was offered, subjects responded to six items meant to serve as an index of the relationship. These questions covered the extent of mutual borrowing and lending that went on between them, whether they confided in one another about personal problems, and the willingness of the pair to support one another against criticism from others. On the basis of these answers the person listed was characterized as a best friend, a friend, or an acquaintance; then the authors reverted to counting the number of each type. (Although the authors state that the subject was asked in each case if the person named was a relative, unfortunately none of these data is reported to clarify the effect of kinship on contact and closeness.)

Sutcliffe and Crabbe found that the absolute numbers of people listed did not vary significantly by location and that there were no clear trends according to type of relationship as one moved from inner city to rural fringe. They did find, however, that the reported percentage of best friends (i.e., people who provide support and sharing) was slightly lower in both the inner city and the rural fringe than in the middle categories. Also, the inner urban students were more likely to go outside their own immediate area for friends than were those living in other places.

A second study, by Stanley Guterman (1969), was directed exclusively at measuring depth of intimacy (rather than frequency or quantity). Using a sample of hotel employees from different cities on the East Coast he asked each one to name the five persons (or married couples) whom the respondent knew best but was not a relative. For each person named, the respondent answered a set of questions: how badly he or she would feel if they lost touch, how long they had known each other, whether the respondent knew the other person's immediate family, whether the other person's best friends were also the respondent's friends, the number of different kinds of things they discussed, and whether the other person had given the respondent a gift over the last year. From these answers a single index of intimacy was constructed to see whether respondents from different settings differed in the intimacy of their stated friendships.

Guterman reports a marginally significant relationship between low intimacy and high population of the city of residence. But a clear interpretation of even this weak finding is precluded by the numerous problems with this study – among them, nonsystematic sampling techniques, high refusal rates unevenly distributed among the community categories, little attempt to deal with the effects of personal and demographic variables, the use of gross population size categories, and the fact that the role of family is unclear. The most critical problem involves the type of questions used, many of which seem to tap the length of the relationship and its connectedness to other relationships rather than the quality of the relationship itself. Given Kasarda and Janowitz's finding that the lengh-of-residence variable is an extremely powerful one, we need to be particularly cautious in interpreting Guterman's findings.

The most comprehensive and carefully conducted piece of comparative research that addresses questions of both quality and quantity and considers and controls for demographic and personal variables has been carried out by Claude Fischer (1982). Fischer conducted a survey of 1,050 people in fifty northern California neighborhoods and communities. Respondents in this survey came from five different types of communities, varying from core urban areas in such places as San Francisco and Oakland to semirural areas far away from any of these cities. Respondents in Fischer's study listed as many key associates as they could think of, specifying the nature of the relationships in a number of ways (for example, what they did together, what kinds of help or support they could count on from one another, whether they were related, and how physically close their places of residence were).

Fischer's findings fill a whole volume, and it is difficult to summarize them adequately here. As for number of people mentioned, however, there were no overall differences between categories of community. There was a tendency for fewer family members (especially extended family) to be mentioned among the urban core, although when they were mentioned there was also a greater tendency for them to be described as friends as well as "just" family. Urban-core residents were less likely to mention neighbors, but again those mentioned tended to be people with whom they were deeply tied. As other research has shown, urban friendships were more spatially dispersed, but they did not seem to be lacking in quality. Measuring quality in terms of available social support, the results indicated that urbanites tended to be slightly better off, although this effect disappeared after controlling for such variables as age and marital status.

From friend to stranger

The apparent paradox that the city is a "world of strangers" and that urban people, nonetheless, have as many close and supportive relationships as others is one that confuses the *ratio* of strangers to friends with the *absolute numbers* of friends that city people may have. It is resolved when we separate people's experience into public and private spheres or, as described by Karen Franck (1980), into the world "out there" of strangers and the world "in here" of friends, relations, and neighbors. It has been suggested by a number of people (e.g., Fischer, 1981, 1982) that we often confuse the urbanite's public gruffness and formality with a disinterest in friends and acquaintances. Conversely, Crowe (1978) and Hummon (1980) comment that we equally often confuse the public familiarity of small-town speech and manner with a private friendliness that may not exist. When absolute numbers are small, people recognize one another and often nod and say hello. Still, it is one matter to make a casual gesture on the street and another to go beyond it by associating socially or providing comfort and support.

What is being suggested is that although the public world does shape some of the experience of the city, the existence of small private worlds is the proof of the pudding when it comes to discovering whether people are satisfied with their relationships. A newcomer to New York City highlights this observation in his comment about urban life:

We get along very well and I really see no difference between these relationships and the ones Nancy and I had with friends in Illinois. The difference is "out there" in the city not "in here" with the people that live in the city. It's peculiar but I haven't met anyone yet who admits to living "out there" – all say they live in here with us humans. Where are the bastards from? [Quoted in Franck, 1980, pp. 52–53]

One issue that is worthy of consideration is the matter of how one gets from "out there" to "in here." In a fascinating study of newcomers to New York City and a small town, respondents were interviewed within two months of their arrival in the fall and again seven to eight months later (Franck, 1980). Franck pointed out that the process of friendship formation in the city took longer and involved more difficulty than the same process in the small town. For instance, in the fall a significantly greater percentage of urban than of small-town residents found it "difficult to meet people here," but by the spring there were no differences. This finding is reflected in actual numbers of friendships made: In the first interview, urban newcomers reported a mean number of 3.50 friends, compared to the small-town group's 6.32. Later in the spring the numbers were almost identical (5.34 for the urban group, 5.12 for the rural group).

The difficulties encountered in forming friendships in the city are associated with a number of factors. One aspect of the problem involves fears for safety and concerns about crime, which lead urbanites to be more distrustful of any given interpersonal encounter. It is consistent with this observation and with our hot–cold orientation that a significant proportion of people in Franck's study reported having not only a number of unpleasant and distressing encounters with strangers but also a large number that were pleasant and helpful. As noted by Milgram (1970), urbanites have a practiced air of outward indifference that makes it difficult to anticipate who will react positively and who will not if and when they are approached. In addition, given the urban norm of noninvolvement (city residents are not likely to volunteer to help unless asked) and the generally conservative nature of interpersonal risk taking (Goffman, 1971), it is not surprising that for many urbanites the motto seems to be "Nothing ventured, nothing lost."

The urban egg, then, has a harder shell to crack. Lacking the occasion or circumstances for making an entrée, many persons who see each other day after day at a bus or railroad station, in a cafeteria or passing in the hallways at work, never become anything more than "familiar strangers" (Milgram, 1972). Also, some people may remain totally on the outside because they lack social skills or initiative. Yet the overwhelming evidence is that because of the diversity of strangers – each one a *potential friend* – and the wide range of lifestyles and interests in the city, people do move from the outside in. And once they are on the inside of one group or network, the possibilities for expanding their connections multiply greatly. As a result, the evidence indicates that the positive opportunities in the city often seem to outweigh the constraining forces, allowing people to develop and maintain satisfying relationships.

Community and neighborhood

Although it has been demonstrated that urban residents do have a large set of people with whom they socialize and upon whom they can call for support, there is still another important perspective from which the attachment question needs to be addressed. This perspective is broader in that it does not ask about the urbanite's commitment to other specific individuals but instead is directed to his or her relationship with larger units, from the local area to the community as a whole. It is concerned with the basis on which attachments are formed and the manner in which consensus, commitment, and cohesiveness are sustained *in* a place and *to* a place as large as a city. In addressing such matters as how patterns of attachment develop and focus, it leads us to ask, Where and how does the notion of *neighborhood* play a role in urban relations, and does it make sense to use the term *community* when referring to the city?

Some definitional matters

In considering the nature and form of community in the city, we immediately come up against the problem that this term has a wide variety of uses and meanings (as far back as 1955 Hillery cited forty-four separate definitions). Each time the concept is discussed or debated – as in "Is community dead in the city?" – the answers vary because not all of the participants are referring to the same thing. Leonard Reissman (1970) has pointed out this difficulty. In making his point, however, he uses the term in both its singular and its plural forms and, therefore, also seems to fall prey to its multiple usages:

. . . cities are communities only because they command allegiance, social consensus and belief, and even at times, a civic spirit. Recognizing this fact makes
invalid the argument that cities have destroyed the old "sense of community."
Except in a very narrow definition of "community." [P. 13]

For the present purposes, it is necessary to identify three major classes of definition of this term. The first manner in which *community* has been used is as a generic term, for places in which people live as they are geographically or administratively defined (as in "communities that range in size from a thousand persons or fewer to a million or more"). The second usage refers also to a place or a group of people, but in this case to a subset of a larger one, and implies in its meaning *local* community. When used in this way, the terms *community* and *neighborhood* are often thought of interchangeably (as in "I know most of the people who live in my community"). The third is really a class of usage, rather than a single definition, which is held together by the fact that it refers to something more psychological or symbolic than physical or geographical. This usage is defined by two elements: (1) the existence of some *shared characteristic* among members of a group, whether interests, values, or skills (for example, in a community of scholars), and (2) a resulting state of interaction, sociability, support, identification, and commitment among the members of the group (as in community spirit). Our major concern here is with community in this third sense. The greatest problem in dealing with the "community question" has been in the confusion between the second and third definitions. The questions of whether solidarity and commitment are (or should be) centered in the local community (i.e., neighborhood) and whether people in cities experience community (i.e., sharing and support) at all are very different ones.

The search for community

Barry Wellman and Barry Leighton (1979) have provided an excellent review of the questions of whether community exists in the city and where it is centered. They present two opposing viewpoints on the issue that will be briefly presented here in order to lay out the arena within which the community question has been discussed. They do offer a third position that places the question in a different perspective, but this option will be dealt with later in the chapter.

The first, labeled the view of *community lost*, is largely the position of the human ecologists. It equates the industrial bureaucratic structuring of formal organization with the structuring of urban life and contrasts this structuring with a more pastoral model. In this view, diffusion of ties is a key negative element of urban life: With the increasing scale of activity, primary ties break down and people become weakly integrated with all forms of support. At best, a person becomes a limited member of many networks, rather than a full member of one. The organization of urban life is seen as not allowing strong local ties to form, with the result that people are forced to go beyond the "local community" (i.e., neighborhood) to seek support and friendship. What they find when they go out there are ties that are characterized as narrowly defined, weak in intensity, loosely knit (few persons within know one another), and loosely bonded. Three major principles underlie this position:

1. The local community is the natural repository for community sentiment.
2. People go beyond it only when they cannot develop satisfying social ties nearby.
3. Ties that are created outside the family and the neighborhood in the city are bound to be inferior in quality.

That is, since community does not exist in the neighborhood and cannot be found elsewhere, the end result is one of *community lost*.

The second position, *community saved*, while reaching an almost opposite set of conclusions about the existence of support and friendship in the city, is still very much based on equating community with neighborhood. This position counters the claims of community lost by demonstrating via surveys and field studies (as in Gans's *Urban Villagers* 1962b; Liebow's *Talley's Corner*, 1967; and Whyte's *Street Corner Society*, 1955) that in spite of the pressures of urban and bureaucratic life, community is alive and well – and is alive and well in the neighborhood. What is suggested here is that urban forces have the opposite effect from that suggested by the human ecologists: In order to counteract the forces that might otherwise pull people apart, urbanites are encouraged or even required to bond together to conserve internal resources, local autonomy, and social control. In this position there is also the implicit acceptance that life "outside" is hostile. But here the suggestion is that the community-within-a-community is possible and, in fact, all the more satisfying because of the hostile world out there.

Herbert Gans, who has provided one of the most vivid descriptions of a vital urban neighborhood in his work in Boston's West End (1962b), has argued that urban neighborhoods and rural or suburban villages are really not greatly different:

For most West Enders, their life in the area resembled that found in the village or small town, and even in the suburb. Indeed, if differences of age and economic level among the residents were eliminated, many similarities between the life of the urban neighborhood and the suburb become visible. . . . The West End was not a charming neighborhood of "noble peasants" living in an exotic fashion, resisting the mass-produced homogeneity of American culture and overflowing with a cohesive sense of community. It was a rundown area of people struggling with problems of low income, poor education and related difficulties. Even so, it was by and large a good place to live. [Pp. 15–16]

In his description, Gans acknowledges the problems of developing community within the urban setting. Nonetheless, here and throughout his writings he points out that the urban neighborhood is a place where comfort, closeness, and security can be found, and therefore he maintains that it is a "good place to live."

The urban neighborhood

As reflected by both of the positions just outlined, in their quest for community people have looked first and often have looked *only* to their neighborhood. In this section we shall ask just what a neighborhood is and why people have looked there. Then we shall briefly review some of what has been found and consider the implications of these findings.

What is it?

Just as with any term used by social scientists to describe the city or some element of it, there are many definitions for the neighborhood (see Keller, 1968; Lee, 1968; Olsen, 1982; and Taylor, 1982 for a set of well-presented but varying discussions). Albert Hunter (1979) refers to the neighborhood as "a social/spatial unit of social organization . . . larger than a household and smaller than a city" (p. 270). It stands between the forces and institutions of society as a whole and the localized routines of the everyday lives of people. This definition captures three essential elements that reveal the importance and failings of the neighborhood as reflected in the literature on urban life.

First, there is *size*. That is, the neighborhood is not too big and not too small; it is something larger than an individual or household and yet smaller than a city. It is a unit of the city that can be conceived of, and dealt with, on a *human scale*.

Second, there is the matter of its basic *nature*. This is to say that the neighborhood is typically defined in both social and spatial terms. Spatially, it can be thought of as part of the city's geography, as a place defined by specific physical boundaries and located on official city maps. Emphasis on this aspect of identifying the neighborhood is reflected in the early work of Robert Park and E. W. Burgess (1925) and of R. D. McKenzie (1926) in their selection and study of "natural areas," parts of the city that can be identified and mapped in concentric circles.

Still, conceptions of the neighborhood go farther. Neighborhoods are defined by their symbolic and cultural meanings as well. More than areas of territory, they are "social constructions." One can easily think of ethnic enclaves, such as Chinatown in San Francisco or the Italian North End in Boston; racially defined neighborhoods, such as Harlem in New York or Watts in Los Angeles; or neighborhoods defined by lifestyle, such as the bohemian sections of Greenwich Village in New York, or Haight-Ashbury in San Francisco. Neighborhoods are most easily defined when physical boundaries coalesce with symbolic meanings. Most important, however, they draw their existence and life from the fact that people within and beyond their "boundaries" recognize them and associate patterns of behavior or particular groupings of people with them. As a result, neighborhoods may or may not exist on formal city maps, but they are meaningful because they are psychologically compelling and exist in many people's *cognitive* maps.

Thus, without any particular reference to geography, Milgram (1977) has defined a "neighborhood" as an "area of comfortable familiarity" (p. 47), noting that the farther you move from your home and toward the edges of your neighborhood, the less familiar and certain the people and places become. One Puerto Rican labor leader in New York has put it more succinctly: "A neighborhood is where, when you go out of it, you get beat up" (quoted in Tripp, 1970, p. 84).

Third, there is the dimension of *function*. The neighborhood, used as a linking concept, is seen as being "interposed" between the individual and society. It serves as a buffer between strong, potentially hostile external forces and the individual. It can serve as a center for mutual aid, a center of economic production and consumption, a political base, or an agency for social control and sociability. In the neighborhood, exchanges of information, services, and approval commonly take place. These may be informal or may be highly formalized, as in old German villages in which each member of a "district" was obligated to respond to a call for help from another member for harvesting or house building (Keller, 1968). Moreover, people are thought to identify with their local area, to be willing to fight to defend it (see Suttles's 1968 work on the gangs of South Chicago), and to grieve over leaving it (see Fried's 1963 work on the West End of Boston).

More formally, Ralph Taylor (1982) and David Popenoe (1973) have described the urban neighborhood as serving six specific functions and needs:

1. Social interaction – as a place to find friendship and support
2. Social control – as a place in which residents see that others adhere to locally accepted norms
3. A sense of security and ease – as a place where fear and threat are minimized
4. Organizational ties – as a place for shared participation, both formally and informally
5. A sense of collective identity – as a place of symbolic attachment
6. Socialization – as a focus for parent–child and child-to-child interaction

In considering this list of functions and thereby the way in which the neighborhood has been conceptualized, we immediately see why it has played such an important role in the literature. It has been defined as the repository for communal ties in the city – or, as Donald Warren (1978) has described the neighborhood, as a *community of place*. The confusion of these two terms, *community* and *neighborhood*, boils down to the fact that what was initially or essentially a physical concept – neighborhood – has accumulated strongly social connotations. And what is most simply a condition of shared social feelings – community – has been thought to exist within a specific physical locale.

When we consider the evidence for the importance of the local neighborhood we face the problem that regardless of the position one prefers to defend, it is relatively easy to summon support. Once again we meet the existence of multiple and contrasting positions, each true for some people at some times. For those who would say that the neighborhood has lost its significance, we have the data cited earlier in this chapter to show that people in cities are likely to go beyond their local areas for friendship and support. In addition, it is undoubtedly true that compared to people in small towns, a larger proportion of urban residents know neither their next-door neighbors nor other people who live in the same building or block.

On the other side of the coin, there are the many studies of tightly knit social worlds existing in cities. Anyone wanting clear evidence of the existence of caring, of support, and of friendships tightly centered around the local area can find endless examples of "neighborhoods that work" (see Schoenberg & Rosenbaum, 1980, for many examples in a book with this very title). Still, we must ask whether these instances are representative of urban life or mere analyses of deviant cases – the exceptions that prove the rule, so to speak.

When we consider the results of large-scale survey studies, such as those by Albert Hunter in Rochester, New York, and Hartford, Connecticut (1975, 1982), we find that the evidence is mixed. Hunter studied 154 households in Rochester's inner urban core in 1974, replicating a study done in 1949. He found that there was a fairly consistent decline over these twenty-five years in residents' use of local (within five blocks of home) facilities for such resources as shopping (down from 77 percent in 1949 to 35 percent in 1974), movies (down from 49 percent to 9 percent), and doctors (from 47 percent to 19 percent). Yet five of the six measures of informal local neighboring (e.g., Do you chat with neighbors at parties and picnics or visit informally?) had increased over time; and questions concerning residents' "sense of community" (e.g., Does your local area have a special name? Does it claim more loyalty than the city as a whole?) also indicated an increase. In addition, Hunter's Hartford results indicate that a feeling of social integration in the neighborhood is also important in moderating people's fear of strangers and crime. These results suggest that neighborhoods may continue to serve psychological functions even when physical use functions decline.

Community transformed

The discussion of community lost versus community saved serves to reaffirm the basic position taken in this book. When we look at the evidence, we find that it does not favor one over the other; rather, both are valid to a large extent. The city is a place big enough for polarities to exist. Each position contains an important kernel of truth, and neither is capable of containing the whole truth. The city is a place where many persons are isolated and lonely and feel as if they have relatively few sources of support. The city is also a place where people who do not know, or perhaps do not even want to know, their neighbors have strong commitments to one another based on interests, values, and common pursuits. And the city is a place where small homogeneous neighborhoods based on kinship and ethnicity continue to exist, offering the people who live in them local source of support, control, and socialization.

Although each of these extremes does exist – and *because* they all exist – it is important to realize that they do not exist in their pure forms. The person in the urban village cannot function in the same way as the person in the rural village; and the urbanite whose friends are spread throughout the city may still use many local facilities and maintain some local acquaintances and commitments. Thus we must approach the matter by asking, to the extent that both of these extremes exist, when, where, and for whom they are each relevant. Also, to the extent that the city involves different kinds of relationships, some of which are spatially based and some of which are not, we must describe the community in various terms that express this hybrid nature of urban commitments.

Community without propinquity

Differing both from the position that community cannot exist in the city and from the argument that community resides in the neighborhood, there are a number of types of compromise. Wellman and Leighton (1979) have labeled one orientation *community liberated*. This stance is represented by David Minar and Scott Greer (1969), who ask "whether community can exist . . . in meaningful ways without the locality as the nexus of loyalties. Must community, in other words, be place oriented?" (p. 47). This position suggests that community exists in the city but that with fast and available transportation, high rates of social and residential mobility, and the separation of working and living places, community is not based on place. Suzanne Keller (1968) has expressed this argument in a manner that parallels the discussion of psychological distance and physical distance: "Nearness and distance, though spatial concepts, depend on more than space. Friends may lie far apart, and yet remain in spiritual communion. Neighbors may be worlds apart, even though they live next door" (p. 23). This kind of arrangement, which is said to pervade urban life, where commitments and attachments are strong but have cultural or personal bases rather than territorial ones, has been termed by Melvin Webber (1963) *community without propinquity*.

According to this view, urbanites are limited members of several social worlds but do not suffer from this dispersal. Rather than being tied to a single, all-encompassing social network, they are attached to a number of different groupings. The people with whom they work, play, and live may all be different, and there may be few connections among these networks. Attachments to some groups and some individuals are strong and broad-based, whereas attachments to others are weak and narrowly defined. In this kind of setup, individuals use different kinds of connections for different purposes. Some are casual, whereas others are meant to create and provide "community": the sense of support, security, and a deep feeling of integration.

The use of the term *liberated* is not without subtle implications. Consulting *Webster's Dictionary*, one finds that it refers to being freed, as from bondage. According to proponents of this orientation, the nonlocalized organization of commitments is said to possess a number of advantages. Whereas the village (whether urban or rural) can provide warmth and support, it can also stifle. It can represent constraint, demands for conformity, and loss of privacy, freedom, and individuality. Having a network of cross-cutting commitments means that no single community can make unreasonable demands; and it provides alternatives and escape routes for those who want or need them.

Proponents of this position also point out that relationships, as defined by kinship, work, or locality, are all to a large extent ascribed: They are relationships that result from circumstance rather than from choice. They are arrangements that we settle for, rather than alliances that we seek out. These theorists suggest that the diversity of modern life and the conditions of urban living allow us to seek out the resources that best fit our needs. Claude Fischer's (1984) subcultural approach, as discussed in Chapter 3, reminds us that the city provides the critical mass necessary for subcultures to form and thrive. The person who fancies seventeenth-century Norwegian woodcarvings or the collector of modern jazz records might be satisfied with friendships developed via proximity. But, it is argued, think how much more pleasing it would be to have friendships based on common interests. Friendships based on propinquity are capable of growing strong and deep, but those based on common interests may be able to provide satisfaction that neighborhood friendships cannot. If distance and the time implied by distance represent "costs" of social relationships, then the fact that friendships continue and grow across distance must represent evidence that these friendships are satisfying and rewarding.

The community of limited liability

The position of community liberated differs from that of community lost in its strong assertion that communal ties exist in the city. At the same time, however, it shares with the community-lost position the denial of the neighborhood as an important element in urban life. In both, the neighborhood is seen as a vestige of an earlier form of social order, and local sentiments are seen as a persisting residue that is of limited significance (Hunter, 1978).

A fourth position differs from each of the previous ones. It posits (1) that community is alive and well, (2) that it can and does reside in the neighborhood for significant elements of the urban population, and (3) that the urban resident is likely to have multiple commitments that do indeed make the neighborhood unlike the rural village. The local community, according to this position, is important, but it is a *community of limited liability* (Kasarda & Janawitz, 1974). In a community of limited liability people develop local attachments, they participate in local activities, but they are still prepared to withdraw physically or psychologically if and when local conditions fail to satisfy their needs and aspirations. That is, city neighborhoods are not seen as self-centered units, nor are they or their residents seen as seeking isolation. Jane Jacobs (1961) suggests that to see the urban neighborhood as the sole source of community or involvement misses the whole point of cities, which draw people to them for the very diversity that they can offer. This final position argues that urban people have real investments in their neighborhood but that these are not the *only* places in which they "live." Instead, an intricate balance is maintained between local and spatially dispersed attachments, a balance that leads to a picture of city dwellers as living in a set of *hierarchical* communities.

Different kinds of communities for different kinds of people

The focus on neighborhoods is an easily understandable one, since proximity remains the simplest and most effortless basis for contacts. But whereas some people make most of their significant contacts and commitments within their neighborhoods (as in the community-saved position), some others have little, if any, investment in their local areas but have extensive contacts throughout the city (as in community liberated), others have significant commitments to neighborhood but also maintain strong and important commitments elsewhere (community found), and still others make few contacts and feel isolated and lonely (community lost). A final critical question we shall address in this chapter asks who seeks community in the local area, who seeks it elsewhere, and what determines whether and where it is found.

Localites and cosmopolites

A number of years ago, Robert Merton (1957) made a simple distinction between two basic types of people that are found in the city. The first group, localites, are those people who seek community immediately around them. They are interested and active in the neighborhood. Through their involvement, they act to create linkages of information and support within the area, thereby strengthening the neighborhood and making it a more attractive focus for others physically and psychologically. The second group, cosmopolites, are those people whose interests and involvement extend beyond the geographical bounds of the neighborhood to a broad range of the urban region. Merton suggests that both groups are important in the city. That is, whereas an area with only cosmopolites would have little internal cohesion, a strong neighborhood needs some cosmopolites to provide links between communities (whether defined geographically or in terms of interest) and to help arouse interest, resources, and support from the outside when they are needed. In fact, Mark Granovetter (1973) has suggested that some urban villages, including Boston's West End, failed to survive when faced with urban renewal, because the local network was so tightly bound within that it never became well connected to the outside. Therefore, it could not exert any great force in the political process, and it perished as a result.

What becomes clearer from this discussion is that the reason the four positions previously presented continue to have strong adherents is that each one is valid – for some people at some times. Up to now we have dealt with generalizations about ''the people'' of the city. At this point it is important to make some finer distinctions within the urban populace and thereby to consider the reasons why community is lost and found and to ask, when it is found, who finds it where.

For instance, when we speak of Merton's cosmopolites, the group of people that come to mind are most likely single or divorced. They tend to be young and to have a higher level of education than the norm, and also higher incomes. These people have (1) the desire to seek out the many and varying attractions of the city, (2) the means to pursue their interests, and (3) few commitments at "home" that would conflict with these pursuits. But depending on their own personal attributes, their social skills, and the nature of the networks they develop, they are thought to run the risk of developing multiple superficial ties with few deep commitments. There is always the possibility that they may end up feeling lonely as a result.

Although we can develop fairly concise images of the attractions beyond the immediate urban locale and of those people who are free to pursue them, the localites Merton describes include a far greater variety of people. We shall consider who they are by analyzing the degree to which they are local *by choice* or *by constraint*: whether they are positively attracted to their areas or whether they are excluded from broader pursuits for one reason or another.

Homogeneous communities

The first group of people who have local commitments are those who feel no need to go beyond the neighborhood. These are people for whom the *community of interest* and the *community of residence* coincide. Such people are most typically found within the ethnic neighborhood, where a homogeneity of values and a critical mass of similar interests are likely to reside already. And they are especially common in early-generation urban neighborhoods, before cultural assimilation leads to wider variation in values and interests. For these people, the neighborhood provides the buffer that was previously mentioned and allows life to proceed on a comfortable scale, among people who are known rather than strangers. This positive sense of community-in-locality is captured in the statement of a resident of Boston's Italian North End, who said only half facetiously that the best way to preserve the neighborhood was to build a fence around it, not to keep residents in but to keep all the outsiders away.

Communities by constraint

Boundaries between communities can be of different sorts and serve different purposes. In the twentieth-century United States, boundaries are often symbolic; they consist of demarcations of differences in lifestyle, ethnicity, or race. Sometimes they are physical, but most often physical barriers result from features of the natural environment rather than being man-made. When physical barriers are actually erected, their purpose is usually to keep outsiders out. In eighteenth-century Europe, however, ghettos were physically walled-off areas meant to keep devalued groups in rather than outsiders out. These places became tightly knit communities, and although people who lived there might have chosen to focus themselves internally anyway, the fact that they could not go elsewhere changed the nature of their existence. When we think of the neighborhood as a place where people are involved because they are excluded from or do not have the resources to become involved in the broader community, we get a very different picture of the meaning of neighborhood.

For groups that are not easily assimilated or face discrimination (e.g., blacks or Orientals), for newly arrived migrant groups who come from a different culture (whether from the farm or from another country), for those to whom physical mobility is a problem (e.g., the elderly or the physically disabled), or more generally, for the urban poor, the neighborhood is often a focal point of life. These people may find the neighborhood satisfying and supportive. Still, in a community by constraint, with high levels of crime and fear and forms of urban design that discourage contact (as will be discussed in greater detail in Chapter 7), there is a greater likelihood that people will withdraw into the home and come to feel isolated and lonely (Fischer, 1982).

Communities by commitment

For some people, community and neighborhood coincide because of their functional relationship to the area. One group in this category would be couples with young children, especially mothers who are not working outside the home. Although it could be argued that such people are related to the neighborhood by constraint (i.e., reduced mobility), people with young children are also likely to have strong commitments to the appearance and safety of their neighborhoods because these things affect opportunities for sociability. Also, the quality of local facilities for recreation and education is likely to be of great interest, enough to lead these people into active involvement and community-based political activity. Another group in this category are people who own rather than rent their places of residence. Because of the financial as well as the psychic commitments involved in owning, these people have a stake in maintaining the current physical level of the neighborhood, in defending it against encroachment, and in organizing both formally and informally.

Block and neighborhood associations sometimes spring up spontaneously in such communities by commitment. Most often, however, they arise in response to some form of threat. Threats can range from a plan to raze a whole area as part of an urban-renewal project, to a plan to put a highway near or through a neighborhood, to an increase in violent crime in the area. The success of community organizations is a complex issue (see, e.g., Wandersman, 1984), but such action must begin with the people who feel that they have both something to gain by the continued existence of an active

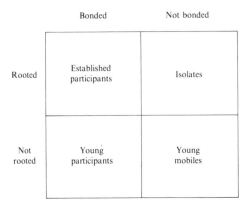

Figure 6.1. Typology of urbanites according to the nature of their neighborhood attachment, as proposed by Riger and Lavrakas. (1981).

neighborhood and something to lose if the quality of life in the locality deteriorates.

Typologies of people and neighborhoods

Research by Stephanie Riger and Paul Lavrakas (1981) contains parallels to this discussion of commitment and further clarifies the issues by providing an empirically derived typology of urbanites according to the extent and kinds of their commitments. Riger and Lavrakas reanalyzed a survey of 540 telephone interviews with adults in Philadelphia, Chicago, and San Francisco to concentrate on the kinds of attachments that people have to their local areas. Using factor analysis, they discovered two factors that separate out somewhat related yet still distinct forms of urban attachment. The first, which they call "rootedness," involves the dimension of physical attachment to locale. It is associated with whether people own or rent, how long they have been living at an address, and whether they expect to be living in the same place in the next two years. The second factor, called "bondedness," is associated with whether people feel that they can tell friend from stranger in the area, whether they feel part of the neighborhood or whether it is just a place to live, and how many children in the area they know by name. By considering whether people were strongly rooted in, or strongly bonded to, the local area, Riger and Lavrakas came up with a fourfold typology, as shown in Figure 6.1:

1. *Young mobiles.* These people are neither bonded to nor rooted in the neighborhood; they constitute 32 percent of the sample. They are well-educated young adults who tend not to join neighborhood groups or read local

newspapers. They live in apartment buildings and sometimes use their neighborhoods for walks and entertainment in the evening. But for the most part,
their homes serve as bases of operations rather than places that they are
permanently attached to or critically invested in. (Kitty Genovese was most
likely a young mobile.)

2. *Young participants.* These people make up 21 percent of the sample.
They are involved in the local area, not only using it for walking and entertainment but also participating in neighborhood activities. These people are
also young but they have less education on the average than the young mobiles
and are more likely to have children. In spite of their current commitment to
the neighborhood, these people are not sure whether they will be there in the
future. Their form of attachment sounds almost like that expressed in the
community-of-limited-liability notion.

3. *Isolates.* This group, 13 percent of the sample, are not bonded to the
neighborhood but are rooted. They are older adults who no longer have
children at home, who do not join or participate in local groups or institutions,
but who have lived in the area a long time and will probably continue to
do so.

4. *Established participants.* These people, who are both rooted in and
bonded to the neighborhood, make up 34 percent of the sample. They are
older than the young participants yet still have children living at home. They
go out at night, are active in local groups, live in a single-family residences,
and consider their current homes permanent.

Riger and Lavrakas's topology is useful in distinguishing two forms of
possible attachment to a neighborhood. But just as we can view people according to their attachment to neighborhood, it would seem equally possible
to reverse the process – to classify neighborhoods according to the commitments of their residents. Donald and Rachel Warren (Warren, 1978; Warren
& Warren, 1975) have done just this. Rather than accept various one-dimensional definitions of the neighborhood as strong or weak, cohesive or non-
cohesive, they have considered three different dimensions in order to come
out with a more complex characterization:

1. Interaction: Do the residents get together often?
2. Identity: Do residents feel that they have much in common?
3. Connections: Are residents involved in political and other such activities
outside the neighborhood?

On the basis of responses to all three questions, they have classified neighborhoods into six categories:

1. *Integral.* This form of neighborhood is high on all three dimensions.
People identify with it, have a good deal of formal and informal interaction

in it, yet have strong ties, interests, and influence in larger political forces. This form of neighborhood is said to be like a vast radar network, picking up information and resources from the outside and dispersing them inside quickly and efficiently.

2. *Parochial.* As in the integral neighborhood, interaction and identification are high here. But this neighborhood faces inward; it is largely isolated from influence over or information from the outside. "We can take care of our own" is the predominant attitude expressed here. Such a neighborhood is satisfying in many ways, but it is vulnerable to external threats.

3. *Diffuse.* In this form of neighborhood, identification with the locale is high, and people are friendly in public. But privacy is greatly valued, and hello's on the street are rarely translated into discussions inside the home. Information flows slowly here, and people indicate that they prefer to rely on the family rather than neighbors should they be in need of aid.

4. *Stepping-stone.* This type of neighborhood is characterized by a high turnover rate. It is often populated by young executives who want to be near their jobs but who are likely to be moving on to other positions within five years. People here are likely to interact and have strong connections with the larger area, but they are less likely to direct their involvements in service of the neighborhood.

5. *Transitory.* In this type of area there is little identification or interaction that can be identified on a neighborhood-wide basis. There are pockets of activity and involvement among some long-term residents, but the population turnover is generally rapid, and there is little sharing or activity on a broader basis.

6. *Anomic.* This is the extreme form of neighborhood, where residents are not involved with one another or with activities in a broader sphere. Such neighborhoods may be either poor or affluent, but in each people remain largely isolated and anonymous.

Temporal perspectives

Typologies are extremely useful descriptive tools. But they breed a tendency to think in discrete categories, when in fact people and places vary along continua. In addition, they offer a static picture of people in communities instead of implying that they can and do change over time. Earlier in this chapter, we considered the transition from stranger to acquaintance to friend. At this point, we might ask whether and how people change in their orientations to their communities and how differing neighborhoods may evolve from one kind to another.

For instance, in Riger and Lavrakas's system, young participants and young mobiles eventually get older, marry, and have children. As they do, it would be interesting and important to note how their orientations to their present neighborhoods change and when or whether they move to other areas to satisfy their changing needs. Similarly, what other circumstances and dispositions change in the lives of established participants as they get older so that some of them become isolates, in Riger and Lavrakas's terms? From the same temporal perspective, we may ask whether it is possible in a diffuse neighborhood for norms and interpersonal orientations to change so that it becomes an integral area, or what can be done in the parochial neighborhood to encourage members to establish ties with the outside when threatened.

Although he does not fully address the ways changes are accomplished, Albert Hunter (1978) does offer a more dynamic model to describe a set of stages by which a sense of community may emerge in the neighborhood. The first stage, that of "residual neighborhoods," captures the sense of vestigial, minimal functioning. The neighborhood described here is a place much like the Warrens' diffuse neighborhood, where people are friendly but, in Fisher's (1984) terms, "just neighbors" rather than "real neighbors."

The second stage, called "emergent communities" or "defended neighborhoods" by Suttles (1972), represents a transition that is motivated not by positive forces from within but by threats that are typically, though not always, external. Such threats may range anywhere from a sharp increase in the number of violent crimes in the neighborhood, to an influx of people who are perceived as undesirable by local residents, to a government-planned change such as the demolition of a group of buildings or the construction of an expressway. Simply because they share a common fate by virtue of physical proximity, members of neighborhoods facing threats band together in order to take more effective action.

The third stage, that of "conscious communities," is one in which the neighborhood has at least partially overcome the threats to it and now begins to assert its existence and importance in a more positive way. According to Hunter, it is at this point that the neighborhood comes to define itself as having a set of central values and characteristics and to plan and organize proactively rather than reactively in order to improve its quality of life. It is not clear why some communities evolve to this point and some do not. Warren and Warren suggest, for instance, that the diffuse neighborhood can be organized against external threats but that the feeling of solidarity that develops often disappears with the threat. External threats bring people together, let them share, and allow them to recognize their similarities. Still, Hunter emphasizes that in order for the positive sentiments to remain vigorous and continue to grow, there must be strong, successful organizing efforts within the community. Such efforts may lead to a fourth stage of "vicarious" or "symbolic" community, in which the attachment and allegiance to an area grow so strong that the area becomes an element of the residents' identities (see Proshansky, 1978; Proshansky, Kaminoff, & Fabian, 1983; Stokols & Shumaker, 1980). At this stage, local ties remain strong even if the area is destroyed or if the resident is required to leave for some reason (see Fried, 1963).

Summary

Throughout this chapter I have assumed, as have other urban commentators, that city people desire contact with others so that they may share feelings, provide and receive support, and engage in joint activities. Yet, unlike many others, I have refused to accept a single conclusion about whether the city encourages or works against the development of close ties. Instead, I have noted that certain features of modern urban life place constraints between people, whereas other features act as resources, providing occasions and opportunities for people to meet one another. I have approached the question of community not only by looking at the local area (i.e., neighborhood) but also by considering where, how, and when it may be found beyond the neighborhood. A review of the empirical literature has suggested that on the average, urban people do not seem to have any fewer or any less satisfying attachments than people who live elsewhere – although the distribution of these attachments may differ.

Whether our questions about social contact involve person-to-person friendships or extend to the nature of communal or community ties, there is an analogy that we can use to help answer them. If we live in a system where there is potential for people to be pulled apart, we can ask, "What is the glue that holds them together?" As educated consumers of cohesion-producing materials, we ought to ask certain questions about this glue. We will want to know (1) whether it is strong, (2) whether it is long-lasting, (3) whether it will break under stress, (4) whether it is messy or costly (e.g., might it gum up the whole works when it is applied?), and (5) whether it is easily available.

The three major "glue" products have been identified, each with its own advantages and disadvantages:

1. *Family.* Kinship ties exist and are nurtured from the day of birth. Therefore, they are strong and automatically available, and usually they do not have any great cost associated with them. Urban people continue to rely strongly on members of the immediate family, although extended family ties seem to be weakened in the city, largely because of spatial separation and the existence of alternative kinds of bonding material. Regardless of the amount of time spent with family, however, at times of particular stress or when aid is needed, urban people report that they feel they can still rely on family members.

2. *Proximity.* This form of glue is also valuable because it is easily accessible and applied with little effort. Urban dwellers rely on neighbors for

friendship and support. Some, however, have said that this glue is used only when no other product is available, whereas others argue that just because it is cheap and easy to use, there is no reason to assume that it cannot provide strong and long-lasting cohesion. It is most often ideal when it is applied to a homogeneous area. As with family, it should not be applied too thickly because it will then produce too constraining a bond.

3. *Common interest.* This product needs to be sought out, as it is not always available in the local neighborhood (although when it is, it is an ideal product). If it must be obtained elsewhere, certain costs are involved. It tends to be preferred by many urban people with special needs and interests and by those with few commitments and relatively great resources. In order for a firm, strong, and meaningful bond to be achieved, it has to be applied in good volume until a critical mass is reached. Although it is highly satisfactory to some, others argue that it does not provide a truly strong bond and that the cohesion may disappear with the passing of time or under stress.

By using this analogy to examine the major positions concerning the nature of communal ties in the city, I have tried to demonstrate that no single position contains an accurate or total description of urban social relations. Community resides in many different forms for many different kinds of people living under many different kinds of circumstances. And for some, especially newcomers, the poor, and those without strong personal resources (i.e., the ill, the psychologically troubled), strong attachments may not exist at all. Therefore, once again, a fully accurate account of urban life requires accounting for a simultaneous existence of multiple realities and experiences, good and bad, black and white, and several shades of gray in between. In Chapter 7 we will look further at how urban experiences vary from person to person and group to group. In this case, however, our interest will focus upon the effects of design and planning. We will consider how the physical environment can be and has been fashioned to promote community and how good design can help pull people together, whereas bad design can help pull them apart.

Suggestions for further reading

Fischer, C. 1982. *To dwell among friends: Personal networks in town and city.* Chicago: University of Chicago Press.

Gans, H. J. 1962b. *The urban villagers.* New York: Free Press.

Keller, S. 1968. *The urban neighborhood.* New York: Random House.

Korte, C. 1980. Urban–nonurban differences in social behavior and social psychological models of urban impact. *Journal of Social Issues, 36,* 29–51.

Warren, R. 1974. *Community in America.* Chicago: Rand McNally.

7

CITIES BY DESIGN: THE PHYSICAL ENVIRONMENT AND URBAN LIVING

Our annual population growth of 4,000,000 people increases the physical pressures, causes us to seek quick remedies, leads us to waste too much wealth on quick-fix projects that provide at best a temporary respite from yesterday's mistakes. The razing of tenements, their instant replacement by high-rise slums, changes the facade – not the features – of the ghetto.
–Secretary of the Interior Stewart Udall, quoted in Spilhaus, 1968, p. 710.

Throughout Part II our focus has been on the quality of life in the city. In Chapter 5 we directed our attention to conditions such as noises and crowds and noted that these are often stressful. Still, for some people at some times high levels of stimulation can be managed successfully and experienced in a positive manner. In Chapter 6 our focus was on the social connectedness of urbanites. We noted that some people in the city feel isolated as a result of not having family and friends physically nearby, whereas others are successful in finding community in the immediate locale and still others find friendship and support among kin and friends scattered throughout the city.

In explaining why the experience of urban life can be so varied and even contrasting for different groups of people, we weighed a number of factors. We began with the ecological realities of urban life: numbers, density, and heterogeneity. We added differences in sociodemographic characteristics such as class or age, and we also considered cognitive styles, personality differences, and past experiences. Yet in all of this discussion we overlooked one critical factor that can and does make urban life better or worse: the immediate person-built environment in which the individual exists. That is, we have taken great account of the *social organization* of everyday urban life, but we have failed to consider the nature and impact of the *physical organization* of cities.

Perhaps one reason we have ignored this area up to now is the antideterminist position taken here, which says that people are not simply creatures of their surroundings: They can react, adapt, and change their environments. But to go too far in the opposite direction is equally wrong; environments do affect people in significant ways. The built environment can facilitate or discourage interaction, foster a sense of identity or alienate people from their surroundings. It can help make people secure when they go outside or lead

156

them to be fearful. In this chapter we will consider some basic requirements and approaches of good, informed design – design with people and their needs in mind. We will consider how good design can help make cities more livable, and we will review some design and policy decision disasters to show how they can have the opposite effect. In all, we will see that people's multiple and contrasting experiences in the city are a function not only of their personal characteristics and their interpersonal associations but also of their varying experiences and interactions with the built environment.

The built environment

As noted earlier in the book, a familiar theme in the discussion of urban life is that the city is "unnatural." It is thought of by some as a form of human organization that interposes man-made limitations and constraints between the person and nature and, therefore, throws the two out of direct contact with one another. Others, however, argue that the city and its buildings and streets are just another form of human invention, no more natural or unnatural than any of the other inventions of human endeavor – no more than, for instance, the tools that a farmer uses to cultivate the soil and grow crops. According to William Ittelson (1976):

To be sure, the environment seen as artifact seems to stand in sharp distinction from the natural world. But as soon as one says this, the internal contradiction becomes apparent. If man and all his products, if technology and its artifacts, are not part of nature, what are they part of? The city may be inhuman but it cannot be unnatural. Design and technology as human process and building and artifact as human product are part of the natural subject matter for study.... Man and his products are as much a part of nature as the birds and their nests and the bees and their hives. [P. 56]

Natural or unnatural, the urban form of life involves existence within a setting that was unknown until approximately fifty-five hundred years ago (Davis, 1965). Urban living requires a great deal of complex organization and coordination, and the city of today is the product of building and planning on a scale never known before. The physical arrangement of rooms, streets, buildings, highways, mass-transportation systems, and even whole neighborhoods translates into the physical arrangement of people; and the nature of these arrangements makes a great deal of difference in how the city is imaged, experienced, and enjoyed.

People relate to the environment via *adaptation* and *change*. Although adaptation is an importation mode that all people employ, the key characteristic that sets humans off from other species is their ability to manipulate the environment and thereby to make changes in it. It has been said that the modern city is the ultimate example of this process. Urban dwellers live and work in buildings that reach to the clouds and travel in tunnels under the ground and water. The creation of cities differs from all previous human transactions with the environment in (1) the extent to which it modifies the environment, (2) the amount of complexity that it has built into it, and (3) the degree to which its implementation is deliberate and self-conscious (Ittelson, Proshansky, Rivlin, & Winkel, 1974).

What urban design does and does not do

It would be inconsistent with our initial discussion in Chapter 1 about the relationship of person to environment to make the mistake of assuming any direct cause-and-effect relationship between the two, thereby using a deterministic model for the relationship between design and behavior. Good design certainly helps, and poor design equally hurts; but neither is able to create or destroy forms of behavior. A number of commentators on the urban process have responded to the simpleminded determinism that occasionally appears in the discussion of urban planning and urban problems. Consider, for example,

Architecture ... has no kind of magic by which men can be redeemed or society transformed. Its primary social function is to *facilitate* people's doing what they wish, or are obligated to do. [Broady, 1972, p. 183, italics mine]

or

Researchers have taken a rather single-minded approach to causality tending to view factors such as building type, site plan, and community size as independent variables or causes which had predictable effects on the quality of life [Abu-Lughod, 1966, p. 157]

What the urban designer or planner does attempt to do is to organize and arrange physical space in such a way as to facilitate certain forms of behavior and to allow for the satisfaction of human needs. The built environment can be thought of as relating to people in each of five ways (Ittelson et al., 1974; Murtha, 1976).

1. *Physical.* The end product of design is the arrangement and building of actual physical structures: houses, apartment buildings, public transportation systems, shopping centers, and so on. These structures encompass and compartmentalize space – and therefore people as well.

2. *Functional.* The reason for designing and building a structure is to help accomplish some purpose. Each structure within a city can be judged by the extent to which it has the necessary components and the appropriate arrangement of them for task facilitation. This may range anywhere from proper

lighting in an office building to an adequate number of toll booths on a bridge to keep traffic flowing properly.

3. *Cognitive*. The city as a whole and each of its component parts from large to small "speak to" people. They provide cues to behavior (i.e., what is appropriate, how best to accomplish one's goals), and these are the intended meanings of design. Furthermore, each environment provides a set of symbolic meanings. It says something about status, values, and lifestyles. Amos Rapoport (1977) refers to the built environment as a form of nonverbal communication. The designer is the "encoder" of meanings, and the user is the "decoder." If they do not share a common language or if the intended meanings are not recognized or are misinterpreted, serious problems can result.

4. *Affective*. Every room, as well as every building, arouses emotions in its users. It is perceived and evaluated against cultural norms and personal standards and judged to be beautiful, cluttered, organized, or comfortable to some degree. Also involved here are feelings of safety and security in the environment. Since people are seen as active rather than passive elements in the environment, this is an important feature. Given any degree of choice, they will use and populate those environments (i.e., public transportation systems, public housing projects) that are evaluated positively and avoid or leave those that are not.

5. *Social*. This element deals not so much with the accomplishment of specific tasks in the environment as with the adequacy of the environment to meet the individual and interpersonal needs of the users. Here we ask such questions as: Does the setting allow people to interact and meet others? Are people afforded enough privacy to feel comfortable? Do they have enough personal space, or do they feel crowded by others?

The effects of good and bad design

Most of the time we take our environment for granted. Good lighting, a comfortable chair, and clean air go just about unnoticed. It is only when we sit down to do work in a dimly lit room or a chair that is too low for the desk, or go outside to breathe the fresh air and have our eyes and noses assaulted instead, that we become strongly aware of what we have always taken for granted. So it is with urban design. The most obvious way we can make a set of points about what good design can do – even though if it is successful we will merely take it for granted – is to demonstrate some of the negative effects that poor design can have on behavior. Brent Brolin (1972) has done intensive documentation of one city in India:

Cattle wander through shopping centers, and lounge in the middle of streets, even though it is illegal for residents to own them. Sidewalk vending is outlawed, yet you can't walk on one without stumbling over peanut vendors, shoe repairmen, and turban washers. There is an expansive park called Leisure Valley, yet hardly anyone takes his leisure there. This is the city of Chantigarh, in Northwest India and it is a complex problem. [P. 56]

Chantigarh is the capital city of the Punjab area of India. Its problems are not those of poverty or overcrowding. The population is not starving, nor is the city run down or deteriorating. Actually, it is an almost completely new city, built from the ground up as recently as the 1950s, and most of its residents are educated government workers. What is more, it was designed by Le Corbusier, one of the world's most noted architects and planning theorists. Unlike a majority of India's population, Chantigarh's residents can boast of many conveniences, including hot and cold running water, closed sewers, and flush toilets. Yet in spite of these amenities there is an underlying malaise, captured in a statement by one of its residents: "In the old cities people are closer; in Chantigarh, we don't share one another's joys and sorrows" (quoted in Brolin, 1972, p. 58).

Its problems are many; the city just does not work. The reason, in a nutshell, is that it was built using a set of Western assumptions about what people need and how they act, and these assumptions were not transferable to India. When the environment and the people who occupy it do not speak a "common language," when there is a lack of fit between the messages that the environment provides and the ways they are read, and between the prevailing needs of the people and the arrangement of space provided to satisfy those needs, the environment will be a "bad" one.

Chantigarh's problems began with its general layout. The city was divided into twenty sectors set out in a rectangular grid. Housing was arranged so that people with similar incomes would live close to one another, in the expectation that this basic similarity would provide a common bond for a sense of community based on proximity. But whereas a community of interest often evolves in a Western city when a critical mass of similar people are placed in close proximity to one another, in India kinship ties are so strong that intense attachments are based almost exclusively on family lines. As a result, many people in Chantigarh are required to travel great distances to overcome proximity and visit their families.

A second characteristic of a typical residential sector, thought to be sound planning on a Western model, was to have each sector (i.e., each neighborhood) basically self-contained. Each was surrounded by high-speed roads, given a centrally placed elementary school, and provided with a small shopping center where the full range of everyday necessities could be bought. What the planners did not realize was that these choices were irrelevant to, or even inconsistent with, an Indian's needs. In India schools are not locally run, and parents may send their children to any school they wish; as a result schools do not provide a focal point for community interest. As for shopping, the initially planned-for variety of stores has been replaced by specialization in each area – hardware and plumbing in one sector, auto repairs in another, dry goods in still a third. The reason for this change involves the way Indians shop. In the West the price is stamped on each item, and this is simply the amount one pays. As in the traditional bazaar, however, in modern stores in India no intelligent consumer will pay the initial price. One bargains and goes back and forth from shop to shop comparing and reducing the asking price. Thus it is necessary to have a number of sellers of the same item near one another so that the process can take place.

Open spaces and parks for recreation, so valued in Western culture, are not important in India. There is simply no tradition of park use. People sew, knit, play cards, and read within close proximity of their houses. Human contact is made along the periphery of the large central park that has been provided, and rarely inside it. The central expanse of land is virtually unused.

Even many nonphysical aspects of the plan for the city show a lack of understanding of Indian culture. Cattle are supposed to be restricted to a few areas of Chantigarh but given the respect paid to them they are allowed to run freely through the streets. Official garbage-collection plans for the city (daily or weekly) have been disrupted by the fact that edible garbage is not thrown away. Instead, it is left out in front of the house for wandering cows to eat, something that the people of Chantigarh feel is part of their religious duty.

Once we get inside the home in Chantigarh the environment's intentions and the users' needs and desires get even further out of kilter. Brolin describes the usage patterns of one family with a relatively spacious apartment. The husband, wife, and six-year-old sleep in one bed in the back bedroom, with a nine-year-old sleeping beside them on the floor. The grandfather (who is with them temporarily) and oldest son sleep together in another bed in what was meant to be the living-dining room. The room intended by the designers to serve as a second bedroom has become the formal entertaining area, because of the belief that visitors should not be able to see the family areas, such as the kitchen and bedroom, that were once restricted to the women of the family. Even now in the homes of college-educated families the women will not join the guests until asked by their husbands. In the house Brolin describes, a curtain is always hung in the middle of the living-dining area to allow the wife to circulate throughout the family rooms without being seen.

Cooking and eating are further examples of lack of fit between design and needs. The kitchen counter is not used for cooking as intended. Rather, food is stored on the counter-top stove, and cooking is done on the floor over a portable kerosene stove. By preference the family eats on the floor in the small kitchen. In the morning the adults eat after the children go to school. In the evening eating is also done in shifts because of lack of room in the kitchen, even though the family members would prefer to eat together. The dining table and six chairs are seldom used unless they are entertaining guests who they feel would think them backward if invited to eat on the kitchen floor. There is no provision of space for the family altar, so it is located in the closet, the only possible place where it can be kept between periods of worship. As a result clothes are kept on makeshift pegs in the closet rather than in the space intended for them.

These are but a few of the many problems of Chantigarh. Although I have chosen an extreme example to make a set of points, there is always the possibility of lack of fit between designers' intentions and users' needs whenever assumptions are made without any attempt to verify them in advance. These misunderstandings need not be between the assumptions of vastly different cultures, such as those described. The meaning and functions of various spaces and structures differ greatly among racial, social class, religious, ethnic, age, and sex groupings as well. In addition, there are a number of studies (e.g., see Lansing & Marans, 1969), that have demonstrated that the "cultures" of designers and laypeople differ in general. What they look at, how they relate to space, and what they value highly can differ greatly – even when planners are designing facilities for clients and users similar to themselves in social and demographic characteristics.

Dealing with basic needs

Although the example of Chantigarh suggests that the means of satisfying people's needs vary greatly, it does not in any way deny the possibility that the needs themselves are still universal. We shall see that whereas many of these needs are equally relevant regardless of the scale of planning, others are more critical to design on a given level. These levels range from the small (i.e., microscopic) scale, such as the design of a single dwelling unit, to mid-level planning that involves, for example, the relationship of buildings to one another, to large-scale (i.e., macroscopic) design, such as the planning of a whole new city. In the rest of this discussion of urban design and planning we will consider how these universal needs can be satisfied at each different scale.

Drawing closely on the work of John Zeisel (1975, 1981), we can identify six needs common to all people that can be addressed by a behavioral approach to urban design:

1. *Security*. The need to feel safe and secure in the place where one lives is one of the most basic concerns of all urban dwellers. It is relevant to all levels of design. People will not be concerned with higher-order needs unless they can feel free from attack and annoyance as they go about their business within their homes and across the city.

2. *Clarity*. As discussed in Chapter 4, the environment must be legible. People must feel confident about their ability to find their way from one part of the city to another, or even from one part of a large housing complex to another. Designs that confuse and disorient urban residents discourage them from moving about.

3. *Privacy*. People desire the ability to regulate the amount of contact they have with others (Altman, 1975). This issue is relevant to some extent on a larger scale, but it is particularly significant at the level of the housing unit. Although differing activities and locations require more or less privacy, depending on the group for whom we are designing, people require some mechanisms (most directly spatial) to sustain a distinction between front stage and back stage (see Goffman, 1959).

4. *Social interaction*. By nature people are gregarious. As I have stated throughout, just as too little privacy (i.e., an overload of interactions) can be disturbing, too much, in the form of isolation, is at least as bad. Environments cannot create friendships or a sense of community. Still, Robert Sommer (1969) has described qualities of certain settings as being sociopetal – having the abilities to orient people toward one another and to encourage interaction – or sociofugal – tending to pull people apart rather than bring them together. Although more often than not smaller-scale environments are described in these terms, these qualities can also be designed into larger environmental units.

5. *Convenience*. Convenience is a more physical than social need of people, yet it is also important. Urban environments at all levels should make the performance of day-to-day and special tasks as easy as possible. This factor, equally important at every level, might range from the arrangement of shelves so that dishes can be stored easily to the planning of a whole metropolitan transportation system that conveys thousands of people from home to work daily.

6. *Identity*. Identity, one of the most difficult to define of needs, refers to the relationship of self to environment. Part of a person's total identity involves identification with places. On a larger scale people have been known to fight, protest, and grieve when part of their identity via place is physically removed, as in the destruction of Boston's West End (see Fried, 1963), or even when it is symbolically removed, as when the Brooklyn Dodgers became the Los Angeles Dodgers. On a smaller scale, identification with one's place is manifested by personalization via symbolic displays within the home. People greatly prefer places that "inspire" or at least allow them to engage themselves emotionally and symbolically with their surroundings (Proshansky, 1978; Stokols & Shumaker, 1980).

By way of summarizing this discussion and relating it to the design process, we can note first of all that the urban designer must be aware of the full range of human needs and not simply plan for some while ignoring others. For instance, one distinction that has been made concerning architects' orientations is an emphasis on the aesthetic rather than on the functional, or vice versa. In our terms, a strictly functional approach is one that neglects the cognitive, affective, and social aspects of the person discussed earlier, as well as people's needs for stimulation. It takes a narrow view of human beings and their needs, relating to people in nuts-and-bolts terms by considering only how various tasks can best be accomplished. Designs undertaken from a purely functional point of view are efficient in controlling sunlight and temperature and are likely to hold up well over time and meet all local building, housing, and zoning codes. But often they are described as sterile, cold, and lacking in complexity and variety.

Purely aesthetic design can be equally problematic. The structure's design may be seen as a work of art by the architect, meant to please the eye and inspire the spirit. Yet typically (though not always), buildings of this sort neglect the more basic and instrumental needs of people in the environment. One example of this problem is the Erich Lindemann Mental Health Center in Boston. A beautiful building that has won design awards, it is round, and most of its passageways and staircases go in circles. This shape makes orientation and pathfinding extremely difficult. At one time I played a weekly basketball game in the gymnasium, and I found that I often got lost going downstairs from the main floor to the gymnasium, more than once going down a circular corridor that eventually led nowhere. When we consider the function of this building and the fact that one problem of its clients in the first place is likely to be disorientation, this design seems particularly inappropriate. Its chapel, beautifully sculptured and dramatically lit, was at first one of the only places patients could find privacy in the building. But it was closed off to both patients and the public in 1976, after three patients sneaked inside and set themselves on fire. Anecdotal reports involving the relationship of disorientation to stress are not unique to this setting. Similar reports have been noted in other attractive but confusing settings (reviewed in Zimring, 1982), and their relationship has also been demonstrated in research over a variety of settings (Peake & Leonard, 1971; Weisman, 1979).

In spite of the importance of being aware of the full range of human needs, the designer must also be aware that not all needs are equally important for all groups at all times. As Abraham Maslow (1970) has pointed out, needs exist in a hierarchy such that concerns for status, convenience, and amenities are hardly salient in the minds of urbanites until their more basic needs have been fulfilled. Lee Rainwater (1966) has pointed out that the home and its surroundings have different meanings for the urban poor, the "traditional working class," and the "modern working class." Urban slum dwellers think of the home as a haven from fear, whereas working- or middle-class people are more likely to take physical safety for granted, seeing the home more in terms of its status or symbolic value. In addition, as was exemplified in the account of Chantigarh, once the most relevant needs of the population to be served have been identified, it is still critical to determine the best means of satisfying them. It is important to recognize that what is best for one group will not necessarily be best for another.

Social science and urban design

Throughout this book my purpose has been to point out the complexity of the urban experience and to emphasize that many elements of opposite polarities exist in the city simultaneously. Some aspects please the residents, while others frustrate their needs and annoy them. Design is one major factor that can affect the urban experience both for good and for bad. I hope to demonstrate this claim in the rest of this chapter by looking at the nature of the planning and design process and also at its outcomes. First, we will consider some of the ways in which social scientists have become involved in the conceptualization and design of urban facilities. Then we will consider two examples of urban mass housing planning, one without social science–planner cooperation and one the product of such collaboration. Throughout, it is important to note how the thinking and perceptions of professionals and laypeople vary and also how people living under differing physical conditions will define their experiences of the whole city very differently as a function of their immediate residential environments.

Filling the user–needs gaps

When social scientists look at a design problem, they ask how the building, the room, the highway, or the neighborhood can satisfy the most important needs of the people who will use it. When considering how to design for human needs a number of problems arise. The first and most basic of these is called by John Zeisel (1981) the ''user–needs gap'' (see Figure 7.1). By this label he means that in a society as complex as ours it is rare for designer and user to be the same person, especially when we are referring to the design of hospitals, schools, playgrounds, and other large-scale undertakings. In such cases – for instance, when a city government commissions housing for the elderly to be built – the *paying* clients and the *using* clients are not even the same group. As a result, although the urban designer may be in direct contact with those in the contracting agency, there is often little direct contact between contracting agencies and potential users and even less (or perhaps no) direct contact between designers and users. And when architects do not know the people for whom they are designing, it is very possible to misread their needs.

Compounding this problem is a second matter. Architects and planners,

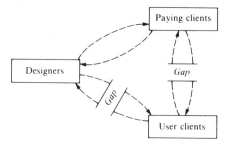

Figure 7.1. The user–needs gap. From *Inquiry by Design: Tools for Environment-Behavior Research* by John Zeisel. Copyright © 1981 by Wadsworth, Inc. Reprinted by permission of Brooks/Cole Publishing Company, Monterey, California.

although they have solid training in the "art" of design and are skilled in the legal, technical, and mechanical aspects of their field, often do not involve themselves in one important aspect of the "science" of design: that of experiment, interview, and systematic observation – the world of empirical research. Given the existing gaps described by Zeisel, lack of design research can mean that assumptions about how an apartment, school, or whole neighborhood will be used or *should* be used will not get tested in advance or even evaluated after the fact. As a result problems in design may not only go undetected in the current project but also remain uncorrected by the planner in the next one undertaken.

This discussion of problems is useful only to the extent that it is followed by suggestions for dealing with them. The most obvious way of dealing with the user–needs gaps is to involve users in planning and design. Robert Sommer (1972) has provided an extensive discussion of what he calls *user-generated design*. Community meetings are one forum for getting users' ideas directly before planners, and other techniques such as role playing may help design professionals place themselves in the users' perspective (Burnette, Moore, & Simek, 1973). Another method involves the systematic collection of data as part of design research jointly executed by social scientist and designer. This research should fit into the basic architectural process and should begin at the first critical planning stage, known as programming.

Programming is a process wherein client and designer make explicit their assumptions and requirements for the project. The end product, a program, specifies just what the building (or park or hospital or whatever) is "expected to do" (Zeisel, 1975, 1981). By determining the goals and constraints of the project before any actual design begins, programming determines not only financial and technical decisions but also such matters as how the project will relate to its physical surroundings and how it will satisfy people's needs. The program specifies how many people will occupy the project and what their spatial and temporal patterns of living, working, or shopping are expected to be. It transfers these specifications into lists involving inches and square feet; the arrangements of rooms, walls, and stairways; and the necessity for particular materials and equipment.

Research that feeds into programming and other design-stage decisions can cover the full range of standard techniques, including focused interviews and standardized questionnaires, as well as various forms of systematic observation. Behavior mapping (recording the distribution of people and activities over time in a given setting) and the recording of physical traces (such as paths or other erosions, displays, and adaptations made by users) are two such observational techniques that have proved highly useful.

Once solid research evidence is available, it must be incorporated into the design process. One approach is to provide a set of design review questions for each aspect of the project being considered. In dealing with how to plan low-rise housing for the elderly, Zeisel and his colleagues (Zeisel, Epp, & Demos, 1977) provided a separate set of questions for each of six levels of design ranging from options for eating, to storage and display in the individual units, to ways of providing indoor and outdoor places for neighboring beyond the apartment, to ways of setting up links between the housing development and the rest of the city. For example, concerning the issue of views to the outdoors from inside the apartments, Zeisel and his colleagues have generated a set of design review questions that the final apartment layout will have to address:

Is there a window in the kitchen, dining or living area beside which residents can sit in a comfortable chair and watch community activities?

Are bedroom windows designed so that furniture can be placed in front of them without obstruction and so that bedridden residents can see out?

Are windows sufficiently separate from outdoor public areas to ensure that resident privacy is not invaded?

Is it possible for residents to see outside while eating in the kitchen?

Are second story living room windows low enough for residents to see ground level activity? [P. 50]

In raising each of these questions, the researchers are clearly cognizant of the special significance such matters will have for the specific group of residents that will use the facility. Zeisel and his associates offer a set of three very different designs, given here as Figure 7.2, each attempting to balance the need to view out with the need for privacy from within. They note the positive and negative aspects of each of these, acknowledging that no single design solution can incorporate all that is positive and avoid all that is negative. Each option necessarily contains some good and some bad. Good planning involves making decisions that are based on systematic knowledge and that maximize the fulfillment of important needs and goals while minimizing the

Performance Criteria

Some older persons do not go out often and are occasionally bedridden. They rely on views from their unit to keep them in touch with what is happening in the outside world. Many enjoy watching activities of others around them. Views of the outdoors can also offer visual relief from an otherwise small and restricted unit. This can be achieved if windows in the apartment unit are located to maximize views of activities while sitting in the living room or lying in the bedroom. At the same time, the possibility of viewing scenic areas must not be forgotten.

POSSIBLE DESIGN RESPONSES

Window Out: In at least one living area overlooking an active area or pathway, locate a window next to which one can put a comfortable chair.

Privacy Invasion: When windows are placed to enable residents to look out, they also can allow others to look in. Often when this privacy invasion forces residents to use draperies to control others' view in, drapes remain closed all day defeating the whole purpose of window views. Privacy from outside must be dealt with in some other way, such as an overhang to create distance, interior bay windows for plants which filter views, or grade changes between unit and pathways.

Window: If possible, provide a window to an activity area near the dining table so older residents can watch activities while eating or relaxing.

Living Room Window & Balcony: Design some living room window sill heights low enough to enable residents to see ground level activity when seated next to windows.

Bedroom Window Heights: While generally window sill heights in bedrooms should allow all walls to accommodate furniture, provide some sill heights so bedridden residents can see out the window easily.

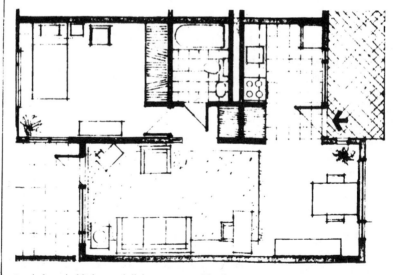

+ windows in kitchen and dining areas provide views
+ back patio provides some privacy to the living room from passersby in the back
+ bedroom has two orientations for natural light and views
– there is the potential for invasion of privacy with the large window in the bedroom

Figure 7.2. Performance criteria and alternative design responses to facilitate visual access to the outside from the apartment unit. From *Low-Rise Housing for Older People: Behavioral Criteria for Design* by J. Zeisel, G. Epp, and S. Demos, pp.

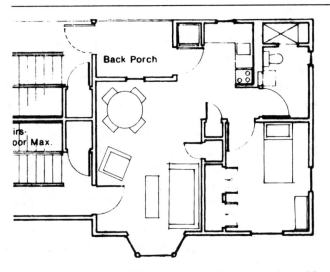

+ large bay window in the living room next to front door can be used for sitting or display
+ bedroom has two orientations for better ventilation and views
+ back porch can be screened in to provide visual privacy while still allowing those inside to see out
− kitchen sink is not located under the window

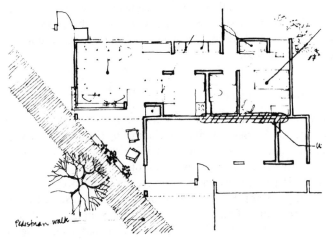

+ corner window from living room to diagonal street permits excellent views of the public pathway
+ there is a view of the pedestrian pathway from the kitchen
+ bedroom looks out on private garden area
− there is a potential problem of invasion of privacy in the living room from passersby
− neighbors can look into each other's units through the corner windows

48–49. U.S. Department of Housing and Urban Development, Office of Policy Development and Research, 1977. Reprinted by permission.

frustration of other needs and goals. The key to planning and design is the ability to make intelligent and informed trade-offs, to find the solutions whose net outcomes will be most positive.

Once a plan or tentative set of plans has been decided upon, research results can be further integrated and tested. That is, whereas traditional design involves the drawing up of schematic plans, an addition introduced by social scientists is the use of behaviorally annotated plans (Zeisel, Welch, Epp, & Demos, 1983). These are simply design drawings in which information about the relationship between the planned environment and behavior is included. Annotation requires people to consider critically the behavioral rationale behind each decision and to confront and question not only the decision itself but the information on which it was based. Figure 7.3 is one example of a site plan for a mid-rise elevator housing project for the elderly. In it we can note how each annotation combines a *physical* aspect of design with a *behavioral* aspect of users' needs.

With this sort of collaboration before the fact, the questions, needs, uncertainties, and assumptions of each of the relevant parties can be tested in advance so that the physical product will be as responsive to people's needs as possible. Moreover, because it explicitly states how each element of the design is supposed to work, it allows for postoccupancy evaluation research designed to feed into future design decisions. As a result, this process – like any other scientific endeavor – becomes one in which knowledge is cumulative and systematically organized.

Urban renewal and its problems

There was only limited collaboration between social scientists and urban planners over a period of many years. Beginning in the 1970s, however, cooperative ventures among psychologists, sociologists, designers, and planners increased greatly. This pattern is the result of converging developments within these areas. In psychology and sociology, the interests of researchers have moved steadily toward the application of theory and research to real-world problems. The efforts of pioneers such as Robert Sommer (1974, 1975) and Robert Bechtel (1967, 1977) have demonstrated that social scientific theory can be used successfully in effecting physical changes in the environment. This demonstration has led more social scientists to pursue environmental studies and design practice and has made the design community more receptive to their inputs.

At the same time, urban-planning theory of the 1950s and 1960s was coming in for much criticism owing to many quiet dilemmas and a few spectacular failures. In particular, the process of urban renewal was not working as planned. Whole sections of the city thought to be unhealthy and unsafe were being torn down and replaced with new, clean, and efficient high-rises; yet

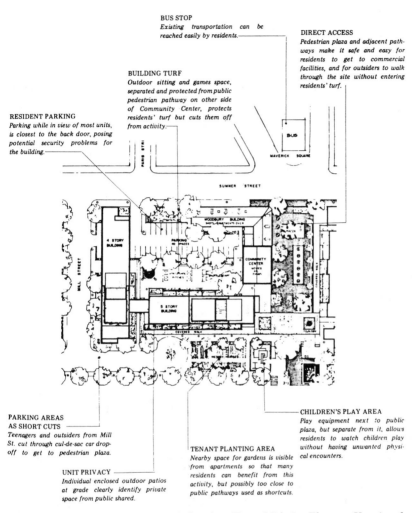

BUS STOP
Existing transportation can be reached easily by residents.

DIRECT ACCESS
Pedestrian plaza and adjacent pathways make it safe and easy for residents to get to commercial facilities, and for outsiders to walk through the site without entering residents' turf.

BUILDING TURF
Outdoor sitting and games space, separated and protected from public pedestrian pathway on other side of Community Center, protects residents' turf but cuts them off from activity.

RESIDENT PARKING
Parking while in view of most units, is closest to the back door, posing potential security problems for the building.

PARKING AREAS AS SHORT CUTS
Teenagers and outsiders from Mill St. cut through cul-de-sac car drop-off to get to pedestrian plaza.

TENANT PLANTING AREA
Nearby space for gardens is visible from apartments so that many residents can benefit from this activity, but possibly too close to public pathways used as shortcuts.

CHILDREN'S PLAY AREA
Play equipment next to public plaza, but separate from it, allows residents to watch children play without having unwanted physical encounters.

UNIT PRIVACY
Individual enclosed outdoor patios at grade clearly identify private space from public shared.

Figure 7.3. Behaviorally annotated site plan. From *Mid-rise Elevator Housing for Older People: Behavioral Criteria for Design* by J. Zeisel, P. Welch, G. Epp, and S. Demos. Building Diagnostics, Inc., Boston, Mass., 1983. Reprinted by permission.

the problems of the people affected seemed to multiply rather than disappear. Apparently, many of the positive functions that these "slum neighborhoods" could and did fulfill were being overlooked, and there was insufficient awareness of the needs that new public housing could not satisfy. We will look here at the damage caused by the destruction of Boston's West End and the new and different problems that St. Louis's Pruitt–Igoe Housing Project brought with it. Then we will look at how mass public housing in the city can be made more livable through the application of social scientific knowledge.

Down with the slum

The section of Boston known as the West End was old, physically deteriorated (especially as viewed from the outside), and crowded. Vacant lots full of garbage surrounded many of the ancient tenement buildings. The people of the area, almost half of whom were Italian, were not well educated and were poor. The Boston Housing Authority decided that the best way to improve the quality of life in this area was to raze the whole forty-eight-acre section and replace it with new high-rise apartment and office buildings. To minimize disruption and problems of relocation, all of the affected inhabitants were guaranteed apartments in the new buildings to be erected.

Overlooked by the planners was the possibility that there could be more than one view of the West End (or of any urban slum). They assumed that *their* view of urban reality was the *only* view of urban reality possible, that their definition of the situation was shared by most if not all of the West Enders. What was missed by the planners was the distinction between a *physical* slum, a place in which the physical environment is old and run down, and a *social* slum, a place in which there is social disorganization and conflict.

The West End was the former, not the latter. It was, as defined in Chapter 6, a community by choice, a place in which personal identity was closely tied to physical location. People described themselves as "West Enders" when asked, rather than as "Bostonians" or "X-Streeters." To marry a non–West Ender was to marry "outside." Strong local relationships and feelings of support were located among kin and friends, most of whom resided in the neighborhood.

Particularly interesting was that while the sense of family was quite strong, the role of neighbors was at least as important. Community life focused not so much on visiting within the home as on an active street life – on the front stoop, the street corner, the local bar. Windows, halls, and steps provided bridges between inside and out, making for a permeability between dwelling unit and street. The neighborhood was seen as an extension of the home, and there was a shared sense of continuity over both time and space. Rather than "renew" this urban setting, the planners pulled apart a place in which there was strong social cohesion. Fried (1963) reported that many of the residents showed signs of grieving, much as they would for a relative or friend who had died. These signs of grief ranged from physical symptoms and depression to visits to the sites of their former homes during and after their demolition. As further evidence of the contrasting definitions of the value of the "slum" for resident and planner, Hartman (1966) has noted that the vast majority of West Enders did not relocate in the new buildings but, rather, sought housing in areas that were physically close and culturally similar to that from which they had been displaced.

In place of the slum

What Boston and other major cities throughout the United States have done to replace the slum is to erect large public housing projects, a form of design that has met with varying degrees of success (e.g., see Farley, 1982; Franck, 1983; VanVliet, 1983). For the most part, mass public housing, like urban renewal, has been beset by problems, and it is also best known for its most dramatic failure. The Pruitt-Igoe Project in St. Louis, Missouri, was intensively studied by Lee Rainwater (1966) and William Yancey (1976). We will consider it in some detail, not for the purpose of criticizing high-rise housing per se but, rather, with two major purposes in mind:

1. To consider what design elements – present or missing – caused problems
2. To note how these designs have been revised and changed by social scientists and architects to deal with these problems

Pruitt-Igoe, near downtown St. Louis, was opened in 1954. It covered fifty-seven acres and housed twelve thousand people. There were forty-three buildings in the project, all eleven stories in height. Its population consisted of the urban poor, including many single-parent families on some form of public assistance. What is most notable about Pruitt-Igoe is its total failure to constitute an environment in which people could live. In 1970, only sixteen years after it had been opened, twenty-seven of the forty-three buildings were totally vacant. Two years later, accepting the nonhabitability of Pruitt-Igoe, officials demolished the entire project. (See Figure 7.4.)

As for the failure itself, it should be clear at the outset that the causes were many, including major responsibility in the political, social, and economic arenas. Design, however, was also a key factor. What was most interesting about the design was that it was not the result of a lack of planning but, rather, the end product of well-thought-out planning concepts that unfortunately had negative consequences for human contact. In fact, the building design was praised by the *Architectural Digest* in 1951 for having "no wasted space." In the discussion to follow we will look closely at Pruitt-Igoe's design and consider how space might be productively "wasted" in the service of human needs.

Individually, the way the buildings were planned discouraged control, support, and confidence. Long, thin hallways and corridors within the buildings, often leading to single elevators, discouraged interaction and promoted anonymity. The stairwells, while doing a fine job of meeting the fire regulations, were so well sealed off that they made a person in any of them an easy target

Figure 7.4. Demolition of the Pruitt-Igoe Housing Project in St. Louis. UPI/Bettmann Archive.

for crime. They were so private that they were used for any surreptitious activity from defecation to sexual intercourse.

Another problem issue was parental control over children. Lower-class mothers typically attempt to restrict the movement of their children to the area immediately around the home, in order to be able to observe the people with whom their children are interacting. Owing to the height of the buildings, as well as their design, mothers in Pruitt-Igoe felt as if they had little control over their children. Once out of the apartment, children were out of sight of their parents. Many parents were seriously concerned, not only for the children's physical safety but also about their own inability to keep their children from being socialized into the drug, sexual, or criminal cultures in the area.

Tied closely to feelings of security is the matter of finding and providing community and a shared sense of support and interest. As noted before, in the lower-class neighborhood close ties with friends and relatives play a critical role in making the area a livable and enjoyable one. Yet rather than encouraging interaction, the design of Pruitt-Igoe (like that of other such developments) had an "atomizing effect" on informal social networks. William Yancey (1976) has summarized some of its major problems:

Pruitt-Igoe represents, in its architectural design, an extreme example of a national housing policy whose single goal is the provision of housing for individual families, with little knowledge about or concern for the development of a community and neighborhood. Unlike normal slums, with their cluttered streets and alleys, Pruitt-Igoe provides no semiprivate space and facilities around which neighboring relationships might develop. There is a minimum of what is often considered "wasted space" – space within buildings that is outside of individual family dwelling units. [P. 452]

What Yancey notes is that whatever the problems of the classic slum, it provides places and spaces in which social networking and social support can take place. The small blocks of the urban slum typically combine residential and commercial uses, providing what has been called semipublic space. These are areas that are not owned by any one person or group, yet people and groups feel that they can exert informal social control over them. In Pruitt-Igoe and many other housing projects, smaller blocks were done away with and residential super-blocks built. In the process a great deal of open space was created externally, but it was not usable space. Having lived in one such New York City housing project for almost my entire youth (ages three to eighteen), I can recall what seemed like vast rectangular grassy areas throughout the project surrounded by chains and filled with "Do Not Walk on Grass" signs. To set foot onto these grassy areas, even to retrieve a ball, was to risk receiving a fine from a housing policeman. The message was clearly "Look but do not touch."

As for the rest of the open space at Pruitt-Igoe, it was equally nonusable: It was too open, too public. People could not congregate in it, nor could outsiders (as opposed to insiders) be recognized throughout it. Jane Jacobs (1961), one of the most influential and outspoken critics of mass urban housing design, has argued that the desire of urbanites for interpersonal contact must be balanced against their desire to maintain privacy as well. She believes that people want varying degrees of contact with their neighbors, so that whereas relations with a few people (who may be physically close or not) may be intimate, relations with many others can be casual, friendly, and supportive – while implying no private commitments. Jacobs has stated:

When an area of a city lacks a sidewalk life, the people of the city must enlarge their private lives if they are to have anything approaching equivalent contact with their neighbors. They must settle for some form of "togetherness," in which more is shared with one another than the life of the sidewalks, or else they must settle for lack of contact. Inevitably the outcome is one or the other; it has to be; and either has distressing results. [Pp. 62–63]

When streets, backyards, and storefronts – semipublic spaces – are not available, the development of strong social networks is inhibited. Faced with many physical threats on the outside and no way to respond to them (collectively, at least, rather than individually), people retreat to the last line of defense, their own apartments. Claire Cooper (1971), for instance, asked residents of two twenty-story buildings where they felt they belonged; 60 percent of these people answered "In my apartment." Data that have been collected on patterns of satisfaction and dissatisfaction with apartment and neighborhood are consistent with Cooper's findings. Pruitt-Igoe residents were generally satisfied with their individual apartments (75 percent satisfaction), but only 53 percent were satisfied with the neighborhood and only 49 percent with project living. In an adjacent slum neighborhood, the pattern was almost reversed: 74 percent of the people there expressed satisfaction with their neighborhood, but only 55 percent were satisfied with their apartments. Thus, while many indoor problems related to matters like heat, plumbing, and potential fires were at least somewhat reduced at Pruitt-Igoe, the amenities of the lower-class neighborhood were largely given up in return. And from all indications, this was a poor trade-off.

Defensible space

Jacobs has provided some cogent insights on the basis of her observations; and Yancey, Rainwater, and others have noted the problems of typical housing-project design and have implied ways of building better urban environments. Having gone the next logical step, Oscar Newman (1972) is credited with (1) developing these ideas into a formal set of principles and guidelines for design, (2) translating these ideas into practice in a variety of settings, and (3) subjecting the ideas to direct empirical test in order to go beyond anecdotal observation in determining the usefulness of his approach.

The reaction to Newman's work is itself another demonstration of urbanites' multiple and contrasting values and viewpoints concerning their needs and the desired shape of their environment. Newman's work has met with great critical acclaim and massive criticism, both of which it deserves. That is, it hardly represents the panacea that some had hoped and assumed it to be. Design does not solve problems, any more than it creates them – and even if it could, any given design would only create certain problems while solving others. Still, the successes, the partial successes, and even the failures generated by Newman's ideas have led to a careful reexamination of a whole concept of design that was used uncritically for many years. At a minimum, Newman's work has led the concept of behavioral design to gain, finally, the attention it deserves.

Newman's thesis is presented in his book *Defensible Space: Crime Prevention through Urban Design*. While we recognize that the arrangement of space is not the cause of crime, nor is the rearrangement of space likely to make a major dent in the overall crime rate of the city, Newman's is an important contribution because it is really about far more than crime. That is, although crime, vandalism, and physical deterioration may have been cited as the most direct causes of the closing down of Pruitt-Igoe, what caused the project to fail was really *social deterioration* – a breakdown of the complex and subtle aspects of interpersonal trust, contact, and support that a lower-class area needs to have in order to be a livable place. What allows crime to take place in general and what encourages it to occur in any given place is a breakdown of social mechanisms.

Referring to public safety, Jacobs (1961) notes that providing more police is not the answer. Safety "is kept primarily by an intricate almost unconscious network of voluntary controls and standards among the people themselves, and enforced by the people themselves" (p. 32). Interest in and use of public areas – what Jacobs calls "eyes on the street" – are what make a difference. She likens the provision of more and better lighting to the stone that falls in the desert. If we lack ears to hear the stone, it makes no noise; if we lack eyes to watch what happens in the light, there is no light.

Problems and principles

In looking at public housing, Newman noticed a set of practices and designs that he believed caused problems for people. He felt that by their design and location, most housing projects were stigmatizing. A negative identity associated with public housing led to self-deprecation and helplessness among residents and exploitation by nonresidents. Referring to the physical layout of the typical housing project, Newman has stated that this "new physical form of urban environment is possibly the most cogent ally crime has" (p. 2).

First among the problems he notes is the fact that builders built vertically. They did so to provide large open areas around the buildings, to make the area aesthetically pleasing, and to give residents areas for recreation and leisure. Cars, which were considered undesirable within the project, were banished, and super-blocks were therefore created. Main building entrances were designed so as to face inside toward the center of the project.

This combination of factors meant that in order to get from public transportation or the perimeter streets, one had to take a circuitous route where no other traffic existed. As a result the center of the project was the most feared external area – avoided at night and even during the day because it provided opportunities for crime. Large, poorly defined areas tended to promote a feeling of anonymity. At all times, but especially at night, a lack of activity and a lack of surveillance invited criminal activity. The more those who traveled the central area were victimized, the more other people avoided it. As a result, lack of activity, lack of surveillance, and the perception that the area was dangerous all tended to reinforce one another. Internally, similar problems of crime and lack of surveillance existed in entrance lobbies, hallways, and corridors.

What was lacking in these projects, according to Newman, was the concept of "defensible space." Defensible space is "a model for residential environments which inhibits crime by creating the *physical* expression of a *social fabric* that defends itself" (p. 3, italics mine). Its goal is to produce an environment "in which latent territoriality and a sense of community in the inhabitants can be translated into responsibility for insuring a safe, productive and well maintained living space" (p. 3). The basic idea works on a set of proposed linkages: Design features encourage a feeling of territoriality in the form of a feeling of shared ownership and responsibility for physically defined areas. This feeling encourages territorial behaviors, such as surveillance and defense, that reduce unwanted intrusion and criminal behavior. As for the *how* of defensible space, Newman offers a set of design guidelines, two of which have been subjected to considerable testing and critical discussion.

First, perceived zones of influence are created when areas of the residential environment are subdivided and articulated. This division of space allows residents of adjacent areas to adopt proprietary attitudes and strengthens their ability to identify with and defend these areas. Newman suggests that this most basic design principle can be made to operate at any level of design. On a small scale, it could be accomplished by clustering a small number of apartments on each floor (somewhat like the dormitory suite arrangement discussed in Chapter 5). On a larger scale, entries, circulation paths, and recreation areas could be arranged so that they were made to "belong" to a small set of apartment residents (see Figure 7.5). Even on the site plan level, the project itself could be placed so as to make it fit into the neighborhood and be cared for by people inside and outside the project. The concept of number is important at each of these levels (number of apartments per hallway, number of units per building, or number of buildings per project). The rule that Newman advocates is always the smaller the better.

While Newman's first guideline involves getting people to care about their immediate environment, his second involves ways of keeping watch over that territory: Physical design can provide surveillance opportunities for residents casually and continuously to watch over nonprivate areas of the environment, both indoors and out. Apartment windows should be positioned to allow all nonprivate areas to be seen by residents. Newman notes that most crime in public housing occurs in visually deprived areas such as lobbies, halls, and stairwells. As a result, he suggests that elevators and mailboxes should not be in obscure places hidden from view; rather they should be located where eyes and ears will be present. A different sort of implementation of this principle is the provision of wide continuous outdoor balconies for residents in high-rise public housing. This design, used in Sheffield, England, allowed for neighboring possibilities and also permitted surveillance of children by parents (Porteous, 1977).

Consistent observation, however, does not work alone. Combined with territorial subdividing, it can help people feel more secure as well as more

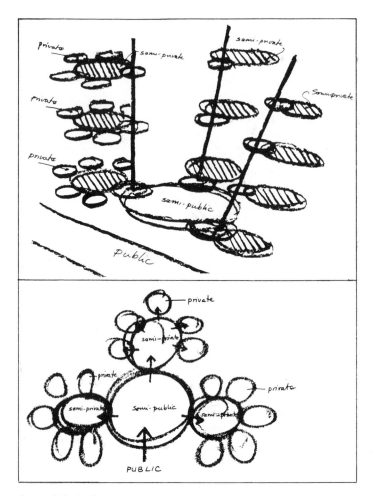

Figure 7.5. Defensible-space hierarchy in a multi/level building (top) and in external areas surrounding a building (bottom). Used by permission of Macmillan Publishing Company and the Architectural Press, Ltd., from *Defensible Space: Crime Prevention Through Urban Design* by Oscar Newman. Copyright © 1972, 1973 by Oscar Newman.

proprietary. Together these features may then reverse the vicious cycle so that high activity levels will create higher levels of observation, which, in turn, will lead to less crime and more use, and so on. The end result is a feeling of greater effectiveness and less helplessness among residents in both roles – as people going about their business as they please and as people who will observe, report, and act when they see something they do not approve.

Figure 7.6. Site plans of the Brownsville and Van Dyke housing projects. Used by permission of Macmillan Publishing Company and the Architectural Press, Ltd., from *Defensible Space: Crime Prevention Through Urban Design* by Oscar Newman. Copyright © 1972, 1973 by Oscar Newman.

Research evidence

The most vivid case that Newman has used to test his ideas is a comparison of two New York housing projects located across the street from one another. The Brownsville project, built in 1947, has buildings of three to six stories and houses approximately six hundred people, twenty-nine per acre. The Van Dyke project, built in 1955, contains some three-story and some fourteen-story buildings, although 76 percent of its population is located in the high-rises. Its total population and density are about equal to Brownsville's, but its problems are far more severe.

The site plans of these two (see Figure 7.6) show the basic design differences

clearly. In design, Brownsville accomplishes many defensible space objectives. Entrances are just off the public street in areas serving about 9–12 families each; 6 families occupy each floor, grouped in 2 sets of 3 around a common vestibule. An open central stairway and skip-stop elevators provide for reasonable surveillance, and parents allow children to play in the hallways and stairs. Van Dyke, however, exemplifies the classically defined high-rise pattern, with a large, open central area and all building entrances on the project's interior. Each of these entrances serves between 112 and 136 families.

While crime and vandalism are common in both projects, Newman reports considerable differences between the two. Relations and cooperation between residents and police are much better in Brownsville than in Van Dyke. The overall crime rate in Van Dyke is 66 percent higher than in Brownsville, including 2.5 times as many robberies. In addition, Brownsville has required 72 percent less repair maintenance, which means that the additional cost of defensible-space designs may pay off not only in improving the quality of life but also, in the long run, financially as well.

In another study by Newman's associates (Kohn, Franck, & Fox, 1975), four housing projects were chosen for review, and actual physical modifications were made at two of these, with the idea of encouraging defensible space. These included changes such as fenced yards to demarcate areas of influence more clearly, the widening and improving of lighting on the central paths to encourage more use and better surveillance, and a better definition of play areas for several age groups. The results of this study were mixed. There were overall differences in safety, neighboring, and self-reported victimization rates between the modified and the unmodified projects. Contrary to expectations, however, residents made more outdoor improvements in the unmodified projects than in the modified ones; and in one project where streetlights were installed, a decrease in crime between 5:00 and 9:00 P.M. was countered by an increase of crime from midnight to 5:00 A.M., with an overall increase in the crime rate.

Defensible-space theory and research have come in for a good deal of close scrutiny and a good deal of criticism. One group has provided primarily methodological critiques (e.g., Patterson, 1977), covering matters ranging from the appropriateness of a number of statistical procedures to the question of whether projects such as Brownsville and Van Dyke were actually comparable on all relevant social characteristics (if they were not comparable socially, for example, then differences between them cannot necessarily be attributed to differences in their physical design; see Mawby, 1977).

A second major area of criticism comes from Newman's use of the concept of territoriality as the mediator of defensible space. Some, such as Bill Hillier (1973), have taken violent exception to the territorial concept itself, arguing that it has been discredited by anthropological research. Others, including the research group at the Johns Hopkins Center for Metropolitan Planning and

Research (Taylor, Gottfredson, & Brower, 1980, 1981), argue that the territorial concept is extremely useful but that Newman has neither defined it nor dealt with it carefully enough. They believe that Newman has used the concept in a way that fails to recognize that territorial behaviors and cognitions can vary widely according to the cultural or subcultural group being dealt with. Therefore, a single set of design solutions, as he has generally advocated, cannot necessarily be expected to have the same effects for lower-class groups of different ethnic and racial origins or to be equally relevant across social class groupings within a culture.

Another related issue is that although Newman has *assumed* that design changes work by creating feelings of ownership and a more positive social fabric, a number of people have pointed out that he has never bothered to assess this key causal link directly. That is, although Newman found in his initial research that crime and vandalism went down, he provided no data to indicate that these changes were mediated or caused by a change in residents' views of their environment. In more recent work in Newark, New Jersey, San Francisco, and St. Louis, Newman and his associate Karen Franck supplemented their usual archival data with a household survey of over twenty-five hundred residents (Newman & Franck, 1982). They also conducted site visits and interviews with project managers. The survey data do confirm defensible-space concepts: Building size (Newman's prime means of operationalizing defensibility of space) affected both crime and fear of crime through residents' control and use of space outside their apartments.

Much of the criticism directed at Newman has derived from the fact that his model often sounds deterministic. In the initial statement of defensible-space theory, design was presented as accounting for various outcomes without considering individuals as active agents in their environments or the effects of such social variables as population heterogeneity. Newman's response to these criticisms has been constructive in that he has begun to consider people more actively (see Newman, 1980) and to test more carefully for the mediating effects of territoriality.

The responses of others interested in defensible-space principles have been of one of two types. The first is a more "scientific" approach aimed at clarifying the model and measuring the cognitive and behavioral linkages involved. The other is the more "practical" approach of making multiple changes in environments, not only in physical design but also in the social and organizational structure of neighborhoods. Each of these responses has its advantages. The more scientific approach is best exemplified by the work of Stephen Gottfredson, Sidney Brower, and Ralph Taylor (1979). Although they were interested in intervention and in creating social change, they focused primarily on providing a discrete test of the defensible-space model and its assumptions. Working in various areas of Baltimore, they (1) interviewed residents in considerable depth about their territorial feelings toward each of six areas around their homes, (2) assessed perceived cultural heterogeneity to test assumptions that groups of people that are (or at least believe they are) highly similar find it easier than other groups to control and appropriate space, (3) examined street characteristics for signs of demarcation and for surveillance opportunities, (4) collected extensive demographic data, and (5) related these data to four outcome measures concerning not only crime but other neighborhood issues.

Their results, like the issues they addressed, are complex. For instance, increasing defensible space had an effect on crime but did not reduce residents' concerns about it. These researchers suggest that increased commitment to an area may heighten concerns about crime and that greater concern, in turn, may lead to increased problem reporting and less crime. The long-term end result is likely to be lessened fear, but this outcome will be found only at the end of the process. Most notably, the results of this research consistently demonstrate that design features affect crime, fear, and a whole range of other outcomes through the territorial attitudes and actions of residents. When areas are subdivided and demarcated, people appropriate them, keep their eyes open for problems, and do something when problems occur.

The more practical approach, exemplified by the attempts to reduce crime in the Asylum Hill section of Hartford, Connecticut (Fowler, McCalla, & Mangione, 1979), was a multipronged attack on urban problems. It involved a number of standard defensible-space design changes. For instance, some neighborhood streets were turned into culs-de-sac, and others were restricted to one-way travel to reduce the volume of motor traffic. Also, visual entrances into the neighborhood from the surrounding streets were created to provide a better definition of the area. In addition to attempts to strengthen the neighborhood and its social control and proprietary attitudes *physically*, other strategies were used as well. The development of formal organizations in the area was encouraged so that residents could work together to solve problems, and a neighborhood police team and police advisory committee were created to strengthen police–community relations and increase police attention to neighborhood problems.

Interventions of this sort (using an array of strategies simultaneously) have a disadvantage from the point of view of knowledge testing. If they work, it is difficult to know which strategy or combination of strategies was most effective. If they do not work, it is difficult to tell whether there were no effects, whether only certain elements of the approach worked, or whether some worked in a negative manner and therefore canceled out the positive effects of others. In practical terms, however, this sort of broad-scale attack on neighborhood problems, employing social as well as physical tactics, is more likely than any narrower focus to have significant effects.

In reviewing this project and trying to gauge the success of each of the strategies, Fowler, McCalla, and Mangione concluded that environmental changes strengthened the neighborhood, encouraging residents to exercise more control and leading them to feel better about the neighborhood. Strengthening informal control also led to reduced fear of crime. As for reducing crime itself, however, both informal social control and more police activity proved necessary to deter crime to any significant degree.

As a result of the writings and interventions of Newman and those who have followed his lead, a more sophisticated view of the interaction of physical and social factors in cities has begun to emerge (e.g., see Greenberg, Williams, & Rohe, 1982; Merry, 1981a, 1981b). As Sally Merry (1981a) suggests, defensible space appears to be a necessary but not sufficient condition for combating urban crime; urban housing projects that do not provide semipublic spaces appear to be centers of crime and fear. Yet even more can and must be done. Architecturally, for instance, well-positioned windows are useful because they enable people to see what goes on in their territory. Still, people will not look out of windows if there is nothing happening below. Activity nodes, accessible places that attract people, must be planned and designed so that there will be people in the street as well as eyes at the windows (Archea, 1977; Bechtel, 1977).

But even the best arrangement of space will not necessarily create a social fabric strong enough to deter crime. Only when urban residents are tied into strong social networks, trust their neighbors, and believe in the effectiveness of the police – as well as themselves – will they be willing to defend their neighborhoods and discourage crime and intrusion. The development of such a social fabric is contingent on a complex set of economic and political factors that residents and social scientists cannot readily affect (see Chapter 8 for some possibilities). Yet since the relationship of the physical, social, economic, and political elements of the environment is a reciprocal one, physical design changes are a step in the right direction. As stated by Newman, they *encourage* and *enable* people to take an active role in the places in which they live, thereby reversing a vicious cycle and turning it in a more positive direction.

Summary

Throughout this book we have asked why some people love the city while others hate it. Part of the answer to this question is a matter of values and the kinds of lifestyles that people are used to or desire. But people do not know whole cities. They know the parts immediately around them (e.g., their homes and their neighborhoods) and generalize from these.

Apartments, buildings, streets, and neighborhoods vary; the perceptions and evaluations of them vary; and this is the starting point for people's multiple and contrasting views about the quality of urban life. In Chapter 6 I presented the ways in which the social fabric of communities may differ. In this chapter the focus has been on the physical characteristics of cities and the impact of design.

I have emphasized here the fact that environments must aim to satisfy a number of needs simultaneously, among them the needs for security, clarity, privacy, social interaction, convenience, and identity. In dealing with design for human needs, there are three important principles to be recognized:

1. No design can simultaneously maximize satisfaction of all basic needs. Intelligent design involves making trade-offs to serve those needs deemed most important while doing the least to frustrate satisfaction of other important needs.

2. The relative importance of needs is not fixed. Needs vary as a function both of the different groups who will use the environment and of the purposes and activities for which they will use it.

3. Whereas needs are universal, the means for satisfying them are not. Privacy, for example, can be accomplished in many different ways. The designer must be aware of the culture or subculture for which a structure is being built in order to create an environment that is congruent with the group's typical or preferred ways.

In this chapter we have highlighted three examples: the Indian city of Chantigarh, the West End neighborhood of Boston, and the Pruitt-Igoe Housing Project of St. Louis. Each of these urban projects was a disaster because it failed to deal successfully with some or all of the principles just stated. In each case, people were moved from their old form of housing with the implicit assumption that what existed previously was *all* bad and needed to be replaced by something completely new and different. Apparently, those in charge were either not able or not willing to incorporate positive features of the old environment into the new and to consider that the new form of design might not meet certain needs and might even frustrate satisfaction of others.

A relevant analogy might be to a doctor prescribing a new medication regimen for a patient. Those who design programs of drug therapy must not only be aware of the problems the new drugs are designed to treat and their advantages and disadvantages compared with the old plan of treatment; they would be thought incompetent if they did not consider the side effects of the medication and the kinds of interactions it might have with other drugs being taken. Urban designs also have indirect effects and unintended consequences, and both advance planning and postoccupancy evaluation are necessary to deal with them.

The final example cited was that of Newman's defensible space. This proposal and the work flowing from it are fine examples of how social scientific knowledge and planning principles can be combined. This work clearly demonstrates that good designs can trigger attitudes and behaviors in people that encourage them to exert more control over their environments and be more secure in them. One basic belief of Newman's that is inconsistent with the premise of this book, however, is that at every scale smaller is better. I believe that it is necessary to question whether smaller is *always* better and whether it is better *for everyone*. Translated up to the community level, some might take this principle to mean that the small town is better than the big city, a conclusion that this book attacks as simplistic. In the final chapter, we will consider the nature of big and small and discuss how communities might be designed to maximize the advantages of each.

Suggestions for further reading

Merry, S. E. 1981b. *Urban danger: Life in a neighborhood of strangers.* Philadelphia: Temple University Press.

Newman, O. 1972. *Defensible space: Crime prevention through urban design.* New York: Macmillan.

Rapoport, A. 1977. *Human aspects of urban form: Towards a man–environment approach to urban form and design.* Elmsford, N.Y.: Pergamon Press.

Sommer, R. 1972. *Design awareness.* San Francisco: Rinehart Press.

Zeisel, J. 1981. *Inquiry by design: Tools for environment–behavior research.* Monterey, Calif.: Brooks/Cole.

8

CAN THE CITY BE A
LIVABLE PLACE?

As we all know, slums, antiquated transport, blight and inadequate plan-
ning are not inevitable features of the urban landscape. They are the heri-
tage of ignorance, mediocrity and the unbridled pursuit of self-interest of a
minority at the expense of the majority.
– Leonard Reissman, 1970, p. 154

We will neglect our cities to our peril, for in neglecting them we neglect
the nation.
– John F. Kennedy addressing Congress, January 30, 1962

We began this book with a set of questions about what a city is and how it
is known by the various people who live in it, work in it, and write about it.
Further, we have asked about life in the city and have investigated the ways
in which people deal with stress, seek social support, and relate to the physical
environment. These questions and the answers to them have highlighted three
variables as key to an understanding of the city. In this final chapter we will
look at some alternatives to the city and then consider the implications of
these three variables for planning, design, and policy. In short, we will ask
how our analysis of urban life can be used in making the city a good or a
better place to live. These key variables are

1. *Size.* All definitions of the city begin with size. Some end there. I have
stated consistently that to understand cities is to go beyond size to understand
what size brings with it for good or bad. Urban living, like any form of living,
involves trade-offs. In this chapter we will consider whether there is such a
thing as an "optimum city size." In line with this question, we will take a
look at other community types, such as suburbs and new towns, to see whether
their sizes or forms have implications for understanding and improving the
city.

2. *Diversity.* Those definitions that go beyond size typically describe urban
life in terms of one or more specific distinctive features: overload, stress,
strangers, subcultures, behavior settings, and so on. The position taken
throughout this book is that each one is an important but partial explanation
of the city and city life. This position serves as the premise of the multiple-
and contrasting-realities view of city life. According to this perspective, the
distinctive feature of urban life is that it has so many distinctive features.
Diversity, heterogeneity, opportunities, and *alternatives* are key words in this
approach. The city means different things to different people. It offers privacy,

187

anonymity, or sociability – or all of these things. It offers tightly knit neighborhoods where people support and help one another and areas where people neither know about nor are concerned with the majority of their "neighbors." The city not only can encompass but even seems to encourage the simultaneous existence of opposites. Whether better or not, this makes it different from communities of smaller sizes.

3. *Control.* Through the discussion of the factors that create stress and most frustrate city people, one theme keeps recurring. It is the issue of control. Whenever people feel that the day-to-day circumstances of their lives are beyond their control, whether in city, town, or suburb, the feeling of helplessness that results deforms their lives. There are those who believe that living in an environment the size of a large city inevitably has these consequences. Others, including me, believe that there are ways of confronting this issue and helping urbanites to feel more in control. In this final chapter we will look for the sources of helplessness in urban life and consider psychological, political, and architectural interventions designed to make city people feel that they have an acceptable degree of power over their own lives.

The search for the ideal community: Is there an optimum city size?

Since people first came to live together in appreciable numbers, great thinkers have posed the question of the best size for a city. Aristotle, although he never named a specific figure, had some ideas about its upper and lower limits. In the *Politics* he stated that "ten people would not make a city, and with a hundred thousand it is a city no longer" (quoted in Lynch, 1981, p. 239). He believed that a city should be large enough to satisfy the general needs of the populace, but still small enough so that it could be taken in as a single view (Howard, 1977). Plato offered an ideal figure of 5,040 "citizens." Since this number did not include women, children, or slaves, it is estimated that a figure of 30,000 would be its total population equivalent. This figure was apparently a reflection of ancient Greek cities, as by the fifth century only three Greek cities (Argos, Acragas, and Syracuse) had populations of 20,000 or more.

In 1902 Ebenezer Howard's *Garden Cities of Tomorrow* (Howard, 1902/ 1965) was published. In it he included a prescription for the ideal city. A firm believer that country and city must be as one, Howard suggested a total figure of 32,000: 30,000 in the city proper and 2,000 in an agricultural greenbelt that would encircle the city. Although support for "smaller is better" continues, some have advocated optimal sizes of greater proportions. The size of Columbia, Maryland, a planned community based on a multidisciplinary and highly sophisticated planning approach, is 125,000. In Russia the planning of new towns has aimed at 180,000–250,000 as optimum to allow for a maximum in public amenities and also town-focused industry (cited in

Howard, 1902/1965). To complete the range of preferences, it should be noted that other influential thinkers have opted for large rather than small or medium. Le Corbusier, the noted French planner and designer, advocated 3 million as the best size (Le Corbusier, 1947); Paul and Percival Goodman (1960) suggested 6–8 million; and Frank Lloyd Wright's plans for Broadacre City (1935) had no upper limit on its size.

What we see from this discussion is that there is no one single size, or even a general range, on which all people can agree. Size increases the likelihood of certain forms of behavior and decreases the likelihood of others. What is best is a matter of personal needs, preferences, and values. Just as we cannot expect to design a single piece of clothing that will suit all the different shapes, sizes, and styles of people, we cannot insist that any one type or size of community is best.

This being so, perhaps the best we can hope to do is to generate a set of criteria by which any community form, large or small, can be judged. The ancient Greeks, for instance, thought that a good city was one in which all the people (i.e., free males) could participate in face-to-face government; any larger size would be unacceptable. In modern times the criteria for evaluation have varied greatly, although more often than not they have been based on economic considerations (e.g., efficiency in production and distribution of goods) rather than "human" concerns (Zimmerman, 1982). One notable exception is provided by Kevin Lynch, who has proposed a set of five general criteria in his book *A Theory of Good City Form* (1981). In briefly reviewing these criteria, we will note that they incorporate a wide range of physical and social concerns and are similar or related to many of the concepts and concerns central to this book. They are.

1. *Vitality* – the degree to which a city supports the vital functions or biological requirements of the individuals in it. Although Lynch is referring to the basic needs of residents for protection and survival, to these I would add higher-order needs for entertainment, excitement, and recreation.

2. *Sense* – the degree to which a city can be clearly perceived and understood by its residents. This criterion clearly follows from Lynch's earlier work on urban imageability and legibility, discussed in Chapter 4.

3. *Fit* – the degree to which the form and capacity of spaces are designed and arranged to match the widely varying needs of residents. Here Lynch recognizes the variety of people and activities in the city and places a premium on creating environments that are adaptable and open to change (see Amos Rapoport's similar suggestions as discussed later in this chapter).

4. *Access* – the degree to which people can reach information, services, and other people. This criterion captures the need for cities to provide not simply *concrete* means of access (e.g., good public transportation) but *symbolic* means of access that give the sense of support, comfort, and sociability.

5. *Control* – the degree to which people feel the ability to manage, modify, and repair existing elements of the city and to effect change in their environments and their lives. This is one of the key concepts of the present book: When a city incorporates each of the first four characteristics it allows people to feel in control; and conversely, those who feel in control experience the city as vital and as providing good access, fit, and sense.

The size of the future: big, medium, or small?

Various theorists (e.g., Chinoy, 1973; Wurster, 1963) have speculated on the shape and size of the community of the future. Claude Fischer (1984) has generated a number of scenarios, each based on a different distribution of the population. The first of these is Supercity, a science-fiction world where a few gigantic urban complexes incorporate the entire population, swallowing up cities and towns en masse and making them all a part of an urban world gone haywire. In Total Dispersal, the opposite of Supercity, the world's population is dispersed far and wide in a "post-city age" (Webber, 1968); high-speed transportation and communications have made a world where physical proximity is no longer necessary or desired. The More of the Same future is a less extreme version of Supercity. In this kind of future, metropolitan areas slowly grow, taking up more land and people; as the suburbs are built up and become a part of the metropolis, the influence of the urbanized suburb increases and the center of the city declines in importance. Finally, the Dispersed Town model is a future of medium-sized cities, none as small as many current small towns or as large as current large cities.

While each of these possibilities is enticing to imagine, it is unlikely that any one of them closely resembles the world of the near future. As stated earlier in this discussion, communities of various sizes will be needed to serve different populations, different needs, and different purposes. Rather than any single one of the proposed possibilities, it is likely that the real future will contain some supercities and many small towns, some large cities and many suburbs around them. There is no single optimum city size, and if some leader of the future decrees that we should all live in communities of size *X*, we will all be worse off as a result. Alonso (1973) has summarized this matter:

The issue is one of finding the most satisfactory constellation of interacting sizes, not finding a single best size. The idea of finding an ideal size to be repeated over and over is comparable to a musical theory that would find the most beautiful note and then compose a symphony by endless and exclusive repetition of that note. [P. 199]

Alternatives to the city

The suburb

For those who do not want to live *in* the city but want to live *near* the city, the suburb has been the answer. Formally defined, it is a part of the metropolitan area that is not within the political boundaries of the city. A suburb is therefore a satellite of a city; by definition, one cannot have a suburb without first having an urb (Abrams, 1971). The development and expansion of the suburb in the United States can be traced to advances in transportation and communication that started in the late nineteenth century. As a community type, the suburb has grown tremendously in popularity over the last twenty-five years and has begun to exert a greater influence worldwide.

Some of the characteristics cited by Gans (1962a) as typical of life in the suburbs are these:

1. Suburbs are like dormitories. They are the homes of commuters who work all day in the city, sleep at home, and then go right back to the city the next day.
2. Being newer than the cities they surround, suburbs are more modern in design and are built for the automobile rather than for the pedestrian or the mass transit user.
3. In the suburbs people live in single-family dwellings that they own rather than in multifamily, rented apartments. Suburbs are therefore horizontal rather than vertical in their layout and are less densely populated.
4. The variety of people one finds in a city is usually not found in the suburb. The population within a given suburb tends to be homogeneous according to class, race, age or socioeconomic status.
5. Residents of suburbs are most typically young, hold white collar jobs, and have a higher income than city residents. In particular, suburbs are thought to be for married couples with children.

Much of the great popularity of the suburb lies in the reasoning that it gives one the "best of both worlds." Suburbanites can work and play in the city, have homes of their own with backyards and gardens, and live in communities that are clean and safe without having to pay taxes to the city nearby. Even after controlling for social class and other relevant differences between urbanites and suburbanites, people who live in the suburbs are happier with their communities and their lives, are less afraid of crime, and feel freer to move about (Lavrakas, 1982; Marans & Rodgers, 1975).

Recently, however, people have come to realize that suburban living is not without its own drawbacks. As more people leave the city and move to the suburbs, the urban problems they were escaping (e.g., crowding, crime) have begun to become suburban problems as well. Living beyond the city limits involves trade-offs that prove to be of net benefit for some but not for all. Suburban workers face the daily commute. They must often leave the house in the morning almost before their children are awake and come home late at night just before (or after) their children go to sleep. Often suburban mothers who do not work outside the home feel a sense of isolation and boredom. For many, homogeneous neighborhoods provide a critical mass of like-minded people who provide support and activity; but many others find that they and their neighbors all share the same problems of a lack of stimulation from the environment.

One important reason that is often cited to explain why people like the suburbs is that living in a suburban setting is something done *by choice*. As Gans (1962a) suggests, people move to suburbs to satisfy their personal needs to live lifestyles they desire. Whenever we compare one living setting to another, all other things being equal the one taken by choice is always the more satisfactory (Michelson, 1977; Rapoport, 1980). This is a point that at once helps to explain the dissatisfaction of many people who live in inner cities (i.e., who are there because they have no other choice) and helps to suggest means for improving the quality of urban life. If choices can be provided for people, if they can be made to feel that they can effect changes in the environment, people can become more satisfied whether they live in city, suburb, or town.

The new-town alternative

Howard's *Garden Cities of Tomorrow* (1902/1965) was destined to have a permanent impact on the shape of the urban planning movement and on the shape of communities as a result. Upset at the crowding and poverty that he observed in British cities, Howard suggested that cities could not ever change sufficiently to meet human needs. He argued that a new form of community, the garden city, had to be planned and implemented. As people were later to say of the suburb, the garden city was to incorporate all that was good from both city and town, while eliminating all that was bad. As a means of graphically presenting his argument, Howard generated the illustration shown as Figure 8.1. The town magnet had many advantages (e.g., highways and entertainment) but also foul air and high rents. The country magnet attracted because of nature, sunshine, and low rents, but wages were low there and it lacked amusements. Town-city, the garden city ideal, had no disadvantages, only advantages.

Howard's plan was for a circular community of thirty thousand people. At the center of the garden city would be a large park, theaters, museums, government buildings, and even a hospital. Shopping would also be included near the center. Just beyond would be housing, recreational areas, and schools,

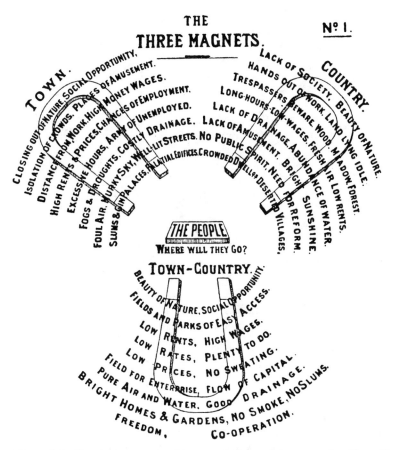

Figure 8.1. The three magnets of town, country, and town-country. From *Garden Cities of Tomorrow* by E. Howard. Copyright 1965 by MIT. Published by the MIT Press. Also reprinted by permission of Faber and Faber, Ltd.

with industry located at the periphery. Throughout the city there would be trees, pastures, gardens, and surrounding the whole community would be an agricultural greenbelt (see Figure 8.2).

Although many people agreed with Howard's general philosophy, his utopian dreams were never realized. Two towns, Letchworth (1903) and Welwyn (1920), were actually built under Howard's plans and direction, but neither succeeded. Among the reasons were a lack of funds, political complications in developing an independent city, and an inability to confront changes brought about by the automobile. However, Reissman (1970) suggests that the ultimate problems of plans such as Howard's go well beyond the political or economic practicalities of creating a new community:

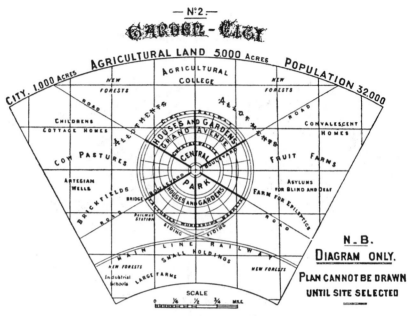

GARDEN CITY AND RURAL BELT

Figure 8.2. Howard's plan for a garden city. From *Garden Cities of Tomorrow* by E. Howard. Copyright 1965 by MIT. Published by the MIT Press. Also reprinted by permission of Faber and Faber, Ltd.

The visionary, like Howard, raised in a milieu of protest against the evils of industrialism, stands fair to be disappointed. His cause may be just, his vision bright, his side that of the angels. Morally and intellectually impelled to transmogrify industrial, urban man into a middle class, provincial, conforming, garden-city species, the visionary claims too much and knows too little. The Plan has him hypnotized into believing that this all is really feasible. But the dream cannot withstand reality, which he seems imperfectly to appreciate. [P. 57]

Reissman poses the same questions for Howard's plans as we have raised throughout for the city: Do people in fact want to live close to nature? Do they want to exchange concrete for meadows? The answer obviously must be that some do and some do not.

Although Howard's efforts were not successful, the seed he planted has grown to great proportions. His idea, that a completely new city can be created to satisfy people's needs, has taken root because of dissatisfaction with the lack of planning evidenced in urban and suburban growth. The haphazard expansion of cities into suburbs and the uneven development of suburban tracts by numerous small private developers (often called the problem of sprawl) brought a call for new communities based on careful planning. Sometimes this planning has been undertaken by government, as in the 1946 New Towns Act of England, by which the building of cities became a part of long-term national policy for the first time in Western history (Rodwin, 1956). Most often, however, well-endowed private developers have entered into this arena. Various forms of new towns can now be found not only in the United States and Great Britain but all over the world.

What exactly is a new town? As J. A. Clapp (1971) points out, defining a new town is not any easier than defining a city. In practice, most new towns are medium-sized communities with populations ranging up to but rarely exceeding 150,000. They are "new," meaning that they are built from the ground up on previously undeveloped land bought especially for the purpose. Although they are sometimes located near urban centers, they are usually more self-sufficient than not. That is, they include both residential and industrial areas. The new town is, therefore, distinguished from the "bedroom suburb" in that people in the former can focus their occupational, personal, and recreational activities solely within the community. However, new towns still retain much of the flavor of the suburb in their emphasis on local contacts and in the presence of many single-family homes and open spaces (i.e., low-density living).

The new town of Columbia

One of the most studied of all new towns in Columbia, Maryland. It is situated on approximately fourteen thousand acres of land previously used for farming and is no more than fifteen or twenty miles from both Baltimore and Washington, D.C. James Rouse, bemoaning the scale of the city ("too big for people to feel part of, responsible for, important in") and dissatisfied with the almost random development of suburban land, argued that one person or one corporation must be solely responsible for developing and planning whole new cities at a time:

Although the business of city building is the largest single industry in America, there is no large corporation engaged in it. City building has no General Motors or General Electric – no IBM, no Xerox; no big capital resources to invest in the purchase of large land areas; no big research and development program unfolding new techniques to produce a better environment. There are no large corporations engaged in the end-product production of the American city. City-building – the development of houses and apartments, stores and offices – is the business of thousands of very small corporations, no one of which has within its own resources the financial capacity to invest millions of dollars in land holding to be planned and developed over, say, 10 to 15 years. [Quoted in Clapp, 1971, p. 5]

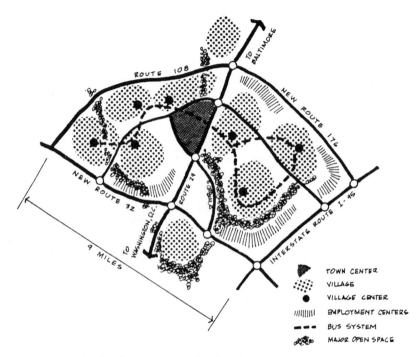

Figure 8.3. Plan for the new town of Columbia, Maryland. From "The Columbia process" by M. Hoppenfeld. In D. Lewis (Ed.), *The Growth of Cities.* Copyright 1971 by Elek Books, Ltd. Reprinted by permission.

In the case of Columbia, Rouse decided to be that large corporation himself. He enlisted the aid of a team of leading consultants on traffic, housing, recreation, family life, health systems, and many more areas. His goals, according to Morton Hoppenfeld (1971), were "to create a social and physical environment which would work for people" and to "preserve and enhance the qualities of the land" while at the same time making a profit. Hoppenfeld, in commenting upon the interdisciplinary discussions and confrontations that took place in the planning of Columbia, points out that the goals of making Columbia a livable place always remained in the forefront of the planners' minds. The guideline for all choices was: "Design decisions based on aesthetic, engineering or economic considerations must vie with the test of social purpose" (p. 39).

Columbia was planned down to the last detail as carefully as any city ever has been. As Figure 8.3 indicates, at its center was a downtown area with commercial buildings as well as recreational and shopping facilities. Eight villages were built around the town, each partially self-contained. Each village had a central area and anywhere from two to five residential neighborhoods. All of the villages were connected to one another by an efficient minibus system so that the whole town could be closely linked. There is a clear resemblance to the early garden city, but these plans are considerably more sophisticated and practical.

Rather than concern ourselves with the specifics of Columbia's design (see Altman & Chemers, 1980; Clapp, 1971; and Lewis, 1971 for excellent discussions of Columbia and other new towns), we will pose the bottom-line question: Does it work? To what extent does systematic and comprehensive planning resolve or eliminate the problems of urban and suburban living? Not surprisingly, the answer is mixed. In addition, although some of the problems of the new town are unique, many others – especially the issues of diversity and control – are shared with the city.

One problem with many new towns is that they are not absolutely certain of their basic identities. How much city and how much suburb are they or do they want to be? While there are advantages to the self-sufficiency that enables people to focus their lives around the town, many of the residents of places like Columbia still work in the nearby big cities. Even if the entire population could be employed locally, could or should the new towns compete and overlap with the cities around them for entertainment and culture?

Second, for whom is the new town? Both the wonder and the misery of the city is the mixture of races, classes, and ethnic groups. Many American new towns are aimed at "the family" and are dominated by the middle class. Is there room there for elderly or young single people, and if so what are the attractions for such groups? Can and should the new town be diverse, mixed, or socially balanced? Concerning the poor, R. O. Brooks (1974) has commented that Columbia neglected to allocate a significant proportion of its units to low-rent housing for fear of getting great numbers of poor blacks from the Baltimore and Washington ghettos. Herbert Gans, who was a consultant to the Columbia project, noted that bringing the middle class and the poor together as neighbors and expecting a social closeness to be created by a physical closeness is naive and deterministic (Gans, 1961). He added that physical propinquity can affect some activity patterns among neighbors; however, homogeneity of backgrounds, interests, or values is necessary before more intense forms of social interaction, such as friendship, will develop. In England as well, the town of Stevenage, with its goal of a balanced community, has had considerably less than total success in bringing about a true mixing of social classes (Reissman, 1970). One suggestion for design of new towns and cities has been for homogeneity at the block level but heterogeneity at the neighborhood or community level (Gans, 1961; Newman, 1980). Still, unless ways can be found to make differing groups interdependent, the available choices appear to be homogeneity or coexistence rather than real diversity and interpenetration.

A third matter facing both new towns and cities is the matter of control. New towns are *planned* communities. Sometimes they are planned by those whose major goal is profit. Others, such as Rouse, have hired highly respected experts to do the planning with people in mind. But rarely have the people themselves been directly involved in expressing their needs and their perceptions. It is even more unusual for the people to have control over the decisions. In general, centralized control over decision making has meant that significant public input could not exist (Brooks, 1974). Columbia has been likened to a company town in which the ruling body may have been benevolent but was nonetheless all-powerful. *Newsweek*, in covering Columbia's growing pains, reported:

To Irwin Auerbach, the most frustrating drawback is the lack of participation in the community's management. The only forum for voicing protest is the "village association," and the residents have no legal right to shape policy. "We are powerless," says the 42-year old Medicare policy analyst. "The real control is in the hands of the developers. I think no man or corporation can own a city. A city belongs to its people." ["Growing Pains," 1969, p. 51]

When we eventually ask whether suburb, new town, or city is "better," we come back to the same conclusion: Each is best for some people at some stages of their lives. The only absolutes we can offer are that planning is to be preferred over haphazard growth, choice is to be preferred over constraint in deciding where to live, control is to be preferred over decision by fiat – even if the decision maker has one's best interests in mind – and affiliation and support are to be preferred over isolation. Whether each positive can be automatically guaranteed by living in a city, a suburb, or a new town is highly doubtful.

The city: Can it be a livable place?

Which is better, big or small? Would you rather go to a large university or a small college, work for a small company or a large corporation, grow up in a big or a small family? Much of the discussion of the city in history, in literature, and in the social sciences implicitly or explicitly has asked this question. The new-town movement, concluding that current big cities are not worth trying to salvage but recognizing some of the advantages of large size, has taken a compromise position and built medium-sized places. The final section of this book is not meant to defend the position that bigger is better but urges that since cities are here to stay, it is important to find ways of working within the framework of urban life to improve its quality.

A number of suggestions and proposals for city design have been offered by imaginative and futuristic thinkers (see Lynch, 1981, for an excellent

Figure 8.4. Safdie's Habitat 67 in Montreal. From *For Everyone a Garden* by M. Safdie. Copyright 1974 by MIT. Published by the MIT Press. Photo by Jerry Spearman.

survey of these). I shall briefly review two of these to show that some suggestions have been imaginative and practical while others, equally creative, have ranged toward the bizarre. In the first case, Israeli architect Moshe Safdie (1970, 1974) has rejected the idea of opposing city living to country living. He has proposed instead a concept of urban design that attempts to combine urban density and diversity with rural peacefulness, thereby incorporating the contrasts of city and country. He has stated, "We want two extremes ... the intensive meeting place, the urban environment, the place where everyone is together and we want the secluded open space where we are alone in the country in nature. We need and want both'' (p. 223).

Safdie designed and had built, as a model of this concept, Habitat 67 in Montreal, a high-rise urban community where people live in boxlike modules (see Figure 8.4). Through highly innovative means of construction, these units can be stacked and arranged in a variety of ways to achieve a maximum of visual complexity. Habitat 67 thereby avoids the uniformity of many urban housing projects and suburban housing tracts and allows people more incentives to explore, identify with and personalize their environment. Safdie also planned these housing units so that people could have terraces and gardens on top of each unit and could thereby bring some country into the city. Although praised by many, Habitat 67 has been criticized for depriving families of easy access to the grounds because of the unique design of the modules

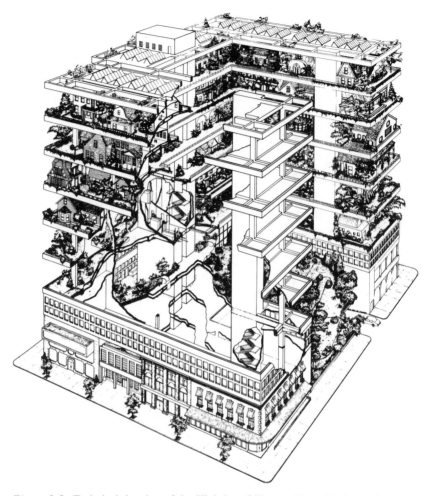

Figure 8.5. Technical drawing of the Highrise of Homes. From *Highrise of Homes* by SITE. Copyright © SITE 1982. Published by Rizzoli International Publications, Inc. Reprinted with permission.

and for the great costs involved in constructing the units in this unusual way (Newman, 1980).

A second proposal that tries to bring an element of suburban living to the city is the Highrise of Homes (see Figure 8.5). The design group SITE (1982) has taken the standard vertical concept of high-rise urban living and put a unique if not bizarre twist on it. The group proposes building concrete frames approximately ten stories high so that the resulting structure looks like a building without walls. On each floor a number of "lots" will be sold to people who will then build suburban-type homes on them. These homes will have yards, gardens, and all of the other accoutrements of the suburban home (although the matter of getting sufficient sunlight to lower floors has not been addressed directly). This proposal does offer a person the chance to own rather than rent and to build as he or she pleases; still, it deals with home ownership as if it were an absolute positive, stripping it from its usual context. Robert Campbell (1982) has noted that homes up in the air lose a good deal of the aesthetic and functional advantages that most homes have. The SITE proposal, though not likely to become popular, is useful in that it requires us to check our assumptions and momentarily change perspectives. It is possible that we have finally found a design solution that incorporates the worst of both worlds.

Maintaining diversity and enhancing control

Although the suggestions just presented are interesting and unique, there are a number of other possibilities for emphasizing the benefits and minimizing the problems of urban living that can be implemented without any revolutionary changes in urban form. These suggestions involve taking the greatest advantage of size where size is an asset and working to counteract the disadvantages of size where size is a liability.

The basic premise here is that of the multiple- and contrasting-realities approach. Cities, by virtue of their size, make possible and even encourage outcomes and conditions that are both positive and negative. Urban living involves trade-offs. Therefore, by careful attention to both poles, we can plan in order to get the best net result. The principal advantage of size is diversity, which brings access to people, opportunities, lifestyles, and resources. Urban people have the freedom to choose among many alternatives. At the same time, they can fiercely guard their privacy against those around them but still receive warmth and support from friends and family throughout the city. Depending on what they prefer, urbanites can seek out community on their doorsteps or among a group of old baseball-card collectors in other sections of the city. In fact, the detractors of the city generally do not disagree about the existence of the positive side; instead, they argue that the number of the negatives makes the exchange a poor one.

Included among the ills of the city are poverty, crime, noise, and pollution. It is beyond the scope and intent of this book to solve the city's ills in one grand plan. What I do propose, however, is that each of these problems has a common denominator, a single mechanism by which it most disturbs urbanites. This is the loss of control. As pointed out in Chapter 5, crowding, noise, and pollution can each be disturbing in itself, but they all work to convey the same set of messages: You cannot do as you please; your actions do not make any difference.

It has been argued that with increasing size, this message becomes stronger and stronger. I do not necessarily disagree with this claim. Rather, I would propose that these messages are not absolutely inevitable, regardless of the size and shape of community one lives in. In these final pages, I will review some suggestions for avoiding or overcoming the sense of helplessness, thereby maintaining the positive while reducing the negative.

The debate between the big city's defenders and its critics has most often involved a centrist-decentrist argument couched in *physical* terms: Build small communities, on the one hand; on the other, large communities are okay. Yet whereas the objective reality of the environment can be measured by *size*, the subjective reality by which each person operates is known as *scale*. If life in a community of any size can be experienced on a human scale, if people can be made to feel that they and their actions have meaning for, and impact on, the environment, they will be satisfied. It is not necessary to live in a village or town to feel responsibility for one's home, one's neighborhood, and one's friends. Informed interventions in architectural design, participation in block associations, and involvement in decentralized political decisions can all help create a sense of living at a scale that is manageable regardless of the size of one's community.

Public involvement and control

Urban residents can be helped to experience a sense of efficacy both in the *process* of planning and in its *outcomes*. As for process, there is a simple rule that is equally relevant for urbanites or villagers: People are more satisfied with decisions in which they have participated than with those handed down to them from some authority. In the United States especially, the value of participatory democracy is a strong one.

The range of citizen participation is presented in Figure 8.6 (Arnstein, 1969). Each step differs from the next in how much decision-making power the members of the community have in comparison to government or local agencies. At one extreme is simple nonconsultation, where agencies or individuals disregard the desires of the community and present decisions in a "take it or leave it" form. At the bottom of the ladder, community members are allowed to participate, but their participation is intended only to inform, educate, or "cure" them. As we get farther up the ladder, the real muscle is still in the hands of others, but token concessions may be made to placate the community and to give the people the appearance of power. At the level of partnership, real power to decide is either shared or completely given over to the people who will be most affected by it.

Porteous (1977) points out that in considering community participation, it is important to make the distinction between real control and pseudocontrol. That is, planners and politicians may use citizen groups, co-opting or manipulating their leaders to justify the very plans they began with in the first

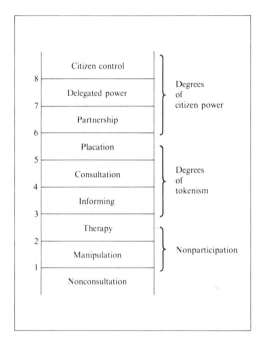

Figure 8.6. Levels of citizen participation and control. From "A ladder of citizen participation" by S. Arnstein. In the *Journal of the American Institute of Planners*, 1969, *35*, 216–224. Copyright 1969 by the American Institute of Planners. Reprinted by permission.

place. Although this form of deception and tokenism is to be deplored because it does nothing to ensure that the community's needs will be met, even tokenism has the paradoxical effect of encouraging people to participate and fight for control, rather than making them feel so powerless that they stop trying.

A number of specific techniques have been advocated not only to enhance participation but also to allow forms of real partnership and control to evolve. Two problems that often limit the layperson's usefulness are a lack of knowledge of choices and an inability to speak the planner's language (Lansing & Marans, 1969). Environmental education and the development of planning workbooks for the public are but two educational methods that have been used with some success (Dixon, 1969; Zinobar & Dinkel, 1981). Community-development workshops and encounter groups in which designers and citizens come together to test ideas, assumptions, and plans often facilitate contact and allow each group to understand the other's needs and constraints (Eugster, 1974). Simulation and role-playing techniques (Rose, 1972) have been especially useful in allowing planners and users to see the project from the other's perspective.

In order to help ensure real control rather than pseudocontrol, some community groups have adopted advocacy planning, an extremely popular technique in the 1960s. In advocacy planning those who will be affected by a plan hire their own expert to represent them and argue for their interests and proposals (Halprin & Burns, 1974; Sanoff, 1975). An advantage of this technique is that it allows urban residents to have a strong, articulate, and expert advocate. On the other hand, it requires the existence of a single community voice (and there may not be one, given urban heterogeneity), and it assumes that the planner can relate to and accurately represent the interests of his or her clients.

Citizen involvement need not be limited to one-project consultation or to a reactive stance to plans for a local change. Decentralization of urban services in the form of Model Cities Programs and the development of street-level governments and citizen boards came of age in the 1960s and has continued with varying degrees of interest and success ever since (Morris & Hess, 1975; Yin & Yates, 1975). Specific goals of political decentralization have been an increase in information flow between service providers and users, improvement in the quality of the services provided, and improvement in the attitudes of providers and users toward themselves and their role complementaries. These goals are, of course, added to that of actual increases in citizen control. The greatest benefit of decentralization, however, is in decreasing the scale of the political process – in making a resident feel that he can call someone to get a huge pothole filled and it will be done, or that she can complain about a streetlight burned out on a busy corner and it will be replaced quickly.

We may ask whether everyone can or does become involved or whether it takes a special kind of person. Abraham Wandersman and his colleagues (Unger & Wandersman, 1983; Wandersman, 1984a; Wandersman, Jakubs, & Giamartino, 1981), using their extensive neighborhood-participation project in Nashville, Tennessee, identified the characteristics of those who become active in neighborhood-level projects. They found that although many different kinds of people do become active, the people who are most likely to join are those who are "rooted" in their home territories (e.g., those who are older, married, female homeowners). This finding is consistent with the implications of Riger and Lavrakas's typology (1981), discussed in Chapter 6, as well as with other research on the nature of local activism (e.g., see Cox, 1982).

Those who organize and form local organizations perceive more problems on their blocks than those who do not, but rather than reflect a feeling that the difficulties cannot be overcome, activists show a heightened level of self-esteem and a strong sense of political efficacy and civic duty. A particular contribution of the Nashville research group is the demonstration that, whereas stable personality and demographic characteristics are useful in predicting activism, other characteristics that are more amenable to change are equally good predictors. That is, *situation-specific* evaluations of a problem and the perceived likelihood of change – variables that a community organizer might affect – strongly determine whether people will get involved or not.

An important point to recognize throughout this discussion is that the degree of control and success achieved need not be great. In fact, the impact of neighborhood organizations on government and on the actual delivery of services is usually moderate at best (Yin, 1977). Still, each attempt that meets with some success brings people together, demonstrates common concerns, and further reinforces the desire to try again. Such efforts reverse the vicious cycle found in learned helplessness. The feeling that one can fight city hall or even that there is a responsive "little city hall" in the area is not quite, but almost, half the battle. People who participate, in contrast to those who do not, find their areas more congruent with their needs, show less distrust and apathy, and most important, have a stronger belief in their perceived ability to exert control over the environment and their lives in general (Rosener, 1977; Sharp, 1978; Wandersman, 1984b).

The possibilities and the rewards are each considerable:

We've got ordinary people who come from public housing projects, retirement centers, and churches, who've never spoken before a crowd who are now sitting down and talking to the governor, to legislators, to the heads of utility companies and who are learning the skills of active citizenship. [Ballou, quoted in Boyte, 1980, p. 39]

You are – if you're willing to put yourself forward as such – a potential community leader who can look forward not only to helping create a better community, but also to satisfying personal growth as your leadership is confirmed and broadened by the responsiveness of a group of your fellow citizens. [Huenefeld, 1970, p. 4]

Open-ended environments

Whether or not planners encourage or accept input from users, all too often the end product is designed down to the last detail. A building or a community is the expression of those who designed it, and it leaves little room for the self-expression of those who live in it. Amos Rapoport (1977) has proposed that instead of asking how completely a new city or new housing development can be planned, we ought to be asking what is the least that needs to be designed and fixed. This approach is known as open-ended design:

Open-ended design is a form of design which determines certain parts of the system allowing other parts, including unforeseen ones, to happen sponta-

neously. This allows for some level of ambiguity, for giving meaning through personalization, for the expression of different values, needs and lifestyles in the environment. It also gets over the problem of tight fit: environments can be used by different groups and individuals. In cities, successive groups can more easily restructure the organization of space, time, meaning and communication.
[P. 356]

This pluralistic view is perfectly consistent with the multiple- and contrasting-realities approach taken here. Different groups have different needs and different views of the world. They need room to express themselves within it. Open-ended design encourages diversity and offers a sense of control. It allows an environment to be flexible enough so that successive groups of occupants can adapt it to their lifestyles and so that the same people can change it as they change themselves. Such an environment may be complex and ambiguous because of the multiple inputs, but the increased involvement of residents should still lead to greater imageability.

Conclusions

What does it mean to live in a big city? The answer offered throughout this book is that with size come a number of consequences, some good and some bad. The city is a physical, political, and economic construction; but it is also a social construction. To say *city* implies the existence of many types of people and many types of experiences. Each person and each group perceive different physical parts and social aspects of the city. People organize, interpret, and evaluate their perceptions differently; and therefore, they behave differently. No single explanation of urban characteristics is encompassing enough to make us understand urban behavior. Therefore, I have argued that we should accept all of the multiple and sometimes contrasting reports, descriptions, and evaluations of urban life as complementary rather than contradictory.

I have suggested here that diversity, the multiplicity of people and experiences, is the city's chief advantage. It is true that heterogeneity can lead to problems in finding and defining one's own niche and may leave one feeling isolated and lonely. But diversity is just as likely to help people find groups of like-minded others, whether locally or among soccer fanatics or rare-coin collectors dispersed throughout the city.

In exchange for diversity, a disadvantage of size is that it can bring alienation and helplessness, the feeling that there is no way to make the environment responsive to one's needs. It is this feeling that makes coping with noise, crowds, and pollution most difficult. Yet just as defensible-space design can make people feel more responsible for, and in control of, the immediate living setting, open-ended design can make them more involved in their general areas. Also people can be given political power – or if they are not given it, they can act assertively to take it. The *big-size* city can still be the *small-scale* city where people are encouraged in, and rewarded for, assuming control over their environment.

The end result is still that the city is not for everyone, nor should it be. The one-environment-fits-all concept is wrong and dangerous. Our future is undoubtedly in a society with a number of community sizes and forms, each available to suit the varying needs of differing individuals and groups. The city will be one of these forms, and it will be an important one. It is possible for urban people to cope with stress, form close relationships, and thrive on the diversity in which they live. It is equally possible for them to feel in control of their lives and their environment, although this will require considerable effort and planning. But with such effort, the city can be carved down to a manageable scale, and it can be a good place to live for the many and different people who reside there.

Suggestions for further reading

Boyte, H. C. 1980. *The backyard revolution: Understanding the new citizen movement*. Philadelphia: Temple University Press.

Heller, K., Price, R., Reinharz, S., Riger, A., & Wandersman, A. 1984. *Psychology and community change* (2nd ed.). Homewood, Ill.: Dorsey Press.

Howard, E. 1965. *Garden cities of tomorrow*. Cambridge, Mass.: MIT Press. (Originally published, 1902.)

Lynch, K. 1981. *A theory of good city form*. Cambridge, Mass.: MIT Press.

REFERENCES

Abler, R., & Adams, J. S. 1976. *A comparative atlas of America's great cities: 20 metropolitan regions*. Minneapolis: University of Minnesota Press.

Abrams, C. 1971. *The language of cities: A glossary of terms*. New York: Viking Press.

Abu-Lughod, J. A. 1966. *The city is dead – long live the city: Some thoughts on urbanity*. Monograph 12. Berkeley, Calif.: Center for Planning and Research.

Alonso, W. 1973. Urban zero population growth. In M. Olson & H. H. Landsberg (Eds.), *The no-growth society*. New York: Norton.

Altman, I. 1973. Some perspectives on the study of man–environment phenomena. *Representative Research in Social Psychology, 4*, 109–126.

Altman, I. 1975. *The environment and social behavior: Privacy, personal space, territory and crowding*. Monterey, Calif.: Brooks/Cole.

Altman, I. 1976. Environmental psychology and social psychology. *Personality and Social Psychology Bulletin, 2*, 96–113.

Altman, I., & Chemers, M. M. 1980. *Culture and environment*. Monterey, Calif.: Brooks/Cole.

Altman, I., Wohlwill, J., & Everett, P. (Eds.). 1980. *Human behavior and environment: Advances in theory and research*. Vol. 5: *Transportation environments*. New York: Plenum.

Angell, R. C. 1951. The moral integration of American cities. *American Journal of Sociology, 57*, 1–14.

Appleyard, D. 1970. Styles and methods of structuring a city. *Environment and Behavior, 2*, 100–117.

Appleyard, D. 1976. *Planning a pluralistic city*. Cambridge, Mass.: MIT Press.

Appleyard, D., & Lintell, M. 1972. The environmental quality of city streets: The residents' viewpoint. *Journal of the American Institute of Planners, 38*, 84–101.

Appleyard, D., Lynch, K., & Meyer, J. 1964. *The view from the road*. Cambridge, Mass.: MIT Press.

Archea, J. 1977. The place of architectural factors in behavioral theories of privacy. *Journal of Social Issues, 33*, 116–138.

Argyle, M. 1981. *Social situations*. Cambridge: Cambridge University Press.

Arnstein, S. 1969. A ladder of citizen participation. *Journal of the American Institute of Planners, 35*, 216–224.

Aronow, W. S., Harris, C. N., Isbell, N. W., Rokaw, M. D., & Imparato, B. 1972. Effect of freeway travel on angina pectoris. *Annals of Internal Medicine, 77*, 669–676.

Ashmore, R., & McConahay, J. B. 1975. *Psychology and America's urban dilemmas*. New York: McGraw-Hill.

Baldassare, M. 1977. Residential density, household crowding and social networks. In C. Fischer (Ed.), *Networks and places: Social relations in the urban setting*. New York: Free Press.

Baldassare, M. 1979. *Residential crowding in America*. Berkeley: University of California Press.

Barker, R. G. 1968. *Ecological psychology: Concepts and methods of studying the environment of human behavior*. Stanford, Calif.: Stanford University Press.

Barker, R. G., & Gump, P. V. (Eds.). 1964. *Big school, small school: High school size and student behavior*. Stanford, Calif.: Stanford University Press.

Barker, R. G., & Wright, H. F. 1955. *Midwest and its children: The psychological ecology of an American town*. New York.: Harper & Row.

Baron, R. A. 1970. *The tyranny of noise*. New York: St. Martin's Press.

Barrett, L. A., & Guest, A. M. 1983. Determinants of neighborhood satisfaction: A metropolitan-level analysis. *Sociological Quarterly*, *24*, 287–303.

Baum, A., Aiello, J. R., & Calesnick, L. E. 1978. Crowding and personal control: Social diversity and the development of learned helplessness. *Journal of Personality and Social Psychology*, *36*, 1000–1011.

Baum, A., & Epstein, Y. M. (Eds.) 1978. *Human response to crowding*. Hillsdale, N.J.: Erlbaum.

Baum, A., & Valins, S. 1977. *Architecture and social behavior: Psychological studies in social density*. Hillsdale, N.J.: Erlbaum.

Bechtel, R. B. 1967. Human movement and architecture. *Trans-action*, *4*, 53–56.

Bechtel, R. B. 1973. Types of cities: The sub-national urban environment and some design implications. In W. P. Preiser (Ed.), *Environmental design research*. Vol. 1: *Selected papers*. Stroudsburg, Pa.: Dowden, Hutchinson & Ross.

Bechtel, R. B. 1977. *Enclosing behavior*. Stroudsburg, Pa.: Dowden, Hutchinson & Ross.

Bellet, S., Roman, L., & Kostis, J. 1969. The effect of automobile driving on catecholamine and adrenocortical excretion. *American Journal of Cardiology*, *24*, 365–368.

Bem, S. L. 1974. The measurement of psychological androgyny. *Journal of Consulting and Clinical Psychology*, *42*, 155–162.

Berlyne, D. E. 1970. Novelty, complexity and hedonic value. *Perception and Psychophysics*, *8*, 279–286.

Berry, B. J. 1972. Latent structure of the American urban system with international comparisons. In B. J. Berry (Ed.), *City classification handbook*. New York: Wiley.

Bissell, R. 1950. *A stretch on the river*. Boston: Little, Brown.

Boyer, R., & Savageau, D. 1981. *Places rated almanac*. Chicago: Rand McNally.

Boyte, H. C. 1980. *The backyard revolution: Understanding the new citizen movement*. Philadelphia: Temple University Press.

Briggs, R. 1973. On the relationship between cognitive and objective distance. In W.

Preiser (Ed.), *Environmental design research*. Vol. 2: *Symposium and workshops*. Stroudsburg, Pa.: Dowden, Hutchinson & Ross.

Broady, M. 1972. Social theory in architectural design. In D. Gutman (Ed.), *People and buildings*. New York: Basic Books.

Brolin, B. 1972. Chantigarh was planned by experts but something has gone wrong. *Smithsonian, 3*, 56–62.

Bronzaft, A. L., & McCarthy, D. P. 1975. The effects of elevated train noise on reading ability. *Environment and Behavior, 7*, 517–527.

Brooks, R. O. 1974. *New towns and communal values: A case study of Columbia, Maryland*. New York: Praeger.

Brudney, J. L., & England, R. E. 1982. Analyzing citizens' evaluations of municipal services. *Urban Affairs Quarterly, 17*, 359–369.

Burnette, C., Moore, G. T., & Simek, L. A. 1973. A role-oriented approach to problemsolving groups. In W. F. E. Preiser (Ed.), *Environmental design research* (Vol. 1). Stroudsburg, Pa.: Dowden, Hutchinson & Ross.

Burton, V. L. 1942. *The little house*. Boston: Houghton Mifflin.

Cahill, S., & Cooper, M. F. (Eds.). 1971. *The urban reader*. Englewood Cliffs, N.J.: Prentice-Hall.

Calhoun, J. B. 1962. Population density and social pathology. *Science, 206*, 139–148.

Campbell, A., Converse, P. E., & Rodgers, W. L. 1976. *The quality of American life: Perceptions, evaluations and satisfactions*. New York: Russell Sage.

Campbell, R. 1982. Bizarre hypothesis applied to housing. *Boston Globe*, October 12.

Canter, D., & Tagg, S. K. 1975. Distance estimation in cities. *Environment and Behavior, 7*, 59–80.

Carnahan, D., Guest, A. M., & Galle, O. R. 1974. Congestion, concentration and behavior: research in the study of urban population density. *Sociological Quarterly, 15*, 488–506.

Carp, F. M., Zawadski, R. T., & Shokrkon, H. 1976. Dimensions of urban environmental quality. *Environment and Behavior, 8*, 239–264.

Carr, S. 1970. The city of the mind. In H. M. Proshansky, W. H. Ittelson, & L. G. Rivlin (Eds.), *Environmental psychology: Man and his physical setting* (1st ed.). New York: Holt, Rinehart & Winston.

Carr, S., & Schissler, D. 1969. The city as a trip: Perceptual selection and memory in the view from the road. *Environment and Behavior, 1*, 7–36.

Cederlöf, R. Friberg, L., Hammarfors, P., Holmquist, S. E., & Kajland, A. 1961. Studier over ljudnivaer och hygieniska olagenheter av trafikbuller samt forslag till atgarder. *Nordisk Hygiènisk Tidskrift, 42*, 101–192.

Chinoy, E. (Ed.). 1973. *The urban future*. New York: Lieber-Atherton.

Choldin, H. M. 1978. Urban density and pathology. *Annual Review of Sociology, 4*, 91–113.

Christian, J. J. 1975. Hormonal control of population growth. In B. E. Eleftheious & R. L. Scott (Eds.), *Hormonal correlates of behavior* (Vol. 1). New York: Plenum.

Clapp, J. A. 1971. *New towns and urban policy*. New York: Dunellen.

Cohen, S., Evans, G. W., Krantz, D. S., & Stokols, D. 1980. Physiological, motivational and cognitive effects of aircraft noise on children: Moving from the laboratory to the field. *American Psychologist, 35,* 231–243.

Cohen, S., Evans, G. W., Krantz, D. S., Stokols, D., & Kelly, S. 1981. Aircraft noise and children: Longitudinal and cross-sectional evidence on adaptation to noise and the effectiveness of noise abatement. *Journal of Personality and Social Psychology, 40,* 331–345.

Cohen, S., Glass, D. C., & Singer, J. E. 1973. Apartment noise, auditory discrimination, and reading ability in children. *Journal of Experimental Social Psychology, 9,* 407–422.

Cohen, S., Krantz, D. S., Stokols, D., & Evans., G. W. In press. *Behavior, health and environmental stress*. New York: Plenum.

Cohen, S., & Weinstein, N. 1982. Nonauditory effects of noise on behavior and health. In G. W. Evans (Ed.), *Environmental stress*. Cambridge: Cambridge University Press.

Cooper, C. 1971. St. Francis Square: Attitudes of its residents. *Journal of the American Institute of Planners, 58,* 22–27.

Cox, K. R. 1982. Housing tenure and neighborhood activism. *Urban Affairs Quarterly, 18,* 107–129.

Craik, K. H. 1971. The assessment of places. In P. McReynolds (Ed.), *Advances in psychological assessment* (Vol. 2). Palo Alto, Calif.: Science & Behavior Books.

Crowe, P. W. 1978. *Good fences make good neighbors: Social networks at three levels of urbanization in Tivol, Austria*. Unpublished doctoral dissertation, Stanford University.

Cutter, S. C. 1981. Community concern for pollution: Social and environmental influences. *Environment and Behavior, 13,* 105–124.

Davis, K. A. 1965. The urbanization of the human population. *Scientific American, 213,* 40–53.

de Jonge, D. 1962. Images of urban areas: Their structure and psychological foundations. *Journal of the American Institute of Planners, 28,* 266–276.

DeLongis, A., Coyne, J. C., Dakof, G., Folkman, S., & Lazarus, R. S. 1982. Relationship of daily hassles, uplifts, and major events to health status. *Health Psychology, 1,* 119–136.

Devlin, A. S. 1976. The "small town" cognitive map: Adjusting to a new environment. In G. T. Moore & R. Golledge (Eds.), *Environmental knowing: Theories, research and methods*. Stroudsburg, Pa.: Dowden, Hutchinson, & Ross.

Dixon, J. M. 1969. Planning workbook for the community. *Architectural Forum, 131,* 32–40.

Downs, R. M., & Stea, D. 1977. *Maps in minds: Reflections on cognitive mapping*. New York: Harper & Row.

Duncan, O. D. 1957. Optimum size of cities. In P. K. Hatt & A. J. Reiss, Jr. (Eds.), *Cities and society*. New York: Free Press.

Eugster, C. 1974. Field education in West Heights: Equipping a deprived community

to help itself. In F. M. Cox, J. L. Erlich, J. Rothman, & J. E. Tropman (Eds.), *Strategies of community organization: A book of readings* (2nd ed.). Itasca, Ill.: F. E. Peacock Publishers.

Evans, G. W. 1980. Environmental cognition. *Psychological Bulletin, 88,* 259–287.

Evans, G. W. (Ed.). 1982. *Environmental stress.* Cambridge: Cambridge University Press.

Evans, G. W., & Jacobs, S. V. 1982. Air pollution and human behavior. In G. W. Evans (Ed.), *Environmental stress.* Cambridge: Cambridge University Press.

Evans, G. W., Jacobs, S. V., & Frager, N. B. 1982. Behavioral response to air pollution. In A. Baum & J. Singer (Eds.), *Advances in environmental psychology. Vol. 4. Environment and health.* Hillsdale, N.J.: Erlbaum.

Evans, G. W., Marrero, D. G., & Butler, P. A. 1981. Environmental learning and cognitive mapping. *Environment and Behavior, 13,* 83–104.

Everitt, J., & Cadwallader, M. 1972. The home area concept in urban analysis. In W. J. Mitchell (Ed.), *Environmental design: Research and practice.* Los Angeles: University of California Press.

Farley, J. E. 1982. Has public housing gotten a bum rap? The incidence of crime in St. Louis public housing developments. *Environment and Behavior, 14,* 443–477.

Fischer, C. 1981. The public and private worlds of city life. *American Sociological Review, 46,* 306–316.

Fischer, C. 1982. *To dwell among friends: Personal networks in town and city.* Chicago: University of Chicago Press.

Fischer, C. 1984. *The urban experience* (2nd ed.). New York: Harcourt Brace Jovanovich.

Fisher, J. D., Bell, P. A., & Baum, A. 1984. *Environmental psychology* (2nd Ed.). New York: Holt, Rinehart & Winston.

Fowler, F. J., Jr., McCalla, M. E., & Mangione, T. W. 1979. *Reducing residential crime and fear: The Hartford neighborhood crime prevention program.* Washington, D.C.: Law Enforcement Assistance Administration, National Institute of Law Enforcement and Criminal Justice.

Francescato, D., & Mebane, W. 1973. How citizens view two great cities: Milan and Rome. In R. M. Downs & D. Stea (Eds.), *Image and environment: Cognitive mapping and spatial behavior.* Chicago: Aldine.

Franck, K. A. 1980. Friends and strangers: The social experience of living in urban and nonurban settings. *Journal of Social Issues, 3,* 52–71.

Franck, K. A. 1983. Comm nity by design. *Sociological Inquiry, 2/3,* 289–313.

Fredericksen, N. 1972. Toward a toxonomy of situations. *American Psychologist, 27,* 114–123.

Freedman, J. C. 1975. *Crowding and behavior.* San Francisco: Freeman.

Freedman, J. C., Heshka, S., & Levy A. S. 1975. Population density and pathology: Is there a relationship? *Journal of Experimental Social Psychology, 11,* 539–552.

Freedman, J. C., Levy, A. S., Buchanan, R. W., & Price, J. 1972. Crowding and human aggressiveness. *Journal of Experimental Social Psychology, 8,* 528–548.

Fried, M. 1963. Grieving for a lost home. In L. J. Duhl (Ed.), *The urban condition*. New York: Simon & Schuster.

Fried M., & Gleicher, P. 1961. Some sources of satisfaction in an urban slum. *Journal of the American Institute of Planners, 27*, 305–315.

Fried, R. C., & Hohenberg, P. M. (Eds.). 1974. *The quality of life in European cities* (2nd ed.) Pittsburgh: Council for European Studies.

Galle, O. R, & Gove, W. R. 1979. Crowding and behavior in Chicago, 1949–1970. In J. R. Aiello & A. Baum (Eds.), *Residential crowding and design*. New York: Plenum.

Galle, O. R., Gove, W. R., & McPherson, J. 1972. Population density and pathology: What are the relations of man? *Science, 176*, 23–30.

Gans, H. J. 1961. Planning and social life: Friendship and neighbor relations in suburban communities. *Journal of the American Institute of Planners, 27*, 134–140.

Gans, H. J. 1962a. Urbanism and suburbanism as ways of life: A reevaluation of definitions. In A. M. Rose (Ed.), *Human behavior and social processes*. Boston: Houghton Mifflin.

Gans, H. J. 1962b. *The urban villagers*. New York: Free Press.

Gansberg, M. 1964. Thirty eight who didn't call the police. *New York Times*, March 27.

Geller, D. 1980. Responses to urban stimuli: A balanced approach. *Journal of Social Issues, 36*, 86–100.

Geller, D., Cook, J., O'Connor, M., & Low, A. 1982. Perception of urban scenes by small town and urban residents: A multi-dimensional scaling analysis. In P. Bart, A. Chin, & G. Francescato (Eds.), *Knowledge for design: Proceedings of the 13th International Conference of the Environmental Design Research Association*. College Park, Md.

Glass, D. C., & Singer, J. E. 1972. *Urban stress: experiments on noise and social stressors*. New York: Academic Press.

Glazer, N. 1984. Paris – the view from New York. *Public Interest, 74*, 31–51.

Glenn, N., & Hill, L. 1977. Rural–urban differences in attitudes and behaviors in the United States. *Annals of the American Academy of Political and Social Science, 429*, 36–50.

Goffman, E. 1959. *The presentation of self in everyday life*. Garden City, N.Y.: Doubleday.

Goffman, E. 1971. *Relations in public*. New York: Basic Books.

Goldstein, M. 1972. Bye bye Miss American pie: Life in Connecticut contrasted to New York City life. *Harper's Magazine, 244*, 80–84.

Golledge, R. G., & Zannaras, G. 1973. Cognitive approaches to the analysis of human spatial behavior. In W. H. Ittelson (Ed.), *Environment and cognition*. New York: Seminar Press.

Goodchild, B. 1974. Class differences in environmental perception. *Urban Studies, 11*, 59–79.

Goodman, P., & Goodman, P. 1960. *Communitas: Means of livelihood and ways of life*. New York: Random House (Vintage Books).

Gottfredson, S. D., Brower, S., & Taylor, R. B. 1979. *Design, social networks and human territoriality: Predicting crime-related and social control outcomes.* Paper presented at the American Psychological Association Convention, New York.

Gove, W. R., Hughes, M., & Galle, O. 1979. Over-crowding in the home: An empirical investigation of its possible pathological consequences. *American Sociological Review, 44*, 59–80.

Granovetter, M. S. 1973. The strength of weak ties. *American Journal of Sociology, 78*, 1360–1380.

Greenberg, S. W., Williams, J. R., & Rohe, W. M. 1982. Safety in urban neighborhoods: A comparison of physical characteristics and informal territorial control in high and low crime neighborhoods. *Population and Environment, 5*, 141–165.

Griffiths, I. D., & Langdon, F. J. 1968. Subjective response to road traffic noise. *Journal of Sound and Vibration, 8*, 16–32.

Growing pains of a new town. 1969. *Newsweek*, July 14.

Guild, W. 1981. *The concept and measure of environmental monitoring.* Unpublished doctoral dissertation, Boston College.

Guild, W., & Krupat, E. 1979. *Multidimensional scaling analysis of the perception of cities.* Unpublished manuscript.

Guterman, S. 1969. In defense of Wirth's "urbanism as a way of life." *American Journal of Sociology, 74*, 492–499.

Haber, R. 1958. Discrepancy from adaptation level as a source of affect. *Journal of Experimental Psychology, 56*, 370–375.

Hadden, J. K., & Borgatta, E. F. 1965. *American cities: Their social characteristics.* Chicago: Rand McNally.

Halprin, L., & Burns, J. 1974. *Taking part.* Cambridge, Mass.: MIT Press.

Harris, C. D. 1943. A functional classification of cities in the United States. *Geographical Review, 33*, 86–99.

Harrison, J. D., & Howard, W. A. 1972. The role of meaning in the urban image. *Environment and Behavior, 4*, 389–411.

Hartman, C. 1966. The housing of relocated families. In J. Q. Wilson (Ed.), *Urban renewal: The record and the controversy.* Cambridge, Mass.: M.I.T. Press.

Hawley, A. 1979. *Societal growth: Processes and Implications.* Riverside, N.J.: Free Press.

Hawley, A. 1981. *Urban society: An ecological approach* (2nd ed.). New York: Wiley.

Heller, K., Price, R., Reinharz, S., Riger, A., & Wandersman, A. 1984. *Psychology and community change* (2nd ed.). Homewood, Ill.: Dorsey Press.

Helson, H. 1964. *Adaptation-level theory.* New York: Harper & Row.

Hillery, G. A., Jr. 1955. Definitions of community: Areas of agreement. *Rural Sociology. 2*, 118.

Hillier, B. 1973. In defense of space. *RIBA Journal*, 539–544.

Holahan, C. J. 1982. *Environmental psychology.* New York: Random House.

Hoppenfeld, M. 1971. The Columbia process: The potential for new towns. In D. Lewis (Ed.), *The growth of cities*. New York: Wiley-Interscience.

Howard, E. 1965. *Garden cities of tomorrow*. Cambridge, Mass.: MIT Press. (Originally published, 1902.)

Howard, W. A. 1977. *Optimum city-size: The persistence of a curious idea*. Paper presented at the Environmental Design Research Association Convention, Urbana, Ill.

Howe, I. 1971. The city in literature. *Commentary 51*, 61–68.

Huenefeld, J. 1970. *The community activist's handbook: A guide for citizen leaders and planners*. Boston: Beacon Press.

Hummon, D. 1980. *Community ideology*. Unpublished doctoral dissertation, University of California, Berkeley.

Hunter, A. 1975. The loss of community. *American Sociological Review, 40*, 537–552.

Hunter, A. 1978. Persistence of local sentiments in mass society. In D. Street (Ed.), *Handbook of contemporary urban life*. San Francisco: Jossey-Bass.

Hunter, A. 1979. The urban neighborhood: Its analytical and social contexts. *Urban Affairs Quarterly, 14*, 267–288.

Hunter, A. 1982. Street traffic, social integration and fear of crime. *Sociological Inquiry, 52*, 122–131.

Ittelson, W. H. 1976. Some issues facing a theory of environment and behavior. In H. M. Proshansky, W. H. Ittelson, & L. G. Rivlin (Eds.), *Environmental psychology: People and their physical settings* (2nd ed.). New York: Holt, Rinehart & Winston.

Ittelson, W. H. 1978. Environmental perception and urban experience. *Environment and Behavior, 10*, 193–214.

Ittelson, W. H., Proshansky, H. M., Rivlin, L. G., & Winkel, G. H. 1974. *An introduction to. environmental psychology*. New York: Holt, Rinehart & Winston.

Jacobs, J. 1961. *The death and life of great American cities*. New York: Random House.

Jonsson, E., & Sorensen, S. 1973. Adaptation to community noise – a case study. *Journal of Sound and Vibration, 26*, 571–575.

Kaplan, S. 1973. Cognitive maps in perception and thought. In R. M. Downs & D. Stea (Eds.), *Image and environment: Cognitive mapping and spatial behavior*. Chicago: Aldine.

Kaplan, S., & Kaplan, R. 1982. *Cognition and environment*. New York: Praeger.

Karan, P. P., Bladen, W. A., & Singh, G. 1980. Slum dwellers' and squatters' images of the city. *Environment and Behavior, 12*, 81–100.

Kasarda, J., & Janowitz, M. 1974. Community attachment in mass society. *American Sociological Review, 39*, 328–339.

Keller, S. 1968. *The urban neighborhood*. New York: Random House.

Key, W. 1968. Rural–urban social participation. In S. Fava (Ed.), *Urbanism in world perspective*. New York: Crowell.

Kirmeyer, S. L. 1978. Urban density and pathology: A review of research. *Environment and Behavior, 10,* 247–270.

Knipschild, P. 1977. Medical effects of aircraft noise. *International Archives of Occupational and Environmental Health, 40,* 185–204.

Koffka, K. 1935. *Principles of Gestalt psychology.* New York: Harcourt, Brace.

Kohn, I. R., Franck, K. A., & Fox, A. S. 1975. *Defensible space modifications in non-house communities.* Unpublished report, National Science Foundation (RANN). Institute for Community Design Analysis.

Korte, C. 1980. Urban–nonurban differences in social behavior and social psychological models of urban impact. *Journal of Social Issues, 36,* 29–51.

Korte, C., & Grant, R. 1980. Traffic noise, environmental awareness and pedestrian behavior. *Environment and Behavior, 12,* 408–420.

Korte, C., Ypma, I., & Toppen, A. 1975. Helpfulness in Dutch society as a function of urbanization and environmental input level. *Journal of Personality and Social Psychology, 32,* 996–1003.

Krupat, E. 1972. *Perceived threat as a function of prior experience.* Unpublished doctoral dissertation, University of Michigan.

Krupat, E. (Ed.). 1980. Urban life: Applying a social psychological perspective. *Journal of Social Issues, 3* (Whole).

Krupat, E. (Ed.). 1982. *Psychology is social: Readings and conversations in social psychology* (2nd ed.). Glenview, Ill.: Scott Foresman.

Krupat, E. 1984. *The perception of city–small town differences.* Poster session presented at the American Psychological Association Convention, Toronto, Canada.

Krupat, E., & Epstein, Y. 1973. I'm too busy: Effects of overload and diffusion of responsibility on working and helping. Paper presented at the meeting of the American Psychological Association, Montreal.

Krupat, E., & Guild, W. 1980a. The measurement of community social climate. *Environment and Behavior, 12,* 195–206.

Krupat, E., & Guild, W. 1980b. Defining the city: The use of objective and subjective measures for community description. *Journal of Social Issues, 36,* 9–28.

Ktsanes, R., & Reissman, L. 1959–60. Suburbia: New homes for old values. *Social Problems, 7,* 187–194.

Kuipers, B. 1982. The "map in the head" metaphor. *Environment and Behavior, 14,* 202–220.

Lamanna, R. A. 1964. Value consensus among urban residents. *Journal of the American Institute of Planners, 30,* 317–320.

Lansing, J. B., & Marans, R. W. 1969. Evaluation of neighborhood quality. *Journal of the American Institute of Planners, 35,* 195–199.

Lapham, L. 1976. City lights – a defense of New York. *Harper's Magazine, 252,* 8–14.

Latané, B., & Darley, J. 1970. *The unresponsive bystander: Why doesn't he help?* New York: Appleton-Century-Crofts.

Lavrakas, P. 1982. Fear of crime and behavior restriction in urban and suburban neighborhoods. *Population and Environment*, *5*, 242–264.

Lazarus, R. S. 1966. *Psychological stress and the coping process*. New York: McGraw-Hill.

Lazarus, R. S., & Cohen, J. 1977. Environmental stress. In I. Altman and J. F. Wohlwill (Eds.), *Human behavior and environment* (Vol. 2). New York: Plenum.

Le Corbusier. 1947. *City of tomorrow and its planning* (E. Etchells, trans.). London: Architectural Press.

Lee, T. R. 1968. The urban neighborhood as a sociospatial schema. *Human Relations*, *21*, 241–268.

Lee, T. R. 1969. Do we need a theory? In D. V. Canter (Ed.), *Architectural psychology*. London: RIBA Publications.

Lee, T. R. 1970. Perceived distance as a function of direction in the city. *Environment and Behavior*, *2*, 40–51.

Levy, L., & Herzog, A. N. 1974. Effects of population density and crowding on health and social adaptation in the Netherlands. *Journal of Health and Social Behavior*, *15*, 228–240.

Lewin, K. 1951. *Field theory in social science* (D. Cartwright, Ed.). New York: Harper.

Lewis, D. (Ed.) 1971. *The growth of cities*. New York: Wiley-Interscience.

Lewis, O. 1965. Further observations on the folk–urban continuum and urbanization. In P. H. Hauser and L. Schnore (Eds.), *The study of urbanization*. New York: Wiley.

Lewis, O. 1976. A poor family moves to a housing project. In H. M. Proshansky, W. H. Ittelson, and L. G. Rivlin (Eds.), *Environmental psychology: People and their physical settings* (2nd ed.). New York: Holt, Rinehart & Winston.

Liebow, E. 1967. *Talley's corner*. Boston: Little, Brown.

Lipsey, M. W. 1977. Attitudes toward the environment and pollution. In S. Oskamp (Ed.), *Attitudes and Opinions*. Englewood Cliffs, N.J.: Prentice-Hall.

Liu, B. C. 1976. *Quality of life indicators in U.S. metropolitan areas: A statistical analysis*. New York: Praeger.

Lofland, L. 1973. *A world of strangers*. New York: Basic Books.

Loftin, C., & Ward, S. K. 1983. A spatial auto-correlation model of the effects of population density on fertility. *American Sociological Review*, *48*, 121–128.

Logan, J. R., & Collver, O. A. 1983. Residents' perceptions of suburban community differences. *American Sociological Review*, *48*, 428–433.

Los Angeles Department of City Planning. 1971. *The visual environment of Los Angeles*. Los Angeles: The Department.

Lowenthal, D. 1972. *Environmental assessment: A comparative analysis of 4 cities*. New York: American Geographical Society.

Lowenthal, D., & Riel, M. 1972. *Structures of environmental associations*. New York: American Geographical Society.

Lowrey, R. A. 1970. Distance concepts of urban residents. *Environment and Behavior*, *2*, 52–73.

Lynch, K. 1960. *The image of the city*. Cambridge, Mass.: MIT Press.

Lynch, K. 1981. *A theory of good city form*. Cambridge, Mass.: MIT Press.

Lynch K., & Rivkin, M. 1959. A walk around the block. *Landscape*, *8*, 24–34.

McCauley, C., Coleman, G., & DeFusco, P. 1978. Commuters' eye contact with the stranger in city and suburban train stations: Evidence of short-term adaptation to interpersonal overload in the city. *Environmental Psychology and Non-verbal Behavior*, *2*, 215–225.

McCauley, C., & Taylor, J. 1976. Is there overload of acquaintances in the city? *Environmental Psychology and Non-verbal Behavior*, *1*, 41–55.

McEvoy, J. 1972. The American concern with environment. In W. R. Burch, W. H. Cheek, & L. Taylor (Eds.), *Social behavior, natural resources, and the environment*. New York: Harper and Row.

McGill, W., & Korn, J. H. 1982. Awareness of an urban environment. *Environment and Behavior*, *14*, 186–201.

McKennell, A. C. 1973. Psycho-social factors in airport noise annoyance. In W. D. Ward (Ed.), *Proceedings of the International Conference on Noise as a Public Health Problem* (EPA 550/9-73-008). Washington, D.C.: U.S. Government Printing Office.

McKennell, A. C., & Hunt, E. A. 1966. *Noise annoyance in central London*. London: Building Research Station.

McKenzie, R. D. 1926. The scope of human ecology. In E. W. Burgess (Ed.), *The urban community: Selected papers from the proceedings of the American Sociological Society*. Chicago: University of Chicago Press.

Magnussen, D. 1981. *Toward a psychology of situations*. Hillsdale, N.J.: Erlbaum.

Marans, R. W., & Rodgers, W. 1975. Toward an understanding of community satisfaction. In A. Hawley & V. Rock (Eds.), *Metropolitan America in contemporary perspective*. New York: Halsted Press.

Marlin, W., & Gelatt, R. 1976. America's most liveable cities. *Saturday Review*, *3*, 9–12.

Maslow, A. 1970. *Motivation and personality* (2nd ed.). New York: Harper & Row.

Mawby, R. I. 1977. Defensible space: A theoretical and empirical appraisal. *Urban Studies*, *14*, 169–179.

Meecham, W. C., & Smith, H. G. 1977. Effects of jet aircraft noise on mental hospital admissions. *British Journal of Audiology*, *11*, 81–85.

Merry, S. E. 1981a. Defensible space undefended: Social factors in criminal control through environmental·design. *Urban Affairs Quarterly*, *16*, 397–422.

Merry, S. E. 1981b. *Urban danger: Life in a neighborhood of strangers*. Philadelphia: Temple University Press.

Merton, R. K. 1957. Patterns of influence: Local and cosmopolitan influentials. In R. K. Merton (Ed.), *Social theory and social structure*. New York: Free Press.

Michelson, W. E. 1976. *Man and his urban environment: A sociological approach.* Reading, Mass.: Addison-Wesley.

Michelson, W. E. 1977. *Environmental choice, human behavior and residential satisfaction.* New York: Oxford University Press.

Milgram, S. 1970. The experience of living in cities. *Science, 167,* 1461–1468.

Milgram, S., 1972. The familiar stranger: An aspect of urban anonymity. *Division of Personality or Social Psychology Newsletter.* (American Psychological Association).

Milgram, S. 1977. *The individual in a social world: Essays and experiments.* Reading, Mass.: Addison-Wesley.

Milgram, S., Greenwald, J., Kessler, S., McKenna, W., & Waters, J. 1972. A psychological map of New York City. *American Scientist, 60,* 194–200.

Minar, D. W., & Greer, S. 1969. The concept of community. Chicago: Aldine Atherton.

Mitchell, R. E. 1971. Some social implications of high density housing. *American Sociological Review, 36,* 18–29.

Moore, G. T. 1974. Developmental variations between and within individuals in the cognitive representation of large-scale spatial environments. *Man-Environment Systems, 4,* 55–57.

Moore, G. T. 1979. Knowing about environmental knowing: The current state of theory and research on environmental cognition. *Environment and Behavior, 11,* 33–70.

Moos, R. H. 1973. Conceptualizations of human environments. *American Psychologist, 28,* 652–665.

Moos, R. H. 1974a. The social climate scales: An overview. Palo Alto, Calif.: Consulting Psychologists Press.

Moos, R. H. 1974b. *Correctional institutions environment scale manual.* Palo Alto: Consulting Psychologists Press.

Moos, R. H. 1976. *The human context.* New York: Wiley-Interscience.

Moos, R. H. 1979. *Evaluating educational environments.* San Francisco: Jossey-Bass.

Moos, R. H. 1980. *The environmental quality of residential care settings.* Paper presented at the Environmental Design Research Association Conference, Charleston, S.C.

Morris, D., & Hess, K. 1975. *Neighborhood power: The new localism.* Boston: Beacon Press.

Murray, H. A. 1938. *Explorations in personality.* New York: Oxford University Press.

Murtha, D. M. 1976. *Dimensions of user benefit.* Washington, D.C.: American Institute of Architects.

Newman, O. 1972. *Defensible space: Crime prevention through urban design.* New York: Macmillan.

Newman, O. 1980. *Community of interest.* New York: Anchor Press.

Newman, O., & Franck, K. 1982. The effects of building size on personal crime and fear of crime. *Population and Environment, 5,* 204–220.

Newman, S. J. 1981. *Residential crowding: A study of definitions*. Ann Arbor, Mich.: Institute for Social Research.

Novaco, R. W., Stokols, D., Campbell, J., & Stokols, J. 1979. Transportation, stress and community psychology. *American Journal of Community Psychology*, *4*, 361–380.

Ogburn, W. F. 1937. *Social characteristics of cities*. Chicago: International City Managers' Association.

Olsen, P. 1982. Urban neighborhood research: Its development and current forms. *Urban Affairs Quarterly*, *17*, 491–518.

Orleans, P. 1973. Differential cognition of urban residents: Effects of social scale on mapping. In M. Downs & D. Stea (Eds.), *Images and environment: Cognitive mapping and spatial behavior*. Chicago: Aldine.

Orleans, P., & Schmidt, S. 1972. Mapping the city: Environmental cognitions of urban residents. In W. J. Mitchell (Ed.), *Environmental design: Research and practice*. Los Angeles: University of California Press.

Osgood, C. E., Suci, G. J., & Tannenbaum, P. H. 1957. *The measurement of meaning*. Urbana: University of Illinois.

Pailhous, J. 1970. *La Représentation de l'espace urbain: L'Example de chauffeur de taxi*. Paris: Presses Universitaires de France.

Park, R. E. 1916. The city: Suggestions for investigation of human behavior in the urban environment. In R. Sennett (Ed.), *Classic essays on the culture of cities*. New York: Appleton-Century-Crofts.

Park, R. E. 1926. The urban community as a spacial pattern and a moral order. In E. W. Burgess (Ed.), *The urban community: Selected papers from the proceedings of the American Sociological Society*. Chicago: University of Chicago Press.

Park, R. E., & Burgess, E. 1925. *The city*. Chicago: University of Chicago Press.

Parr, A. E. 1973. City and psyche. In J. Gabree (Ed.), *Surviving the city: A sourcebook of papers on urban livability*. New York: Ballantine Books.

Patterson, A. H. 1977. Methodological developments in environment–behavior research. In D. Stokols (Ed.), *Perspectives on environment and behavior*. Monterey, Calif.: Brooks/Cole.

Peake, P., & Leonard, J. A. 1971. The use of heart rate as an index of stress in blind pedestrians. *Ergonomics*, *14*, 189–204.

Popenoe, D. 1973. Urban residential differentiation: An overview of patterns, trends, and problems. *Sociological Inquiry*, *43*, 35–46.

Porteous, J. D. 1977. *Environment and behavior: planning and everyday urban life*. Reading, Mass.: Addison-Wesley.

President's Council on Environmental Quality, Environmental Protection Agency. 1978. Washington, D.C.: United States Government Printing Office.

Proshansky, H. M. 1978. The city and self-identity. *Environment and Behavior*, *10*, 147–170.

Proshansky, H. M., Kaminoff, R., & Fabian, A. K. 1983. Place identity: Physical world socialization of the self. *Journal of Environmental Psychology*, *3*, 57–83.

Quinn, R. P., & Staines, G. L. 1979. *The 1977 quality of employment survey.* Ann Arbor, Mich.: Survey Research Center.

Rainwater, L. 1966. Fear and house-as-haven in the lower class. *Journal of the American Institute of Planners, 32,* 23–31.

Rankin, R. E., 1969. Air pollution control and public apathy. *Journal of the Air Pollution Control Association, 19,* 565–569.

Rapoport, A. 1972. *Some perspectives on human use and organization of space.* Paper delivered at the meeting of the Australian Association of Social Anthropologists, Melbourne.

Rapoport, A. 1977. *Human aspects of urban form: Towards a man–environment approach to urban form and design.* Elmsford, N.Y.: Pergamon.

Rapoport, A. 1980. Environmental preference, habitat selection and urban housing. *Journal of Social Issues. 36,* 118–134.

Redfield, R. 1941. *The folk culture of Yucatan.* Chicago: University of Chicago Press.

Reiss, A., Jr. 1959. Rural–urban and status differences in interpersonal contacts. *American Journal of Sociology, 65,* 182–195.

Reissman, L. 1970. *The urban process.* New York: Free Press.

Rietzes, D. C. 1983. Urban images: A social psychological approach. *Sociological Inquiry, 53,* 314–332.

Riger, S., & Lavrakas, P. J. 1981. Community ties: Patterns of attachment and social interaction in urban neighborhoods. *American Journal of Community Psychology, 9,* 55–62.

Rodin, J. 1976. Density, perceived choice and response to controllable and uncontrollable outcomes. *Journal of Experimental Social Psychology, 12,* 564–578.

Rodwin, L. 1956. *The British new towns policy.* Cambridge, Mass.: Harvard University Press.

Rose, S. W. 1972. RESIDE: A gaming method for improving environmental interaction. In W. J. Mitchell (Ed.), *Environmental design: Research and practice.* Los Angeles: University of California/EDRA 3.

Rosener, J. 1977. Citizen participation: Tying strategy to function. In P. Marshall (Ed.), *Citizen participation certification for community development.* Washington, D.C.: National Association for Housing and Redevelopment Officials.

Rosenthal, A. M. 1964. *Thirty-eight witnesses.* New York: McGraw-Hill.

Rotton, J. 1978. *The psychological effects of air pollution.* Unpublished manuscript. Florida International University.

Rotton, J. 1983. Affective cognitive consequences of malodorous pollution. *Basic and Applied Social Psychology, 4,* 171–191.

Rotton, J., & Frey, J. 1982. *Air pollution, weather and psychiatric emergencies: A constructive replication.* Paper presented to the American Psychological Association Convention, Washington, D.C.

Rotton, J., Frey, J., Barry, R., Milligan, M., & Fitzpatrick, M. 1979.The air pollution experience and physical aggression. *Journal of Applied Social Psychology, 9,* 397–412.

Rubin, Z. 1973. *Liking and loving: An invitation to social psychology.* New York: Holt, Rinehart & Winston.

Sadalla, E. K., & Magel, S. G. 1980. The perception of traversed distance. *Environment and Behavior, 12,* 65–79.

Sadalla, E. K., & Staplin, L. J. 1980. An information storage model for distance cognition. *Environment and Behavior, 12,* 183–193.

Saegert, S. 1978. High density environments: Their personal and social consequences. In A. Baum & Y. M. Epstein (Eds.), *Human response to crowding.* Hillsdale, N.J.: Erlbaum.

Saegert, S., Mackintosh, E., & West, S. 1975. Two studies of crowding in urban public places. *Environment and Behavior, 7,* 159–184.

Safdie, M. 1970. *Beyond habitat.* Cambridge, Mass.: MIT Press.

Safdie, M. 1974. *For everyone a garden.* Cambridge, Mass.: MIT Press.

Sanford, N. 1962. *The American college.* New York: Wiley.

Sanoff, H. 1975. Son of rationality. In B. Honikman (Ed.), *Responding to social changes.* Stroudsburg, Pa.: Dowden, Hutchinson & Ross.

Schmitt, R. 1957. Density, delinquency and crime in Honolulu. *Sociology and Social Research, 41,* 274–276.

Schneider, M. 1975. The quality of life in large American cities: Objective and subjective social indicators. *Social Indicators Research, 1,* 495–509.

Schoenberg, S., & Rosenbaum, P. 1980. *Neighborhoods that work.* New Brunswick, N.J.: Rutgers University Press.

Schopler, J., & Stockdale, J. E. 1977. An interference analysis of crowding. *Journal of Environmental Psychology and Nonverbal Behavior, 1,* 81–88.

Seligman, M. E. P. 1974. Depression and learned helplessness. In R. J. Friedman & M. M. Katz (Eds.), *The psychology of depression: Contemporary theory and research.* New York: Wiley.

Seligman, M. E. P. 1975. *Helplessness.* San Francisco: Freeman.

Selye, H. 1956. *The stress of life.* New York: McGraw-Hill.

Selye, H. 1976. *Stress in health and disease.* Woburn, Mass.: Butterworth.

Sharp, E. B. 1978. Citizen organization in policing issues and crime prevention: Incentives for participation. *Journal of Voluntary Action Research, 7* (1–2), 45–58.

Sherrod, D. R., & Downs, R. 1974. Environmental determinants of altruism: The effects of stimulus overload and perceived control on helping. *Journal of Experimental Social Psychology, 10,* 468–479.

Sherrod, D. R., Hage, J. N., Halpern, P. L., & Moore, B. S. 1977. Effects of personal causation and perceived control on responses to an aversive environment: The more control, the better. *Journal of Experimental Social Psychology, 13,* 14–27.

Simmel, G. 1950. The stranger. In *The sociology of Georg Simmel* (K. Wolff, trans.). New York: Free Press.

Singer, J. E., Lundberg, V., & Frankenhaeuser, M. 1978. Stress on the train: A study of urban commuting. In A. Baum, J. Singer, and S. Valins (Eds.), *Advances in environmental psychology* (Vol. 1). Hillsdale, N.J.: Erlbaum.

SITE. 1982. *Highrise of homes*. New York: Rizzoli.

Sommer, R. 1969. *Personal space*. Englewood Cliffs, N.J.: Prentice-Hall.

Sommer, R. 1972. *Design awareness*. San Francisco: Rinehart Press.

Sommer, R. 1974. *Tight spaces: Hard architecture and how to humanize it*. Englewood Cliffs, N.J.: Prentice-Hall.

Sommer, R. 1975. A social scientist tells what he has learned from working with architects. *American Institute of Architects Journal*, 42–56.

Spilhaus, A. S. 1968. The experimental city. *Science, 159*, 710–715.

Sproul, H., & Sproul, M. 1956. *Man–milieu relationship hypotheses in the context of international politics*. Princeton, N.J.: Princeton University Center of International Studies.

Stea, D. 1969. The measurement of mental maps: An experimental model for studying conceptual spaces. In K. Cox & R. Golledge (Eds.), *Behavioral problems in geography*. Evanston, Ill.: Northwestern University Press.

Sternlieb, G., & Hughes, W. 1983. The uncertain future of the central city. *Urban Affairs Quarterly, 18*, 455–472.

Stokols, D. 1972. On the distinction between density and crowding: Some implications for future research. *Psychological Review, 79*, 275–278.

Stokols, D. 1976. The experience of crowding in primary and secondary environments. *Environment and Behavior, 8*, 49–86.

Stokols, D., & Novaco, R. 1981. Transportation and well being: An ecological perspective. In I. Altman, J. Wohlwill, & P. Everett (Eds.), *Human behavior and environment: Advances in theory and research* (Vol. 5). New York: Plenum.

Stokols, D., & Shumaker, S. A. 1980. People in places: A transitional view of settings. In J. Harvey (Ed.), *Cognition, social behavior, and the environment*. Hillsdale, N.J.: Erlbaum.

Strahilevitz, N., Strahilevitz, A., & Miller, J. E. 1979. Air pollution and the admission rate of psychiatric patients. *American Journal of Psychiatry, 136*, 206–207.

Strauss, A. L. 1976. *Images of the American city*. New Brunswick, N.J.: Transaction Books.

Sutcliffe, J. P., & Crabbe, B. 1963. Incidence and degree of friendship in urban and rural areas. *Social Forces, 42*, 60–67.

Suttles, G. D. 1968. *The social order of the slum: Ethnicity and territory in the inner city*. Chicago: University of Chicago Press.

Suttles, G. D. 1972. *The social construction of communities*. Chicago. University of Chicago Press.

Sweetser, F. L. 1982. *Community size and neighborhood differentiation*. Paper presented at the meeting of the International Sociological Association.

Taylor, R. B. 1980. Conceptual dimensions of crowding reconsidered. *Population and Environment, 3*, 298–308.

Taylor, R. B., 1981. Perception of density: Individual differences? *Environment and Behavior, 13*, 3–21.

Taylor, R. B. 1982. Neighborhood physical environment and stress. In G.W. Evans (Ed.), *Environmental stress*. Cambridge: Cambridge University Press.

Taylor, R. B., Gottfredson, S. D., & Brower, S. 1980. The defensibility of defensible space: A critical review and synthetic framework for future research. In T. Hirschi & M. Gottfredson (Eds.), *Understanding crime: Current theory and research*. Beverly Hills, Calif.: Sage.

Taylor, R. B., Gottfredson, S. D., & Brower, S. 1981. Territorial cognitions and social climate in urban neighborhoods. *Basic and Applied Social Psychology, 2,* 289–303.

Taylor, R. B., & Verbrugge, L. M. 1980. Consequences of population density and size. *Urban Affairs Quarterly, 16*, 135–160.

Thorndike, E. L. 1939. *Your city*. New York: Harcourt, Brace & World.

Thorndike, E. L. 1940. *144 smaller cities*. New York: Harcourt, Brace & World.

Tracor, Inc. 1970. *Community reactions to airport noise* (Vol. 1) (NASA CR. 1761). Washington, D.C.: National Aeronautics and Space Administration.

Tripp, R. T. (Ed.). 1970. *The international thesaurus of quotations*. New York: Crowell.

Turner, C. W., Layton, J. F., & Simons, L. S. 1975. Naturalistic studies of aggressive behavior: Aggressive stimuli, victim visibility and horn honking. *Journal of Personality and Social Psychology, 31*, 1098–1107.

Unger, D. G., & Wandersman, A. 1983. Neighboring and its role in block organizations: An exploratory report. *American Journal of Community Psychology, 11,* 291–300.

Ury, H. 1968. Photochemical air pollution and automobile accidents in Los Angeles: An investigation of oxident and accidents, 1963 and 1965. *Archives of Environmental Health, 17*, 334–342.

VanVliet, W. 1983. Families in apartment buildings: Sad storeys for children. *Environment and Behavior, 15*, 211–234.

Verba, S., & Nie, N. 1972. *Participation in America: Political democracy and social equality*. New York: Harper & Row.

Wandersman, A. 1984a. Citizen participation. In R. Hellin, R. Price, S. Reinharz, S. Riger, & A. Wandersman, *Psychology and community change* (2nd ed.). Homewood, Ill.: Dorsey.

Wandersman, A. 1984b. Personal communication.

Wandersman, A., Jakubs, J. F., & Giamartino, G. 1981. Participation in block organizations. *Journal of Community Action, 1*, 40–48.

Wapner, S., Kaplan, B., & Cohen, S. B. 1973. An organismic-developmental perspective for understanding transactions of men and environments. *Environment and Behavior, 5*, 255–289.

Ward, L. M., & Suedfeld, P. 1973. Human response to highway noise. *Environmental Research, 6*, 306–326.

Warr, P. B., & Knapper, C. 1968. *The perception of people and events.* London: Wiley.

Warren, D. I. 1978. Explorations in neighborhood differentiation. *Sociological Quarterly, 19,* 310–331.

Warren, D. I., & Warren, R. B. 1975. Six kinds of neighborhoods. *Psychology Today, 9,* 74–80.

Warren, R. B. 1974. *Community in America.* Chicago: Rand McNally.

Webb, S. D., & Collette, J. 1975. Urban ecological and household correlates of stress-alleviating drug use. *American Behavioral Scientist, 18,* 750–769.

Webber, M. M. 1963. Order in diversity: Community without propinquity. In L. Wingo (Ed.), *Cities and space.* Baltimore: Johns Hopkins Press.

Webber, M. M. 1968.The post-city age. *Daedalus, 97,* 1091-1110.

Weisman, G. 1979. *A study in architectural legibility.* Unpublished doctoral dissertation, University of Michigan.

Wellman, B., & Leighton, B. 1979. Network, neighborhoods and communities: Approaches to the study of the community question. *Urban Affairs Quarterly, 14,* 363–390.

Westin, A. 1970. *Privacy and freedom.* New York: Atheneum.

White, M., & White, L. 1962. *The intellectual vs. the city.* Cambridge, Mass.: Harvard University Press.

Whyte, W. F. 1955. *Street corner society.* Chicago: University of Chicago Press.

Wicker, A. W. 1979. *An introduction to ecological psychology.* Monterey, Calif.: Brooks/Cole.

Widgery, R. N. 1982. Satisfaction with the quality of urban life: A predictive model. *American Journal of Community Psychology, 10,* 37–48.

Winsborough, H. 1965. The social consequences of high population density. *Law and Contemporary Problems, 30,* 120–126.

Wirth, L. 1938. Urbanism as a way of life. *American Journal of Sociology, 44,* 1–24.

Wohlwill, J. F. 1966. The physical environment: A problem for a psychology of stimulation. *Journal of Social Issues, 22,* 29–38.

Wohlwill, J. F. 1973. The environment is not in the head. In W. F. T. Preciser (Ed.), *Environmental design research.* Vol. 2: *Symposia and workshops.* Stroudsburg, Pa.: Dowden, Hutchinson & Ross.

Wohlwill, J. F., & Kohn, I. 1976. Dimensionalizing the environmental manifold. In S. Wapner, S. B. Cohen, & B. Kaplan (Eds.), *Experiencing the environment.* New York: Plenum.

Wright, F. L. 1935. Broadacre City: A new community plan. *Architectural Record, 77,* 234–254.

Wurster, C. B. 1963. The form and structure of the future urban complex. In L. Wingo (Ed.), *Cities and space.* Baltimore: Johns Hopkins Press.

Yancey, W. L. 1976. Architecture, interaction and social control: The case of a large-scale housing project. In H. M. Proshansky, W. H. Ittelson, & L. G. Rivlin (Eds.),

Environmental psychology: People and their physical settings (2nd ed.). New York: Holt, Rinehart & Winston.

Yin, R. K. 1977. Goals for citizen involvement: Some possibilities and some evidence. In P. Marshall (Ed.), *Citizen participation certification for community development.* Washington, D.C.: National Association for Housing and Redevelopment Officials.

Yin, R. K., & Yates, D. 1975. *Street-level governments.* Lexington, Mass.: Lexington Books.

Zeisel, J. 1975. *Sociology and architectural design.* New York: Free Press.

Zeisel, J. 1981. *Inquiry by design: Tools for environment-behavior research.* Montery, Calif.: Brooks/Cole.

Zeisel, J., Epp, G., & Demos, S. 1977. *Low-rise housing for older people: Behavioral criteria for design.* Washington, D.C.: U.S. Government Printing Office.

Zeisel, J., Welch, P., Epp, G., & Demos, S. 1983. *Mid-rise elevator housing for older people: Behavioral criteria for design.* Boston: Building Diagnostics.

Zimmerman, D. 1982. Small is beautiful, but: An appraisal of the optimum city. *Humboldt Journal of Social Relations, 9,* 120–142.

Zimring, C. 1982. The built environment as a source of psychological stress: Impacts of buildings and cities on satisfaction and behavior. In G. W. Evans (Ed.), *Environmental stress.* Cambridge: Cambridge University Press.

Zinobar, J. W., & Dinkel, N. R. (Eds.). 1981. *A trust of evaluation: A guide for involving citizens in community mental health program evaluation.* Tampa: Florida Consortium for Research and Evaluation.

Zlutnick, S., & Altman, I. 1972. Crowding and human behavior. In J. Wohlwill and D. Carson (Eds.), *Environment and the social sciences: Perspectives and applications.* Washington, D.C.: American Psychological Association.

Zuckerman, M. 1971. Dimensions of sensation seeking. *Journal of Consulting and Clinical Psychology. 36,* 45–52.

AUTHOR INDEX

SUBJECT INDEX